German
Rescuers
of Jews

German Rescuers of Jews

INDIVIDUALS VERSUS
THE NAZI SYSTEM

* * *

Mordecai Paldiel

ISBN: 1541251172
ISBN 13: 9781541251175

Contents

Introduction

*   *   *

IN 1993, AUDIENCES THE WORLD over sat spellbound watching Steven Spielberg's movie *Schindler's List*, which told the story of a German, a member of the Nazi Party, who went out of his way to save over a thousand Jews, and of the men and women who worked in his firms in German-occupied Poland and the similarly occupied Moravia region – today part of the Czech Republic. People have often wondered whether, apart from Oskar Schindler and perhaps a few more isolated cases, there were to be found more brave Germans who saved Jews at considerable risks to themselves. The positive response to this question – literally, numbering in the hundreds of so-far authenticated rescuers – has raised surprised eyebrows. In this study, I propose to examine this subject in greater depth and to explore in what ways help was extended to Jews by Germans during their country's rule by the Nazi regime, based on records stored at Yad Vashem, Israel's national Holocaust memorial. These records were compiled under a special program to honor non-Jews who risked their lives to save Jews from the Nazis. Most persons appearing in this study were indeed awarded the title of "Righteous Among the Nations," though not all, for reasons explained in Appendix A, which discusses the criteria and issues for that honorific.

Before delving into the story of German rescuers of Jews, however, the reader is to be reminded that we are dealing with persons who were citizens of one of the most horrific regimes in mankind's history, whose appearance in the twentieth century and the fealty of millions of followers to its dehumanizing agenda, still leave many historians grasping for credible explanations. Back in 1987, at a scholarly symposium in Jerusalem, this *Sonderweg* (unique event) gave rise to lengthy debates, known as the Historians' Debate

(*Historikerstreit*). Historians and others questioned whether the Nazi phenomenon was an outgrowth of the specific German character and its history, and was only applicable to that country. Antisemitism has had a long and widespread history, and at the beginning of the twentieth century was in fact more prominent in countries such as France during the Dreyfus Affair, Romania, and Czarist Russia – but was there something about German history and the proliferation of certain ideas that made the Holocaust waiting to happen only in that country? Or are the reasons to this riddle to be found elsewhere?[1]

This ongoing debate, relevant to this book's study, is also of special interest in light of the ongoing, spirited controversy sparked by Daniel Goldhagen's 1996 "Hitler's Willing Executioners," in which he submitted that large segments of the German public favored an "eliminationist" type of antisemitism; in other words, the physical removal of Jews from Germany, which consequently cleared the way for Hitler's extermination of Jews.[2] Goldhagen argued that most Germans had, previous to the ascent of the Nazis, adhered to a virulent form of antisemitism, which did not diminish with passing years, and which only waited for a detonator, in the form of Hitler, to take it to its explosive culmination. Hitler, according to this argument, "leaped across the moral chasm that ordinary Germans on their own could not cross," and by creating an efficient killing machinery, made possible the carrying out of this supposedly public will. The German people's prior antisemitism "created the necessary enabling condition for the so-called eliminationist program to unfold, of which they, with sadly few exceptions, approved in principle, if not wholeheartedly."[3] So goes the Goldhagen argument.

Many historians of the Holocaust, while agreeing in principle on the complicity of numerous people in Germany in the killing process, disagree with Goldhagen's sweeping assertion of a supposedly all-embracing, deadly "eliminationist" desire of most Germans with regard to the Jews. In this study, while steering clear of this scholarly debate, we will keep it in the back of our minds as we recount the heroic deeds of Germans who saved Jews from certain death.[4] We will show how a sizable, though perhaps not overly significant, number of Germans were able to stand clear of this presumed "eliminationist" drive, and even risked their lives to save Jews, each one according to his capacity – whether one, several, or many. We will examine the role and scope of German rescuers from many walks of life, some of whom even donned military and police uniforms, who acted to save Jews in various circumstances. Then we will discuss the possible motivations of these rescuers, and in the concluding chapter, try to draw some lessons, with an eye on the aforementioned scholarly debate. But, before we begin, a few words about human behavior within a social context.

Post-war studies in human behavior and social conformity (Stanley Milgram, Elliot Aronson, and Solomon Asch, among others) have highlighted the social context in which individual persons act and respond to outside stimuli. According to Milgram, for instance, human behavior is predicated on certain hierarchical social value structures that cause individual impulses and egos to be diluted, even suppressed, in favor of group and social pressures.[5] These studies also reveal the degree to which people comply with social behavioral pressures and submit to higher authority, even when no overt coercion is exercised to enforce conformity, no promised rewards for "team play" are offered, and no punishments for individual-type behavior are threatened. Such obedience is explained by the well-known observation that people want to be recognized and accepted by the larger group, and not be stigmatized as an "outsider." This situation prevails even when the individual person, while toeing the group line, simultaneously continues to secretly harbor doubts and disagreements about the wisdom of the larger group's action.[6]

When group pressure rises to an intensive level, these studies suggest that the individual sees himself as an instrument in carrying out the wishes of others, and his entire set of activities is pervaded by his relationship to his superiors – a condition that Milgram defines as an Agentic State. In such a setting, a person's moral judgments are largely suspended, the obedient subject divests himself of responsibility by attributing all initiative to legitimate authority – "I was just doing what I was told." Milgram also noted that only a few people will have the strength to disobey orders, even when these are incompatible with fundamental standards of morality. A variety of inhibitions come into play and keep the hesitating person in place. Understandably, not all social scientists necessarily agree with these conclusions.[7] At the same time, studies also have shown that pressure to conform to the judgment of others does not necessarily carry over to the private judgments of the conforming individual. This is also supported by the fact that many of the persons who saved Jews, at least outwardly, expressed allegiance to the Nazi state, even if in private they held opposing viewpoints.

An additional observation worth noting is that proximity to suffering persons, disasters, and other emergency situations, as was the case with German rescuers of Jews, may prompt otherwise impassive bystanders to step in and help, and bring out the best in them. Confrontation with totally helpless persons can, moreover, momentarily even neutralize socially inbred prejudices and opinions. In addition, the sight of violence and sheer inhumanity on an unprecedented scale may trigger the release of a humanitarian "sleeper," to borrow a term coined by George Steiner (defined as a latent innate human reaction, activated under certain conditions), and launch one in a rescue operation, as will be amply illustrated in the case histories of Oskar Schindler, Hans von Dohnányi, and Hans Georg Calmeyer.[8]

In such inordinate situations, in a world of morally reversed values such as during the Holocaust, certain questions may run through the bystander's mind: "Is the situation really that morally serious? Can I in clear conscience turn down the pleadings of the suffering party? Can my personal intervention make a difference? Will my help benefit the victim?" Clearly, the first prerequisite for helping is to define the situation as an emergency, both in physical and moral terms, which during the Holocaust was obvious to anyone witnessing the Nazi onslaught on the Jews. Second is any would-be rescuer's crystal-clear realization that one's involvement will definitely have an immediate, remedial impact on the persons in desperate need of help; hence, for those willing to take up the challenge, the greater the impulse to intervene.[9]

So, keeping in mind the earlier-mentioned scholarly debate on the degree of support by the German public for their government's antisemitic policy, and in light of the studies on human behavior in a social context, it is no wonder that many ask whether there were to be found Germans in great numbers who were prepared to undergo risks to themselves in order to save Jews from the grip of the authorities. The answer to this remains inconclusive and requires much further study, but we do know of a number of salient, documented and significant instances of such positive behavior. This study will examine the nature of their humanitarian deeds against the setting of an unprecedented reign of terror by the rescuers' own government on the Jews, the regime's main targeted victims.

Rescue operations by Germans were prompted by various sets of circumstances. In most cases, for those originating in Germany, rescuers and rescued knew each other previously on a personal basis. Others had their origins in work-related contacts. In both these instances, the "proximity" factor triggered a rescue initiative when the need for such an intervention arose. Others, shocked by the brutality of the Nazi regime, may have been induced to help when approached by third parties or due to a sudden and impromptu encounter with Jews on the run. The sufferings of Nazi-defined half or quarter Jews and of Jews married to non-Jewish spouses (more about this further in this study) may also have prompted some to come to their rescue. In the cases narrated in this book, a few persons in positions of authority and influence found the courage to subvert the system's discriminatory laws in order to help. Some rescuers, who openly flouted the regime's antisemitism, paid the dire consequences of their disobedience.

The cases studied here comprise rescuers from both Germany and Austria (which, since March 1938 up to the end of the war was part of the German state) and persons from these two areas who operated in countries under Nazi or Fascist rule. I have culled most of these stories from records of rescuers honored by Yad Vashem under the "Righteous Among the Nations" program, a project begun in 1963, and that I headed in my 24-year tenure as director of the Righteous Among the Nations Department at Yad Vashem from 1982 to 2007 – as well as a few cases not awarded this honor.

Before commencing, however, the historical setting needs to be addressed, so as to better understand the situational context in which rescuers operated. The following chapter briefly details the evolution of Nazi policy vis-a-vis the Jews, from 1933 onwards, and the response by German public bodies and of the public at large to the rising crescendo of anti-Jewish measures, culminating in the deportation of Jews to the death camps.

CHAPTER 1

The Historical Setting

* * *

A) FACTS AND FIGURES

"HOLOCAUST" IS A TERM USED to describe the planned murder of the Jewish people by Nazi Germany, under the leadership of Adolf Hitler. Once considered the fount of civilized nations, Germany is the country where Nazism came to birth, one of the most destructive political movements in history, with a pseudo-religious racist ideology as its guiding platform. The aim was as bold as it was mad – the wish to fully transform German and eventually European society based on the leadership of the so-called Nordic or Aryan race, of which the Germans were the outstanding and superior representatives, followed by the subjugation of other races considered "inferior" to the Germanic one, and the creation of a vast empire populated by ethnic Germans at the expense of the "inferior" Slavic nations in the east. At the bottom of the racial scale were the Jews – considered an "anti-race" – who supposedly posed a threat not only to the Germans but to the rest of the world, for the Nazis claimed that the Jewish teachings contested the nature-given "aristocratic" distribution of races. As with bad weeds in a garden, the only solution conceivable to the Nazis was to uproot and forcibly remove the Jews from all their present habitations – for the benefit, so they claimed, of mankind.

This virulent form of antisemitism was not a footnote in the Nazi ideology, but one of its constituent components and genuinely believed in, and it became institutionalized as official government policy in Nazi Germany. The "Jew" symbolized to the Nazis all that was "wrong" in the world: from Western liberalism, democracy, and Wall Street capitalism to socialism and communism, as well as

Christianity (considered by Hitler as a Jewish front, a belief he did not articulated openly but only in so-called confidential "table talks" with his confidants), although paradoxically Christian historical teachings of theological antisemitism and demonization of the Jews had prepared the ground for Hitler's anti-Jewish genocidal crusade. Hitler believed that what he termed "International Jewry" was spearheading a worldwide conspiracy against Germany, the fountainhead of the pure races, and therefore called forth the most drastic countermeasures imaginable, including, eventually, mass murder of the entire Jewish people – all Jews, without distinction, everywhere where the Germans and their collaborating countries dominated.[1]

The Final Solution, the largest officially sanctioned murder operation known in history, was ordered by the Nazi leadership and carried out by an obedient bureaucracy, not necessarily all die-hard Nazis. Hitler and his closest aides considered the destruction of the Jews as a well-nigh sacral act; the Second World War was to them a crusade against a so-called International Jewry (usually association with "Bolshevism," in other words, worldwide communism), whom they accused of being behind the nations at war with Germany. While millions of innocent people were consumed by Nazi barbarity, as has been pointed out, not all the victims were Jews, but all Jews were victims. Jews were to be punished for simply being, for having been born. At the same time, a reign of terror was unleashed against political and religious opponents from within and, with the conquest of other countries, against all who opposed Nazi expansionist policies on the European continent – as well as those who tried to prevent the destruction of Jewish lives.

While antisemitism of one sort of another was prevalent throughout many segments of the German population, it may not have extended, as claimed by Goldhagen, to the urgent wish to see them physically harmed and eliminated, but rather favored sweeping discriminatory measures against Jews, including, for some, their forcible expulsion from the country.[2] Prior to Hitler, not a few public figures spoke denigratingly about the Jews (including historian Heinrich von Treitschke, who a century early bemoaned the Jews as "our misfortune," a so-called stigma vastly amplified by Nazi propagandists), but this took mostly the form of social distancing, not the violent pogroms known in Poland and other Eastern European countries, which most culturally sensitive Germans abhorred. Briefly put, while the Nazi brand of radical antisemitism was probably not shared by a majority of the population, many persons in Germany favored extensive restrictive measures against the Jews – but short of physical violence.

Historically, Jews began to settle in Germany during the late Roman period (third century C.E.), such as in Cologne in the fourth century. Over the succeeding centuries, Jews knew periods of growth and tranquility, interspersed with savage persecutions, culminating with the wholesale massacre of Jewish communities along the Rhine River by the Crusaders during the eleventh century. During the Middle Ages, Jews lived under severe economic and legal restrictions, and in the sixteenth century, Protestant reformer Martin Luther fulminated against them, and called for their expulsion and the burning of their synagogues. Finally, by 1870, in the newly united German kingdom, Jews had been fully emancipated and granted equal civic and economic rights. However, in 1880, Wilhelm Marr coined the term "anti-Semitism" as a label for those opposed to the integration of Jews in the life of the nation.[3] Before the Nazi period, while antisemitic movements arose and advocated the disenfranchisement of Jews, they were never able to attract more than at most 14% of the electorate in Germany. In nearby Austria, however, the antisemitic party headed by Karl Lueger actually won the mayoral elections in Vienna, in 1897, but paradoxically, under his tenure, Viennese Jewry continued to flourish and prosper. The Weimar republic, which rose after Germany's defeat in World War One, witnessed the flowering of Jewish activity in practically all spheres of the country's life. It seemed to all observers that the danger for Jews in Germany had passed into history, for good.[4]

German Jews, who numerically counted some 550,000 persons at the start of Nazi rule, in January 1933, with 180,000 alone residing in Berlin, represented less than 1% of the country's population. They were mostly well assimilated, with many considering themselves as principally Germans, and only afterwards as Jews. They prided themselves on having contributed more than their share to the German military during World War One, and proudly displayed the high military decorations they were awarded for bravery on the battlefield. Up to then, Jewish integration into German life had continued at a fast pace, judging by the rate of intermarriages between Jews and non-Jews that steadily rose to an alarming rate, endangering the future growth and stability of the Jewish community. An additional concern was the growing number of Jews who left the Jewish fold. In 1927, for instance, up to 1,000 Jews officially converted to Christianity.

Then came the Nazi accession to power in 1933, and a reverse process was set in motion – beginning with a gradual but swiftly mounting total segregation, and culminating in wholesale murder. At the start, laws were drafted that disenfranchised Jews, and reduced them by degrees to the status of a pariah people. Following the 1933 Law for the Reestablishment of the Professional Civil Service, which prohibited Jews from holding public office, all Jews were subsequently dismissed from influential positions and professions: academia, law, public administration, the media, entertainment, and public health. This was soon followed by the Law Against Overcrowding of German Schools, which restricted the number of Jewish children in higher institutions to the proportion of Jews in the population. Additional laws further restricted Jewish freedom of movement and professional employment possibilities. They were also barred from train dining cars, public resorts, and beaches.

On September 15, 1935, came the most radical legislation so far enacted, known as the two Nuremberg Laws – the Citizenship Law, which declared Jews no longer citizens of Germany but merely subjects, and the Law for the Protection of German Blood and Honor, which forbade marriage and sexual intercourse between Jew and Aryans (a term designating members of the Germanic and kindred race, such as Scandinavians), and prohibiting Jews from keeping non-Jewish household maids below the age of 45, as a preventive measure against "race defilement" (*rassenschande*). An ironic offshoot of this law was the Nazi creation of a new race, consisting of the offspring of mixed marriages, better known as *Mischlinge* (mixed offspring), which was to give no rest to Nazi racists for years to come. There were some variations under this category – a first-degree *Mischling* (Grade A) was a person with only two Jewish grandparents and subject to certain restrictions; a second-degree *Mischling* (Grade B) was one with only one Jewish grandparent – also discriminated against but not as severely as a first-degree *Mischling*. A person with three or four Jewish grandparents was considered a "full" Jew, even if he was baptized at birth into the Christian faith – and starting in 1941 he or she was also slated for destruction.

The increasing tension between the Nazi government and the Catholic Church (which first had come to an acceptance of the regime in the July 1933 Concordat) culminated, in 1937, with the papal encyclical of Pius XI, "With Burning Anxiety" (*Mit Brennender Sorge*), condemning race glorification as a new paganism, but glossing over the persecution of the Jews. The following year saw a vigorous increase in anti-Jewish measures, with all Jewish men required to add the middle name "Israel" on their identifications, and all Jewish women, "Sara." Passports held by Jews were marked with a bold "J." In the meantime, already starting in 1933, Jewish enterprises were gradually liquidated by being forced to sell at below-market-value prices – a policy known as Aryanization. At the same time, the Nazi policy at that point – strangely, in light of what took place at a later phase – was not to kill but to force the Jews out of the country through legal or other forms of emigration, and consequently continued to encourage Jews to leave; close to half of the original Jewish population indeed left the country.[5]

Then, on the night of November 9–10, 1938, the regime instigated a massive pogrom against Jews across the whole country (which by then included annexed Austria and the Sudeten region of Czechoslovakia). Hundreds of synagogues, shops, businesses, and dwellings were vandalized, looted, and torched. Known as Kristallnacht ("night of broken glass"), it was the first (and ironically the last) public display of violence against Jews on German soil, with official approval. During that officially sanctioned pogrom, close to 100 Jews were killed and some 30,000 men were rounded up and sent to concentration camps, to be released only upon the promise to leave the country immediately, by whatever means. To add insult to injury, the government, the instigator of this riot, capped it all by imposing on the Jewish community a one-billion-mark fine for damages sustained on its property by a government-organized pogrom.

More heightened anti-Jewish measures were henceforth to proceed inside Germany, but in an orderly manner, so as not to upset the sensibilities of the populace that the Gestapo reported were keen on preserving law and order, at least publicly. By the end of 1938 Jews were forcibly transferred from their homes into specially designated "Jewish houses," with sometimes eight people crowded into a single small room, and up to 20 in larger apartment dwellings; these homes were marked with a Star of David. Jewish lawyers and medical doctors were forbidden to practice their profession, even for Jewish clients. Jews were also ordered to turn in their radio sets and telephones; household items, such as typewriters, bicycles, cameras, and binoculars, were confiscated – even household pets – and Jews were banned the use of public telephones. They were also restricted from using public transportation other than those travelling to forced labor locations, at least seven kilometers away from their home. On the eve of World War Two, Jews had been made "socially dead" (in the words of Goldhagen), before actually being made physically dead.[6] This was a portent of worse things to come. In his annual speech before the Reichstag on January 30, 1939, Hitler threatened the extermination of the Jewish people throughout Europe should another war erupt, a statement that he referred to in later years in public and in closed sessions with party and army heads when the extermination campaign was in full swing.

At the start of the war, in September 1939, there were still some 245,000 Jews remaining in Greater Germany, which included 185,000 in Germany proper (the *Altreich*) and 60,000 in annexed Austria.[7] Immigration restrictions in most other countries prevented a greater exit of Jews. In November 1940, all Jewish men and women aged 18–55 who were fit to work were mobilized for forced labor in war-essential plants, where they were segregated from the non-Jewish labor force, and assigned the dirtiest and most menial jobs. The work canteen was denied to them.

A year later, in September 1941, Jews aged seven and over were ordered to wear a yellow star on their outer clothing, when stepping out. A month later, the emigration of Jews, until then still possible in very limited cases, was officially banned for the duration of the war. This was the signal for the start of systematic deportations, which began on October 15, 1941. A few thousand Jews had already been dumped earlier in defeated France. This was followed in November 1941 with regular transports of Jews, who were taken from Germany and Austria to ghettos and concentration camps in German-occupied Poland and Lithuania, or to be shot over open pits in various East European locations. Those designated as prominent or talented (among them persons who had rendered significant services to the country), especially the elderly among them, were first dispatched to the "model" camp of Theresienstadt (today, Terezin), located in the annexed Sudetenland region of dismembered Czechoslovakia, thence to Auschwitz where most were gassed. Included among these were Jewish war veterans, who bore some of the country's highest military decorations.[8] Already a bit earlier – starting on June 22, 1941, and coinciding with the German attack on the Soviet Union – specially organized killing battalions, known as Einsatzgruppen, were shooting tens of thousands of Jews before open pits and natural ravines, on a wide arc stretching from the Baltic to the Black Sea, in the newly conquered vast expanses of that country.

By January 1943, Auschwitz gradually replaced all destinations to the half dozen death camps on Polish soil, where most persons were gassed upon arrival. The deportees were required to leave their apartments in good order, pay their household bills, surrender their keys, and take with them only a limited supply of personal possessions. They had to declare and surrender their money (except 50 marks), their valuables, and their property. Those not yet deported were forbidden to leave their assigned place of residence, and their food rations were severely reduced: no milk, fish, fowl, rice, and cocoa.[9]

February 27, 1943, saw a massive raid, the so-called Factory Action, carried out in broad daylight, when the remainder of Berlin Jews working in war-essential factories were rounded up and dispatched to Auschwitz. By November 1941, over 90% of the estimated 200,000 Jews in the country (including Austria) had been deported to the death camps. On May 19, 1943, the Nazi regime triumphantly declared Berlin and the rest of Germany as *Judenrein* – (surgically) "cleaned out of Jews." In fact, the authorities were well aware that not all Jews ("full" Jews by Nazi definition) had been netted, and many had gone into hiding. In addition, an estimated 28,000 Jews intermarried with Aryan spouses were momentarily not touched, and the "half-Jews," the *Mischlinge* (some place their figure as high as 80,000), were also left unharmed – after the Nazis, following marathon discussions, could not agree on their fate.[10]

Across the frontiers, with the advance of German armies throughout Europe, the extermination of Jews proceeded apace, with Poland serving as the main slaughtering house, to which Jews in the tens and hundreds of thousands were dispatched by trains from most other occupied countries. Of the estimated close to seven million Jews under Nazi rule, some six million perished – murdered through a combination of gassing and mass shootings, as well as deaths caused by hard labor, starvation, infectious diseases, and death marches. The actual killings, which started in June 1941 with the German invasion of the Soviet Union, continued uninterrupted until the last day of the war – May 8, 1945.

The final death toll for German and Austrian Jews is approximately 200,000 killed (this figure includes the tens of thousands who had fled to neighboring countries and were later caught up in the Final Solution when their new host countries came under German domination). Of the 137,000 Jews deported from Germany proper, only an estimated 9,000 survived the depredations of the camps. Inside Germany, some 20,000 survived, of which an estimated 15,000 were intermarried with non-Jews, and some 5,000 were in hiding – this without counting the *Mischlinge*, those classified as part-Jewish, whose number ran into the thousands. (An additional unspecified number of thousands of Jews survived in camps on German soil, brought there from concentration camps in Poland, in the latter phase of the war).[11]

In Austria, of the 185,00 Jews in the country in 1938 (including 170,000 in Vienna alone), most managed to leave before emigration was officially banned in November 1941. The rest, a total of 65,000, perished in the camps (including those who fled to neighboring countries but were later caught there for deportation by the Germans), leaving only an estimated 1,700 survivors. Inside the country, up to 1,000 eked out a secret existence, mostly in Vienna, and several thousand others were spared deportation due to their marriage to non-Jewish spouses (precise figures are sketchy).[12] As for the Jewish death toll in countries under German occupation, Poland tops the list in both absolute figures and in population rate. Between 2.9 to 3 million out of a prewar Jewish population of 3.3 million Polish Jews (87–91%) perished in the Holocaust. The respective figures for other countries are no less disheartening, and they add up to a grand total of close to (or slightly more, according to other estimates) six million Jewish victims.[13]

Never before had the world witnessed such wholesale, ongoing, and senseless destruction of human lives for reasons that still baffle and boggle the mind. Was this the result of an unavoidable, radical form of lethal Jewish hatred in Germany, which of necessity had to lead to the gas chambers? The historical record does not justify such a rash conclusion, and historians are still debating this point.

B) ANTISEMITISM AND PUBLIC OPINION

As already noted, few students of Nazi Germany and of the Holocaust concur with Goldhagen's sweeping statements, according to which most Germans had already, before Hitler, clung to an "eliminationist" type of antisemitism, which called for even the use of physical violence against Germany's Jews.[14] According to historian Ian Kershaw, although of vital importance to the top Nazi leadership, antisemitism was far from being the principal motive in bringing Nazism to power, and seems to have been secondary to the main appeal of the Nazi message among the populace. Kershaw quotes in this regard W.S. Allen's remarks that people "were drawn to anti-Semitism because they were drawn to Nazism, not the other way around."[15] Millions of Nazi voters, though probably antisemitic at heart, were in no sense dyed-in-the-wool Jew-haters, and most Germans did not necessarily have Jews on their mind (the so-called Nazi trumped-up "Jewish Question") when they cast their votes for the Nazis.[16]

At the same time, these same Nazi voters could not have been oblivious of their party's antisemitic platform, and together with non-Nazi voters shared the anti-Jewish prejudices in one form or another of the majority of the population. After the Nazi takeover, many people felt that it was correct to deprive the Jews of many of their civil rights and separate them from the rest of the population, but it is unclear whether they supported the drastic methods employed against them later by the Nazis. Witness the Gestapo-reported public abhorrence of violence on the streets and the senseless destruction of property (as took place during the Kristallnacht pogrom), though it is unclear whether they would have been equally repelled by more drastic measures, but hidden from public view. In some places, people stood up for "their" Jews, usually resident neighbors, while at the same time sanctioning measures against all "other" Jews.[17] Consequently, the forcible dismissal of Jews from many influential posts in administration, science, and the arts met with no negative reaction from the German public. On the contrary, most people (though abstaining from violent outbreaks) subscribed to the idea that Jews had played an inordinately large and harmful role in the life of the country, and therefore even staunch anti-Nazis, such as the author Thomas Mann, mildly condoned such measures.[18] As for the Nuremberg Laws of September 1935, here the record shows that they met with wide approval, though opinions were divided if this law went far enough, or perhaps too far, in creating a legal framework for a lasting solution to the separation of Jews and non-Jews.[19]

The November 1938 Kristallnacht riots, which were orchestrated and directed by the Nazi party, constituted the only occasion during the Third Reich when the German public was confronted directly, on a nationwide scale, with the full savagery of the regime's anti-Jewish animus. Never before and never again did the persecution of the Jews stand at the forefront of the public's attention as on the morning of the November 10, 1938. In some places, prominent citizens participated in this orgy, such as in Düsseldorf, where doctors of the municipal hospital and presidents of the District Courts took part in setting the synagogue on fire. In Leipzig, there was a mixture of numbed bewilderment and silent disgust, and expressions of shame, and in general it seems that the pogrom aroused widespread unpopularity. Within the Nazi party, only a small group approved of the pogrom. Vienna, newly incorporated into the Reich, was one of the few cities of Greater Germany where no traces of opposition to the pogrom were encountered. Whatever the underlying reasons, after Kristallnacht, in the words of a German witness, "no German old enough to walk could ever plead ignorance of the persecution of the Jews." The general uneasiness caused by this pogrom persuaded the Nazi leadership that such open manifestations of lawlessness should never again be copied, and that further anti-Jewish measures inside Germany should be done in a more orderly fashion and removed from public view as much as possible; no similar limitations, however, applied in other countries under German rule.[20]

The Yellow Star decree of September 1941 also produced mixed reactions. Some people were frankly surprised at the number of Jews still remaining in Germany (of which 70–80,000 lived in Berlin) and asked for their removal, while others openly sympathized with their plight through symbolic gestures, such as standing up for Jews on trams and the elevated trains. The weight of evidence (including eyewitness accounts by foreigners in Germany at the time) confirmed the public discomfort with this new decree glaringly displayed on the city streets, to the extent that Josef Goebbels (the Nazi Propaganda Minister) reacted angrily, as noted in his diary: "This nation is simply not yet mature; it's full of all kinds of idiotic sentimentality."[21] Again, it was not so much a case of empathy for the beleaguered Jews. As long as Jews were segregated and not perceived, many could remain emotionally distant and claim ignorance of what was happening to them, and thereby avoid feelings of shame and guilt. But labeling the victim, through the public display of the Jewish badge, forced upright citizens to face squarely the injustice perpetrated on the stigmatized Jews, and this outraged the self-righteous sensibilities of many "upright" citizens.

The population could also not avoid witnessing the mass deportations, which began in September 1941. In some places, the deportees were marched through the streets to the assembly point, as in the case of Frankfurt am Main. In Bielefeld, there was public support for vacating the town of its

Jewish inhabitants, with some people only objecting to the inclusion of such-and-such person they personally knew, or in Berlin, to the degrading manner the deportation was carried out in one particular raid. In Goettingen, when news spread of an anticipated raid against local Jews, government agencies were flooded with petitions asking for allotment of the soon-to-be vacated apartments.[22]

As to the fate of the deportees, although not openly acknowledged and advertised by the authorities, the mass killings were public knowledge in Germany. Concrete details were often lacking, but everyone was cognizant that dire things were happening to the Jews who were being deported to unknown destinations in the east. Soldiers home on leave told of mass shootings in specially designated camps; railway workers related stories of train after train, packed with several thousand persons, moving inside the camps, and leaving empty. Leaflets dropped by Allied planes over German cities, during 1943–1944, gave details on the extermination of Jews in some camps. Ironically, in spite of these reports and the continuous deadly anti-Jewish propaganda throughout the war years, the Nazi leadership stopped short of disclosing to the German population the true nature of the Final Solution. SS chief Himmler's words before top SS officers in Posen in October 1943, in which he described the Holocaust as a "never to be written glorious page of our history," whose secret it was better to carry to the grave, coupled with the very secrecy of the Final Solution, clearly demonstrate that the Nazi leadership felt unsure whether it could rely on popular backing for its extermination policy.[23]

The mass killings of the Jews did provoke a different kind of anxiety – of the retaliatory measures to be expected should Germany lose the war. These fears became concretized in people's minds, especially after the massive German defeat in the Stalingrad battle, when thousands of German soldiers were taken prisoner by the Russians, and the incessant and mounting air bombings of German cities. As articulated by Lutheran Bishop Theophil Wurm, at the end of 1943, "the German people deeply feel the sufferings caused by enemy air bombings, which it has to bear, to be a retribution for what has been done to the Jews." Paradoxically, the sight of their cities flattened and torched by Allied planes confirmed in the minds of many Germans the antisemitic charge of a worldwide Jewish conspiracy, which was the real power behind the Allies, and that these bombings were nothing but Jewish reprisals against the extermination of their brethren.[24]

c) ACADEMIA AND CORPORATIONS

As noted earlier, social scientists agree that individuals will rarely display disapproval of the ruling group's policies, especially in a dictatorial
regime, unless their protest has the backing of one or several of society's
institutionalized bodies – and such institutional protests were not heard
in Nazi Germany with regard to the Jews. In Western democracies, public figures including lawyers and judges are the mainstay of individual
rights vis-a-vis the governing powers. In Nazi Germany, people such as
these abdicated their duty to uphold these rights and toed the regime's
line. Members of the bar, moreover, were in the forefront among those
who administered the anti-Jewish measures, and were even to be found
among commanders of the Einsatzgruppen killing units. Already before
the Nazi takeover, some jurists made no secret of their anti-Jewish prejudices.[25] April 1, 1933, barely two months after the Nazi takeover, state
ministries of justice suspended all Jewish judges, public prosecutors, and
district attorneys. This was followed a week later with the removal from
the civil service of all Jewish judges, and soon thereafter the removal of all
Jews from the bar.[26]

    As to the dispensing of justice by German jurists, the following ex-
amples, just a few of many, will suffice. A Hamburg court condemned a
Jewish male to six years in jail for having written love letters to his non-
Jewish female companion. In the court's opinion, the defendant's action allowed for no mitigation, since his behavior was a clear example of "Jewish
effrontery, Jewish contempt for German laws, Jewish lasciviousness, and
Jewish unscrupulousness." In 1937, another court condemned a Jewish male
for having spoken in the street to a girl, "clearly and immediately recogniz-
able as being of German blood"; this, the court added, in spite of the man's
knowledge of the current race laws, and "the unbending determination of the
German people to secure its future for all time by maintaining the purity of
its blood." Two years later, another Jewish male was sentenced to prison for
staring across the street at the fifteen-year-old "German blooded" Ilse S., "if
not importunately, then at least so as to attract notice." This mere glance, in
the eyes of the Frankfurt county court, represented "a grave lack of respect
for her sense of honor, . . . even if the defendant pursued no further intentions" with regard to that girl. In Nuremberg, a Jewish man was sentenced
to death in 1941, for maintaining a friendship with a non-Jewish woman,

although nothing sexual had occurred between them. The presiding judge, Dr. Oswald Rothaug, referred to the defendant as a "syphilitic Jew" and an "agent of world Jewry" who was responsible for the war. These unjustified harsh sentences should come as no surprise, in light of the oath taken by every new attorney: "I swear to remain loyal to Adolf Hitler, the leader of the German nation and people, and conscientiously to fulfill the duties of a German attorney."[27]

There is on record only one case of a judge refusing to bend to Nazi laws – Dr. Lothar Kreyssig, in Brandenburg. He was charged with numerous acts of "insubordination," such as departing early from a ceremony when a bust of Hitler was unveiled in a courthouse, and he was forced to retire from the bench. In the words of Benno Müller-Hill, in his study of German jurists during the Nazi period, Kreyssig's case shows that the worst a judge had to fear for noncompliance to Nazi justice was early retirement. However, "no matter how hard one searches for stout-hearted men among the judges of the Third Reich, for judges who refused to serve the regime from the bench, there remains a grand total of one: Dr. Lothar Kreyssig."[28] Clearly, Jews could look for no succor from German courts.

Nor could Jews expect consideration of their plight from German academic institutions. Martin Heidegger, head of the University of Freiburg and the most acclaimed philosopher at the time, joined the Nazi party in 1933, and exclaimed: "The Führer himself, and he alone, is the German reality of today, and of the future, and of its law." Professor Konrad Lorenz, known for his studies of animal behavior, also enlisted in the Nazi party. In 1940, he defended the euthanasia program of killing the mentally ill. Werner Sombart, the famed economist, also joined the Nazi party and called for rooting out the Jewish merchant mentality from Germany's economic life – whatever that meant.[29]

The medical field was also inundated with Nazi ideas. About half of all physicians joined the Nazi Physicians League, although the party did not insist on this. The prestigious Kaiser Wilhelm Society for the Advancement of Science, which specialized in genetics, advocated human evaluation based on blood and race, not culture and education. The institution's head, Dr. Otmar von Verschuer, requested and was granted permission to do research on prisoners at Auschwitz camp. Another institute professor, Kurt Hallervorden, researched the brain composition of child victims in the camps. The notorious Dr. Josef Mengele was an assistant professor at the Kaiser Wilhelm Institute under Verschuer, and in that capacity he selected victims at Auschwitz for the racial genetic studies of his mentors in Berlin.[30]

The corporate world also took advantage of the opportunities offered by the dispossession of Jewish businesses and the availability of cheap slave labor. Banks and financial institutions rushed to compete for a grab of confiscated Jewish holdings. Corporate executives sought and received unlimited slave laborers from the conquered territories and from the concentration camps. Krupp, Siemens, I.G. Farben, Telefunken, and Daimler-Benz are a few of the companies that used slave laborers from nearby concentration camps (such as Auschwitz, Dachau, Buchenwald, and Mauthausen). Not a few companies even set up plants within the camps.[31]

d) The Churches

With all major civil and economic institutions toeing the official line, the only bulwark left facing the Nazis were the churches. Both Protestant and Catholic churches were the only non-Nazified bodies still functioning in Germany, and their influence would have been considerable on the formation of public opinion, had they been willing to counter the Nazi propaganda. Paradoxically as it may sound, even in the police state that was Nazi Germany, widespread public dissent against a particular policy could lead the authorities to compromise and even retract, in the face of a strong opposition. Such as when in October 1934, the regime's hand was forced on the issue of the non-interference of the State in Church affairs. Protestant Bishop Hans Meiser had been placed under house arrest and dismissed from his post, in Munich, for refusing to toe the line of the official Church hierarchy headed by the Reich-appointed Bishop Ludwig Müller. The massive emotional demonstrations that followed this action convinced Nazi authorities to forego an open confrontation with the churches. Meiser was reinstated, after Hitler personally intervened and reassured worried churchgoers of the neutrality of the Nazi party and State in Church affairs. In the words of historian Kershaw, "it was a spectacular display of what popular protest could achieve even in the restrictive conditions of a repressive police state." At the same time, one ought to keep in mind that the same people who vehemently protested the State's interference in Church affairs did not by the same token question their loyalty to the Führer and the Nazi state. The protest was not against the system, but a particularly unattractive sideline issue, one that was not of major importance to the Nazis, such as was the Jewish issue, which sadly did not prompt a similar public protest by the churches.[32]

Seven years later, in the summer of 1941, in the midst of the war, two more incidents arose that strained relations between the Nazi state and the Catholic Church. Here too, the Nazi leadership gave in to Church demands in the face of public outcries that threatened to undermine the confidence of the Catholic population (estimated at a third) in the Nazi leadership.

The first of these was over the attempt by local Nazis to remove crucifixes from Catholic schools in Bavaria and substitute religious prayer with Nazi slogans and songs. As public protest mounted, the situation threatened to become chaotic, and in October 1941, the Nazi leadership ordered the reinstatement of the crosses. This came about after the authorities learned of a strongly worded pastoral letter by Cardinal Michael Faulhaber, archbishop of Munich, to be read from the pulpit several weeks later, in which he implied that the crucifix decree might affect the morale of Wehrmacht soldiers currently engaged in the war against the Soviet Union. This was followed with demonstrations by angry crowds in various towns and villages. The government retracted, censured the local Nazi leader, and ordered the reinstatement of the crucifixes and the release of the 59 priests arrested for protesting against Nazi interference in Church matters. It was a total defeat for the Nazi party, and a triumph of popular opinion.[33]

The Catholic Church also came out victorious on the euthanasia issue, after Bishop Clement von Galen of Münster, in a celebrated sermon on August 3, 1941, denounced in strong terms the "murder" of the mentally sick, a government-sanctioned policy that had already claimed some 70,000 lives. Not willing to embroil himself in an open conflict with the Catholic Church – at least not while in the midst of an ever-widening war – Hitler ordered a halt of the euthanasia program for the duration of the war. In reality, it was not fully stopped, but continued at a lower and more secretive scale. Still, in the words of historian Kershaw, "It was a victory without parallel during the Third Reich for the force of popular opinion in a matter which lay not far from the heart of the Nazi racial-eugenic creed of Social Darwinism." This, together with the crucifix incident, convinced the Nazis to stay clear of any further clashes with the churches, at least for the duration of the war.[34]

These actions by the churches stand in sharp contrast to their thunderous silence on the antisemitic measures of the Nazi state against Jews, and even Jewish converts to Christianity. It is worth reiterating that the teaching of racism, so central to Nazi ideology, was irreconcilable with the basic Christian tenets of the equality of all men before God. One would therefore have expected that this direct challenge to basic Church beliefs would have met with an unequivocal response by the Church leaders. But here too, the record is dismal, especially with regard to the Jewish issue.[35]

The churches in Germany were still blinded by a rejectionist theology of Judaism and the Jewish people and generally followed the traditional theological anti-Jewish bias, coupled with newer accusations: that the Jews were somehow responsible for the liberal spirit, too liberal, to many eyes, in many sectors of public life in the post-World War One Weimar Republic, which many people believed benefitted mostly the Jews. A significant part of the Protestant churches in Germany, known as the German Christians, not only condoned but even gave enthusiastic blessings to the new racist teaching emanating from Nazi spokesmen.[36] The Church's public silence in the early war years at the deportation of the Jews, when at the same time they were exposing the horrors of the euthanasia program, prevented any possibility of antisemitism from becoming a public issue and a nuisance to the Nazi leadership, as happened in the euthanasia example.[37]

Some clerics were not beyond aping the virulent antisemitism of the Nazis and quoting passages from the New Testament that spoke disparagingly of Jews who refused to acknowledge Jesus as the Messiah. A spate of theologians followed suit to approve the Nazi anti-Jewish measures. Gerhard Kittel, a distinguished New Testament scholar and a leading authority on ancient Judaism, joined the Nazi party and favored laws forbidding marriages between Jews and Gentiles. He maintained that a Jewish convert to Christianity still remained a Jew after his baptism. He may now have become a Christian brother, Kittel added with tongue in cheek, though never a German brother. Paul Althaus, another leading theologian (Lutheran Church), stated that the German people had come to recognize the threat to them from the emancipated Jews in their midst and had taken appropriate steps to combat it by removing Jews and half-Jews from office. In 1934, Althaus played a leading role in the formulation of a declaration that stated: "We as believing Christians thank the Lord God that He has in our need presented us with the Führer as pious and faithful overlord, and that in the National Socialist political system he will provide us with good government, a government with discipline and honor. We therefore acknowledge before God our responsibility in our profession and calling to assist the work of the Führer."[38] Bishop Otto Dibelius, the post-World War Two General Superintendent in the Lutheran Church, admitted in 1933 to being an antisemite, and stated in that year: "One cannot fail to appreciate that in all of the corrosive manifestations of modern civilization Jewry plays a leading role."[39] Other Protestant church leaders thanked the Lord for having sent to them Hitler, "a divine gift and miracle," and gladly took the oath of allegiance to him. Practically all Protestant denominations, with the notable exceptions of the Confessing Church (*Bekennende Kirche*) and the Jehovah's Witnesses, synchronized much of their teachings with the spirit emanating from Hitler's office.[40]

Dietrich Bonhoeffer, a leading figure in the Confessing Church (which opposed the Nazi idea of the primacy of race), was a man of great integrity and moral courage and a strenuous opponent of the Nazis, who eventually put him to death in April 1945; he wrote in 1933 condescendingly about the new anti-Jewish laws. He began by describing the Jews as living "under a curse" since their rejection of Jesus, for which they undergo sufferings – a divine punishment that is to last until the Jews confess their "sin" and join the Church in acknowledging Jesus as their divine Messiah. It was not the Church's business, he continued, to either praise or to censure the new antisemitic laws, he affirmed. Since the State was part of God's order of preservation in a godless world, it was justified in adopting new measures when dealing with the Jewish Question, and the Church should not meddle and criticize these actions from some humanitarian standpoint. Taking a step backwards, he added that the Church was obliged to extend help to the victims of this new persecution by the State and to oppose the State's interference in Church affairs, and especially her treatment of baptized members, for the Jewish problem was not the same for the Church as it was for the State. Such was the mellow opposition to the new antisemitism of Nazi Germany by a staunch opponent of Nazism.[41]

Martin Niemöller, another leading Confessing Church pastor, also joined the chorus of Jewish denunciations. At first a supporter of Nazism, he then became a staunch opponent and spent many years in a concentration camp. He has since become a symbol of moral and religious courage in the face of tyranny. But he too had less kind words to say about the Jews. In 1935, Niemöller stated (as did his colleague Bonhoeffer) that he had doubts whether the Church had the right to sit in judgment over the State in regard to its treatment of the Jews, for the State was every bit as much part of the divine economy as was the Church.[42] In a sermon that same year, Niemöller used sharper words, stating that a dark mystery enveloped the sinister history of the Jews, which can neither live nor die, because it is under a curse that forbids it to do either. "We speak of the 'Eternal Jew' and conjure up the picture of a restless wanderer who has no home and who cannot find peace, and we see a highly gifted people which produces idea after idea for the benefit of the world, but whatever it takes up changes into poison, and all that it ever reaps is contempt and hatred." However, Niemöller added, we have no license empowering us to supplement God's curse with our hatred. Even Cain received God's mark, that no one may kill him; and Jesus's command "Love your enemies!" leaves no room for exceptions. "We cannot, however, alter the fact that until the end of time the Jewish people must go its own way under the burden which the Word of Judgment of Jesus has laid upon it. . . . The Jews have caused the crucifixion of God's Christ. . . . They bear the curse, and, because they rejected the forgiveness, they drag about with them as a fearsome burden the unforgiving blood-guilt of their fathers."[43] At his trial in 1938 before a Nazi court, for public criticism of Nazi beliefs, Niemöller reiterated his anti-Jewish bias, stating that he found it an unpleasant fact that God has seen fit to reveal Himself in the Jew, Jesus of Nazareth. "This painful and grievous stumbling-block has to be accepted for the sake of the Gospel," Niemöller regrettably added.[44]

The Catholic Church, originally wary of the Nazi party, rushed to grant recognition to the new dictatorship, through its Concordat with Hitler in July 1933, the first significant international recognition of its kind. Though more constrained than many Protestant ministers in aping Nazi racist teachings, not a few Catholic prelates continued to drum the ancient theological anti-Jewish animus. Munich archbishop Michael von Faulhaber, who did not hide his opposition to Nazi ideas, claimed that the Jews were not the progenitors of the Bible, but were opposed to it. Interestingly, one-fourth of the SS were practicing Catholics, yet none were denied communion for their murderous acts, nor for that matter were concentration camp guards and members of other units involved in the killing of Jews and other "undesirables."[45] With all the anti-Jewish rhetoric emanating from church pulpits, it is no wonder that Martin Sasse, the Bishop of Thuringia, exulted in the November 1938 Kristallnacht pogrom, since the burning of the synagogues was, in his words, the crowning moment of the Führer's divinely blessed fight for the complete emancipation of the German people, the Jewish race being the fundamental and supreme enemy of Christianity. None of the Catholic and Evangelical Church leadership came out openly against that government-instigated pogrom.[46]

Among the thousands of clergy of all the churches in Germany, there are only several known cases of public denunciation of the Nazi anti-Jewish measures. These include the village pastor Julius von Jan, of Oberlenningen in Württemberg, who condemned the Kristallnacht pogrom of November 1938 from the pulpit, and the Catholic prelate Bernhard Lichtenberg in Berlin who condemned the Nazi persecution of Jews – and both were made to suffer the consequences of their courageous stand. Their story is described in greater length in chapter 8.[47]

Pastor Hermann Hesse, another lone protester, in a June 1943 sermon, was also forthright in condemning the persecution of the Jews. "As Christians we can no longer tolerate the silence of the Church in Germany over the persecution of the Jews . . . . Every non-Aryan, whether Jewish or Christian by faith, is today in Germany the one who has fallen among thieves. The Church has to confess that as the true Israel in Guilt and in Promise she is inextricably bound up with Jewry. . . . When Israel is assailed, she and her Lord Jesus Christ Himself are also attacked." Hesse was jailed and, by order of Himmler, sent to Dachau camp.[48] These constitute isolated, very isolated, voices in an otherwise moral desert. After the war, Martin Niemöller admitted: "One of the most glorious opportunities to make proof of Christian profession through Christian action was, taken as a whole, missed and unexercised. . . . We ought to have recognized the Lord Jesus in the brother who suffered and was persecuted despite him being a communist or a Jew."[49]

Even Jewish converts to Christianity fared badly in the hands of Christian theologians. A German Christian mass rally in Berlin proclaimed: "Those of Jewish descent can no longer be tolerated in the pulpit and in ecclesiastical office. . . . We will allow no person of alien blood, and especially no Jew, to assume the office of elder or parochial church counselor." Priests bowed to pressure from the congregation, who did not wish to hold services, let alone be seated, next to Jewish converts.[50]

Since many earnest Christians remained captive to the Church's age-old anti-Jewish diatribe, they failed to appreciate the dangerous nature, not only to Jews, but to themselves, of the Nazi racial teaching. As admitted by Lutheran Church head Theophil Wurm, who before the war upheld the opinion trumpeted by others on "the disintegrating effect of Jewry in the spheres of religion, morals, literature, economics and politics": "A spell was laid upon us, and it was as if our mouths were kept shut by an invisible power."[51]

We will never know whether a widespread and decisive outcry, spearheaded by religious leaders, may have convinced the Nazi leadership that there were limits to what the people, the great majority of whom subscribed to the Christian faith, would tolerate. It might have averted, or severely limited, the subsequent massacre of millions. In the words of Niemöller, spoken in 1970: "There was not one single voice to be heard affirming in public that murder is murder."[52] Here, too, the Jews could look for no succor from the Christian churches.

e) The Rosenstrasse Protest

The only public demonstration against the deportation of Jews, not spearheaded by social or religious leaders but spontaneously organized by angry citizens, occurred in late February 1943; it was launched by non-Jewish wives of Jewish men arrested during the massive Factory Action at that same time. Known as the Rosenstrasse protest, after the site where most of the Jewish men were interned (in a building that previously served the Jewish community in Berlin) before being processed to the camps, it included hundreds of women who gathered every day and, facing armed SS soldiers, shouted: "Give us our husbands back!" Soldiers threatened to open fire on the defenseless women if they did not clear the streets. As the days wore on, the Nazi leadership, worried that such an open display of anti-government protests might prompt others to take to the streets to likewise protest other issues in the midst of the beginning of a losing war (one month after the terrible debacle of German arms in Stalingrad), and not wishing to open fire on "Aryan" women in the streets of Berlin, it decided to capitulate and release the imprisoned Jewish spouses, a total of some 2,000 men, including 120 who had already been deported to Auschwitz and were promptly released. Jewish spouses were henceforth not harmed, and only in late 1944, with defeat staring it in the eyes, did the Nazi leadership again move to deport the Jewish spouses to the camps. In the interval, the endangered Jews had had ample time to plan their escape by hiding with friendly non-Jewish persons.

The Rosenstrasse incident is a clear example where collective action proved effective in staying the government's hand on a matter of crucial importance to its racial policy. In the words of historian Nathan Stoltzfus, "nothing demonstrates the sturrborn power of the private sphere in the face of Nazi terror better than Jewish-Gentile marriages. A dictatorship committed to the complete biological extinction of the Jewish people was compelled to stop short of a boundary drawn by the traditional regard for marriage."[53] The success of this and previous Church-sponsored protests was also due in large measure to the fact that the protests were overt, broad-based, and non-violent, and avoided the appearances of questioning the Nazi regime's legitimacy. It was, furthermore, perhaps easier for the Nazis to yield to the protesting women, since they did not, at least openly, condemn the antisemitic policy as such, but just wanted their loved ones back, and this struck a chord in the heart of many people, even among staunch Nazis. In the words of a Gestapo agent who observed the protesting women: "This is German loyalty." Still, there is no telling how the Nazis would have reacted to a broad-based public protest against the deportation of Jews – as no such protest ever took place.[54] In Nazi Germany, every significant institution upheld a negative image of the Jews, and this ruled out any public effort on their behalf. In the words of Kershaw, "the road to Auschwitz was built by hate, but paved with indifference." While "dynamic" Jew-haters probably formed only a small percentage of the population, "active" friends of the Jews formed an even smaller proportion.[55]

* * *

The previous somewhat lengthy narrative of the poisonous antisemitism that engulfed such a wide spectrum of German public life was necessary in order to underline the significance of the few who stood out in defiance of a government-orchestrated and publicly supported antisemitic agenda by acting to defend Jews – done at considerable risks to the rescuers. Jews could only hope for help from isolated cases of individual Germans of goodwill, prepared to take up the cause of humanity on a person-to-person basis, without the support and in isolation of any religious or secular group backing. The rescuers described in this book drew sustenance neither from their civic leaders (who were either Nazis or Nazi appointees) nor from their religious ones, who were blinded to the events of their day by a centuries-old theological antisemitism, with the sole exception of a breakaway church fellowship known as the Confessing Church. It was a case of every individual rescuer versus the society as a whole. Citizens of a country headed by a virulent antisemitic regime, and the moral abnegation of the country's mainstream civic and religious leadership – the rescuers decided to swim against the stream, so to speak. Their sole support came from within themselves, from the inner core of their souls and being. It was, indeed, a lonely struggle, of a relatively small group of courageous people against all others – Nazis and bystanders alike.

German rescuers were to be counted from all walks of life. Many were prompted to help due to an earlier friendship or close acquaintance with the rescued party, originating in a business or work relationship, before or during the war years. An additional factor was the sight of suffering of an unprecedented scale to which the rescuer became witness and the realization that he, or she, could do something about it. Many rescuers were also at heart opposed to the Nazi philosophy, or if not fully then at least to the evolving brutalization correlated with that philosophy, and by helping Jews they found an outlet for their revulsion of these horrific methods. Facing them was a regimented society and a brutal totalitarian regime, not hesitant to punish severely those that tried to subvert their antisemitic agenda. I have, therefore, subtitled this book: Individuals Versus the System.

A few final words on the methodology of this study. Aside from this opening chapter (which draws heavily from scholarly sources), further references of individual rescuers are based on files at Yad Vashem (Israel's national Holocaust museum and archives center) for those honored with the title of Righteous Among the Nations – from Germany and Austria, but also for rescuers in both countries who were not necessarily awarded the Righteous title, for reasons explained in Appendix A. Yad Vashem's honoring of non-Jewish rescuers of Jews was launched in 1963, with the creation of a public commission, mandated to set criteria and conditions for the Righteous title. But already a year earlier, starting May 1, 1962, trees were begun to be planted in Yad Vashem's Avenue of the Righteous by such rescuers from various European countries upon their visit to Israel. The records of these rescue stories are mostly in the form of personal eyewitness testimonies by the rescued party, as well personal accounts by rescuers and other persons, official documentations, and scholarly and journalistic sources.

Our study does not provide clues as to how many petitions and appeals of help by Jews to non-Jewish acquaintances were recorded or disclosed in the post-war period, and otherwise how many Germans, inside the country and in the occupied countries, responded to these appeals or declined help to Jews when challenged to do so. We are consequently presently left with bowing our heads in gratitude to those relatively few, but significant, recorded stories of persons who took up the human challenge of helping one, several, or more Jews to survive, and thus upholding the image of man as a morally sensitive being.

CHAPTER 2

Friends, Acquaintances and Various Relationships

* * *

BY THE TIME MASS DEPORTATIONS to Poland began in October 1941, most remaining Jews in Germany had already for some time seen the handwriting on the wall, and many had already made plans to go into hiding – "to submerge," or *U-Boot* (submarine), in the coded language of the time. Some still hesitated, and only after receiving the dreaded summons to report for deportation did they summon the courage to do whatever necessary and possible to avoid reporting. Statistically speaking, of the approximately 150,000 Jews remaining in Germany in October 1941, some 12,000 to 15,000 Jews (8%–10%) opted for an illegal way of existence, mostly in hiding. Figures are not available on the number of Jews who managed to outwit and elude the Gestapo, although many did not make it. About 75% were seized by the Gestapo, according to a study by Avraham Seligmann. In Berlin alone, some 5,000 Jews sought hiding places. Of these, about 1,400 survived; the rest, or 75%, were caught by the Gestapo either on the street or after being informed on. In other words, the few thousand German Jews who lived to witness the fall of the Nazi regime in 1945 represent only a fraction of the many more who chose to go into hiding. But these figures are at best sketchy, and it is not clear whether they include the thousands of baptized Jews and semi-Jews (*Mischlinge*). The estimated 5,000 Jews in Berlin who chose a clandestine existence had to be often on the move – making sure to be one step ahead of the police. Some people, to distract the Gestapo, left behind suicide notes. All together, some 3,500–4,000 Berlin Jews (25–28%) survived while the rest were apprehended and deported.[1]

Apart from a few exceptions (such as Pastor Grüber's Bureau and the Confessing Church, to be discussed later, who both initially aided mostly baptized Jews), no organized non-Jewish rescue networks existed to help Jews find safe havens. For most Jews, it was everyone for himself. Most hiders in Seligmann's study spent the entire period of hiding in at least two main places, moving from one to another for added security. Others found it necessary to change hiding places more frequently. The first refuge was generally with a friend or acquaintance or with persons of mixed marriage (who were temporarily exempt from deportation) whom they knew from before. However, of those hiding inside Germany, only an estimated one quarter succeeded in remaining with one main rescuer throughout most of the hiding period, or with someone to whom they could always return. In many instances, when the first hiding place no longer proved safe, the initial rescuers themselves helped find a new hiding place for their fleeing Jewish wards.

An additional, though not surprising, revelation is that most persons on the run preferred the big cities, where detection was more difficult, since people in large cities do not usually know each other as intimately as in smaller localities. A hiding place could be an unused back room, an airless attic, a cold dark cellar, a special shelter beneath a staircase where air was in short supply and which was too small to permit anything more than lying down, or a bombed-out building (especially after the start of the large-scale carpet bombings of German cities in 1943). Some of those in hiding did not emerge for long periods, fearing detection by neighbors and occasional passers-by, while others, who were passing as "Aryans," were compelled to leave early every morning, as though going to work, returning only late in the evening, and spend the intervening hours wandering about the streets and parks or in cinemas, and anxiously taking precautions not to be detected. For those in hiding throughout the day and night, a special effort was required to maintain personal hygiene and to remove rubbish without arousing attention.[2]

During the saturation bombing of German cities, when many personal archival data were destroyed, new papers with false information could be obtained with relative ease. Saying that one had come from a bombed area made it easier to obtain official papers, including travel permits to places seemingly safer from aerial bombings, and this facilitated the movement of Jews on the run. Thus, as the war progressed, the number of hiding places in smaller towns and villages increased. On the other hand, persons of military age, passing as non-Jews, had to carry personal documents (mostly false) stating the reason for their exemption from military service. Without such papers, they stood the risk of arrest and being shot, not for passing as Jews, but for desertion from the army![3]

The majority of those who chose to hide were, as expected, of a relatively younger age, not too elderly – between 20 and 50. Surprisingly, 28% of the married couples in hiding were in Seligmann's study persons in a mixed marriage, especially those targeted for deportation in the latter part of 1944, as the curtain was coming down on the Third Reich. Also, 44% of those in hiding managed to obtain false papers with an assumed non-Jewish-sounding name – so as to be on the safe side as much as possible, even while originally contemplating going into hiding, or stepping out of their hiding places for brief sojourns to meet with friends.[4] As for those in charge of the hidden Jews, 27% of rescuers in Seligmann's study were pensioners or housewives (sometimes with husbands, or a grownup son, away in the army). In most instances the rescuers did not belong to any organization, save the few who were affiliated with the Protestant pastors in the Confessing Church (the sole church organization that stood back from supporting the Nazi regime).[5] Of interest, many of the rescuers had belonged to left-wing parties before the war. Also of note is the smaller number of rescuers who once supported right-wing parties but who had become increasingly appalled by their government's actions as the war progressed (and, especially, as the German army was steadily losing ground). Such latter rescuers comprised more than a third of the second main rescuers – persons who offered shelter to Jews after they found it necessary to leave their original hiding place.[6]

We will now illustrate rescue stories that originated in a previous reciprocal relationship – acquaintance or friendship. Not surprisingly, many of the sheltered Jews in Germany knew their rescuers from before the Nazi period, or at least before the start of the deportations in late 1941. Some even entertained close and friendly relations since bygone days, when none imagined that a day would come when one side would desperately seek the help of the other in order to survive.

A) CASUAL ACQUAINTANCES

Some of these links had as background a mere casual relationship, or so it seems from the record, such as in the case of the Jewish Meta Sawady and the non-Jewish Emma Richter, who had known each other since 1924, when both worked as saleswomen in a Berlin store. During the massive Factory Action of February 1943, when Jews doing forced labor in vital installations (and hence felt momentarily protected from deportation) were suddenly rounded up, Mrs. Sawady made her escape and headed for Richter's small apartment, where she stayed for six months. Then, due to the danger of detection, Emma moved her at night to a home in Volten, outside of Berlin, which she visited every day (over an hour train ride), bringing food and provisions and keeping Meta's spirit high through the constant air raids, and sometimes staying overnight with her. Evidently, Richter's help to Mrs. Sawady became known to some people, although they did not know the precise location of Mrs. Sawady's hiding place, as Richter began receiving anonymous threatening letters and phone calls, headed with the captions such as "On the Disgrace List with Jews Lovers," or "We are watching you." Sure enough, Emma Richter was called in by the police for questioning but denied all allegations. The two women made it safely through the war, and they boarded together again and even jointly operated a tobacco shop.[7]

Another work colleague setting is the story of Erna Puterman, child of a Jewish orthodox family, and the non-Jewish Frieda Adam. Both women met in a Berlin factory where they did knitting and sewing assignments. In 1940, Erna was forced to switch to a different work site – the Siemens Company. When Erna was obligated to don the Yellow Star sign, in September 1941, Frieda Adam turned up at Erna's place and walked with her on the street in demonstration against the Star edict. Later, in November 1942, when Erna's mother was picked up during a raid orchestrated by the Austrian Nazi Alois Brunner and deported to Auschwitz, Erna took flight and, appearing at Adam's house, she naively asked whether she should also willingly report for deportation. Frieda Adam's response was to invite Erna to stay with her for shelter (she had three children of her own), stating to the frightened Erna, "If there's food enough for 4 persons, then there is enough also for six" (including Erna's brother). Frieda's three children were told that Erna was a refugee from a bombed-out place. Frieda's soldier husband did not take kindly to his wife's guests, and harassed her about it. In order not to cause additional tension, Frieda's wards left for other temporary sheltering arrangements in the large metropolitan Berlin area.[8]

A similar casual acquaintance that later blossomed into a rescue operation is the story of Gerhard Hagemann, who worked as an economic affairs aide for the Catholic diocese of Berlin, which required him to make long daily journeys by train from his hometown in Havelberg to Berlin, a distance of some 150 kilometers. At times, he stayed overnight in Berlin, where he met Jacob Kahane during his business rounds. As Nazi anti-Jewish measures increased, Gerhard repeatedly assured Jacob that in case of need, he would be prepared to help. The Kahanes managed on their own until 1943, when Jacob Kahane and wife Lina fled from Berlin (their daughter Sonja-Jenny was in hiding and a son, Max, had earlier left for France, where he was incarcerated in Gurs camp). Hagemann found for the two Kahanes a room in a nearby place, which he rented under his name. There the two Kahanes and their daughter Jenny stayed for two years. Thanks to his contacts with a municipality clerk, Hagemann acquired for them false credentials, including food rations coupons, under assumed names. While risking his own safety in case of discovery by continuously assisting the Kahane family, two of Hagemann's sons were away in the army, fighting Germany's war – a curious and significant detail also present in other narratives where a close relative of a rescuer family (son or sibling) was a soldier in the German army.[9]

In another Berlin story, Angela Pohl and the Jewish Erna Niedermayer had been friends at school, which lasted through 1936, when Erna left for the U.S.A. Then, in November 1942, Erna's step-sister, Elsa Klein, who had also known Angela, appeared at Angela's Berlin home and asked to be hidden with her husband Artur for only a few weeks, since they had made plans to flee to Sweden across the Baltic Sea. Angela Pohl at the time was living alone with her mother Agneta in Rahnsdorf, an East Berlin suburb, which was close to a forest. Mother and daughter set aside a room for the Klein couple. Later, two more of Klein's relatives and a two-year-old son were added. All sheltered persons hoped to make good their escape to Sweden, but this plan proved impractical and had to be abandoned. The five hidden persons were now stuck in Pohl's home. Every morning, they would leave for downtown Berlin, ostensibly on their way to work, trying all sorts of schemes to pass the working hours unobserved, before heading back to Pohl's home. At times, they spent evenings with city friends. They also stayed away on Sundays to avoid meeting people who might drop in for a visit. Luckily for the Klein family, they all survived the Nazi period undetected, thanks to Angela Pohl and her mother.[10]

Similar stories abound, of helpers who knew their wards from before the period of hiding, such as Mina Kuttelwascher who hid Erna Kohn in her Vienna home, while her husband Otto was in the *Luftwaffe* (German Air Force). Erna remained hidden for three years. Mina had also offered to shelter Erna's sister and mother, but they declined and were eventually deported to the camps. In Vienna as well, postal clerk Konstantin Müller helped the Jewish Julia Schwarzstein (whom he married after the war) and her friend Franzi Weiss, who for a time was an English-language private teacher to Konstantin before the Nazi takeover of Vienna. Together with his mother, Anna, he sheltered the forlorn Julia in his mother's home and other places from 1941 to 1944. In October of that year, Julia was arrested while making a phone call outside her hiding place but managed to escape and return to the Müller home, where she remained hidden until Vienna's liberation by the Russians in April 1945. When she reappeared in Anna Müller's home, her son, Konstantin, was no longer there, having been drafted for military duties. Further to the north, in Berlin, Charlotte Weiler admitted Bernhard and Hedwig Senger into her Berlin flat after the two were evicted from their home in March 1943 – and she cared for them until they had acquired false credentials with which they were able to leave for a different location, far from Berlin where too many persons knew them from before (they had owned a successful linen wholesale store).[11]

Even persons who knew each other only casually, such as neighbors, could later become involved in their rescue. Thus Walter Czok sheltered his neighbors Josef and Emilie Stappler in his Vienna flat from 1941 onwards. The interesting narrative about Czok is that not only was he a member of the Nazi party, but he also wore the uniform of a Stormtrooper (SA). Czok is reported to have helped several other Jews in distress.[12] Similarly, Heinz and Diana Brieger in Berlin, who in March 1943, desperate at the prospect of deportation, at first contemplated suicide, were fortunate to be offered shelter by Valeska Buchholz in an annex of the porter lodge in a block of apartments over which her husband served as caretaker. Years earlier, the Briegers had been neighbors of Valeska Buchholz in a different section of the city. As in some other stories, her husband was away in the army during the period of the sheltering of the Jewish Briegers.[13]

The fact that a husband or son could serve in the German army while their loved ones were sheltering Jews raises interesting questions about the

motivations of these rescuers. In such cases there could not have been otherwise than a combination of two important reasons: a previous link with
the person needing help combined with a strong humanitarian instinct
that was triggered into action when persons they had known from before
(even if only casually) stood in danger of their lives by the same regime
in whose military the rescuers' loved ones served. The significance of the
context of these unusual rescue stories cannot be overstated.

Our final story in this section, another of many similar examples, takes
us to Elisabeth Jacoby, born 1923, who lived in Berlin with her parents,
Bruno and Ella, and her elder brother by two years, Hans Martin. Her father
was a freelance journalist for the *Berliner Tageblatt* and had also served in
the German army during World War I and was awarded the Iron Cross, first
class. In February 1943, Elisabeth and brother Hans Martin returned home
after their day's forced labor assignment at the Siemens factory, only to find
their apartment sealed. The parents had fallen victim to the Factory Action
of that month. As Elisabeth learned after the war, they were first deported
to Theresienstadt camp, thence to a field near Riga, Latvia, where they were
shot with other Jews. With nowhere else to head, Elisabeth and her brother
first found shelter in a home of a former nanny. When her house was bombed,
the two left and slept in empty cellars or bombed-out houses. Brother Hans
Martin was arrested that same month and deported to Auschwitz, never to
return. Elisabeth was still a bit luckier as she walked the streets aimlessly
("during the day I kept on walking and walking as best I could"), and spent
nights sitting on a toilet seat at the Bahnhof-Zoo train station.

On one of her street forays, she suddenly heard someone calling her.
"Lilo, Lilo (that was the name my friends called me), let me talk to you." It
was Eva Cassirer, a former high school classmate – the daughter of Hannah
Sotscheck and husband Alfred Cassirer, a Jew. The two had divorced, and
Alfred died in 1932. There was no time for a lengthy conversation on a busy
Berlin street, as one had to be constantly on the move. So Eva quickly invited
Elisabeth to come to her house in the evening; perhaps she and her mother
could help her. Elisabeth hedged. "I knew Eva as the girl in school who was
driven to and from the Bismarck Lyceum in a chauffeured car," Elisabeth
recalled. "She was only an acquaintance, not a friend. Would her mother take
the risk of bringing me in their house? I still remember walking up to that
house on a cold night; my thoughts were filled with apprehension and with
hope." Mrs. Sotscheck met her at the door and brought her in, and Charlotte

stayed there until liberation – over two years. She was given new false papers, under the name of Liselote Lehmann, supposedly an art student. She lived openly in the house with her new identity, and was explained as being a domestic maid in order to make extra money, but officially she did not sleep there since, otherwise she would have had to register with the police. When guests dropped over, Elisabeth slipped out through the garden and stayed in the air raid shelter, near the house. "The bunker was small, the size of a large closet. I remember sitting on the steps, waiting and listening, but I also remember being young and wanting to live. When I thought it was safe, I quietly walked up the bunker stairs and looked at the center bedroom window on the third floor. Open shutters was our signal it was safe to return."

After the war, in 1947, she married Ernst Joseph, another Berlin Jewish survivor, whom she had sometimes met in Berlin when he too was looking for a safe hiding place with his parents. He too was lucky to find a sheltering place through a third party, the home of Paul and Leni Pissarius. There he stayed with his parents for over two years. Elisabeth recalls meeting Ernst at a prearranged place. "He told me he was hiding but did not disclose the place. I did not tell him of my hiding place." In those years, it was best not to know too much of someone else's secret life.[14]

b) Friends to the Rescue

Needless to emphasize, help to Jews in distress could also evolve, not due to a mere acquaintance, but out of a long-standing friendship between both sides. Although non-Jews were forbidden to fraternize with Jews under various edicts and especially the harsh 1935 Nuremberg Laws, not a few Germans maintained the close and friendly relations that they had cultivated with Jews in the pre-Nazi era. The case of the Wolffenstein sisters is typical of many in this category. Although converts to Christianity since birth, they now felt threatened by the Nazis who considered them "full Jews" since all their grandparents were born Jewish. Valerie and Andrea were at first helped by friends in the Confessing Church in Berlin. As danger mounted for the two sisters in May 1943, their close friend, Esther-Maria Seidel, invited the two to her home in Munich, to where she had recently moved with her husband Hans, who was working for the local BMW car company. In a coded letter, Esther wrote them that that two "doggies" could be brought over. The response was that only one of the "doggies," the one "with brown eyes," would come. It was Valerie. In consideration of the safety of her three small children, Esther arranged for Valerie to be sheltered by another woman. The two women met at a trolley station in Munich and took a stroll in a nearby park to discuss the matter, while Valerie anxiously waited for the outcome in a nearby train station. This woman, Mrs. Ammann, told Esther-Maria Seidel that as a young schoolgirl she had befriended a Jewish girl who, in the meantime, had emigrated and that she now missed her very much. A Jewish person in her home would allay this longing for her lost friend – certainly, a reckless idea to entertain at the height of the Nazi Final Solution of the Jews. A year later, in September 1944, Valerie left Mrs. Ammann's home and moved into Seidel's own home, which was now located near a distant lake, after the Seidels were forced to evacuate their city home due to the aerial bombings. False credentials were provided for Valerie. Many years after the war, Esther-Maria Seidel told that her longstanding friendship with Valerie Wolffenstein is what prompted her to extend help, in spite of the risks to herself. In her words: "During the 1930s it was often discussed how one should react [to the anti-Jewish measures]. I then said, I will not stand in the middle of Potsdam Place and scream 'I am against it,' thus sealing my doom. My responsibility as a mother of small children did not allow me this. Should it, however, ever involve my friend Vally, I was prepared to risk something."[15]

A friendly relationship similarly was a lucky break to a Jewish man and his son, who were already inside a concentration camp. Originally from Germany, Max Schloss was first deported to Latvia and was then shuffled through several camps. Surviving these rigors, in September 1944 he found himself again on German soil near Bochum, in a Buchenwald-subsidiary labor camp. Through a third party, Max was able to link up with his old friend Heinrich Wilmes, who lived in nearby Gelsenkirchen-Hessler. Happy at this rediscovery, Wilmes managed to smuggle vital foods inside the Bochum camp. Toward Christmas 1944, Wilmes passed word to Schloss that he would welcome him in his home if Schloss could make good his escape. Father and son, indeed, fled in March 1945, and walking at night, arrived at Wilmes' home and knocked at his door. As told by Schloss, "He opened the door, at first very cautiously, not recognizing us due to our physical condition, and also having company at the time; he took us in and introduced us as distant bombed-out cousins of his. He fed us and gave us clothing to wear and kept us with him for several weeks." Hosting bombed-out relatives was a common phenomenon in those days, so the Schlosses' presence did not arouse suspicion. Still, to be on the safe side, after a while Heinrich Wilmes moved the two to Essen, where they were hidden by his brother Theo. There they stayed until liberated by the US Army in April 1945.[16]

As for Ludwig Walz, he was by all accounts a bit idiosyncratic. Mayor of Ridelingen, near Biberach (Stuttgart region), in 1934, he was known for his profound religiosity and for his friendly relations with the nearby Jewish community in Buttenhausen (Wurttemburg) and especially with its religious head, Rabbi Naphtali Berlinger. Although Riedlingen was 35 kilometers away, during the early years of the Nazi period, Walz travelled in inclement weather to bring food and clothing for the whole congregation in Buttenhausen, entirely free of charge. Following Kristallnacht, in November 1938, he brought money for distribution among the Jews of Buttenhausen. Earlier, in 1934, Walz tore off the Nazi flag from the top of his church. When called up to the army, he refused. He continued to maintain close contacts with his Jewish friends, including Rabbi Berlinger, until the latter's deportation to Theresienstadt in 1942. Because he was considered a crank because of his fanatical belief in the Bible, the Nazis did not press for punitive measures, other than confiscating his property and taking away his three sons who were inducted in the Hitler Youth. One of his sons fell on the Russian front. For the remainder of the Nazi period, he lived in isolation and dire poverty. After the war, he was reinstated as mayor of Ridelingen. He reportedly had been greatly influenced by the writings of the nineteenth-century Jewish religious thinker, Samson Raphael Hirsch. A born Catholic, Walz went so far as to observing the Sabbath – for so he argued it was commanded in the Bible! In his writings, he saw himself a stranger in "Egypt" and a "wanderer in the wilderness." Walz's help to Jews originated in a combination of friendship and philosophical attraction toward Judaism, and came to fruition as a result of his friendship with a rabbi.[17]

Continuing with cases of help to Jews prompted by a pre-Nazi friendly relationship, we note the case of Maimi von Mirbach, an accomplished cellist, who invited her fellow Jewish musicians to rehearse in her Berlin home, to some of whom she extended temporary shelter. In one instance, she allowed a semi-Jewish piano student to give birth in her home in 1944. To those of her musical colleagues who were deported to Theresienstadt camp, she sent regular food packages. Mirbach related that once her mother, in 1936 or 1937, asked her in a serious vein: "Do you still practice music with non-Aryans?"

To which she facetiously responded: "Each week . . . a quartet with 2 'full Jews' and 1 'half Jew'; every two weeks, a piano trio with 2 full Jews."[18] In Berlin as well, Paula Hülle found an ingenious way to protect her Jewish friends from Nazi raids. Starting from Kristallnacht, in November 1938, she paid off a local Nazi neighborhood leader (*Ortsgruppenleiter*, later *Kreisleiter*) in return for his promise to forewarn her of any anticipated raids of Jews on her block. The bribe was in the form of a monthly payment, supplemented with various tobacco items from a shop she owned. Jutta Schaefer, one of the protected Jewish persons, testified that "on many occasions I would deliver those items to his home." Jutta also witnessed Paula handing the Nazi official rolls of money during his visits to Paula's home. "On one occasion, I overheard a conversation between Frau Hülle and Mr. Karl Bratzke [another Nazi section leader], during which she offered him any amount of money, if he would help Margot [another Jewish protégé of Hülle]." But he replied that since that woman did not live in the area of his jurisdiction, he could not guarantee her safety. In December 1943, Paula spirited several *Mischlinge* and Jews married to Aryan spouses, to a safe place in Silesia province, after being tipped off by her Nazi accomplice of an approaching raid. They stayed there until he informed Paula, in April 1944, that it was safe for these persons to return to Berlin.[19]

Still in Berlin, Erich Büngener was a longtime friend of Max Mandel, and owned a furniture store. Max was married to a non-Jewish woman who had converted to Judaism. In the eyes of the authorities, the couple's son Gert was considered a Mischling Grade A. In 1939, Max's wife left for Brazil to visit relatives, and as a first step to get her own family out of Germany. However, the war put an end to this plan, as Max could no longer leave. When the authorities discovered belatedly in 1944 that Max's wife had not returned, he, as a Jew but without his Aryan-born wife, stood in real danger of deportation. At this juncture, Erich offered to hide Max and son in a corner of the store display room, which was on the second floor of the same building where Erich and Erika Büngener lived with their two small children. Gert helped defray the additional expenses by selling personal items on the street. The Büngeners also sheltered in their home Max's sister Erna and husband Kurt Kantorowicz. When using the public air shelter, Erika introduced Erna as a distant friend who had come to help out with the children. Three of the four sheltered persons survived. As for Erna's husband Kurt, his luck on occasional street forays ran out, when he was caught by the Gestapo on his way to buy medicaments, and was deported.[20]

In Vienna, Rudi Kraus managed to leave for Iran in time, as a first step to set free his wife and daughter. However, the war intervened, and Regine Kraus with her daughter Lucia remained trapped behind. At this critical juncture, Rudi's friend, Reinhold Duschka, came to the rescue. He was a professional art craftsman and operated a two-room atelier on the fourth floor of a workshop building, where he stored brass and other metals that he needed for his work. There, in one of the rooms, he hid his friend's wife and daughter. Lucia recalls the tense moments of utter silence and immobility when customers visited the premises. At night, mother and daughter slept on the stone floor, covering themselves with blankets. During daytime, the two helped Reinhold with his work, and with the money earned, he was able to buy extra food on the black market. When air raids increased over the city, Duschka moved the two to a small summer house outside Vienna, telling neighbors they were relatives from Germany who had dropped in for an extended stay. He felt his friendship with the now distant Rudi Kraus obligated him to save the man's wife and daughter, a responsibility to which he dedicated himself meticulously and with miraculous success.[21]

Danger lurked for sheltered Jews and their rescuers mostly due to denunciations by hardline Nazis, plain antisemites, or persons hoping for a reward for fulfilling a "patriotic" duty by denouncing Jews in hiding. But danger could also come from another quarter, of quite a very personal nature, as in the following Berlin story. Walter Rieck's wife's jealousy almost brought calamity to the persons sheltered by him and her. Before the Nazi period Walter, a principal in a Berlin high school, had befriended Martin Deutschkron, who served as a teacher, and both were members of the Social Democratic party. Much later, when Martin's wife Ella and daughter Inge felt threatened with deportation (Martin had managed to leave for England on the eve of the war), the Riecks found a safe place for mother and daughter in a Potsdam suburb home. But then, as a result of Walter Rieck's infidelity (he was amorously linked with a younger woman), his wife, fuming with rage, swore revenge. One day, in January 1945, Walter was called in for questioning by the Gestapo and shown an anonymous letter accusing him of sheltering two Jewish women. Walter immediately recognized his wife's handwriting. Using his oratory skills to the fullest, he managed to convince the Gestapo agents of the nonsensical nature of this charge, as it originated in marital jealousy. The Gestapo, busy at the time, which was very late in the war, with more serious matters caused by the constant bombings of Berlin, shelved the case. In the meantime, Walter managed to tip off the Deutschkrons, and they hurriedly left their hiding place in the middle of the night and moved to a flat in Berlin belonging to Walter's friend, who happened to be out of town. Ironically, it was at his wife's urging that Walter had originally decided to help out the Deutschkrons, but then, unable to overcome her jealousy, she now tried to entrap him. After the war, she begged the Deutschkrons their forgiveness for her irrational and erratic behavior. She had meant no harm to them, she stated, only to her husband, for his infidelity.[22]

We end this section, about help given due to a previous friendship, with a similar Gestapo investigation, but one that unfortunately ended tragically for the rescuer. Marie-Luise Hensel was married to a law professor, who in 1933 was dismissed from his post at Königsberg University due to his Jewish parentage (his mother was Jewish), and he soon thereafter died from a heart stroke. In August 1942, she decided to aid several Jewish friends to cross into Switzerland. Taking along one of her sons (the other was in the army), she left for Schiemmburg, on Lake Constance, facing the Swiss border, ostensibly on vacation, and took a room in a nearby inn. There, she rendezvoused with a friend, and both decided to contact professional border smugglers. The escape plot was somehow discovered and Mrs. Hensel was hauled off for questioning. Not able to withstand further torture, and fearing for her children's safety, she hanged herself in her Konstanz cell. She left a note to her sons stating: "My sons, I will never again do something which could harm you." Her teammate, Kaethe Jung, was also arrested but survived imprisonment.[23]

c) Previous Work-Related Relationship

Some rescue stories were prompted by previous work-related ties between the two parties, such as a doctor-patient relationship, as in the case of Leo Witkowski. His father-in-law, a medical doctor, had treated the Zubeil family. Later, during the Nazi period, after eluding a police raid on their Berlin apartment during the February 1943 Factory Action, Leo Witkowski and his wife headed to the home of Gustav and Agnes Zubeil, who lived on a boat home on the Spree River. There, the Witkowskis remained hidden for about six months; they then moved to another sheltering place.[24] Similarly, a professional relationship aided the Jewish Dr. Arthur Arndt, who had previously treated the daughter of Max and Augusta Gehre for diphtheria, for which her parents, ordinary working-class people, remained thankful. As a token of deep appreciation, the Gehres hid Dr. Arndt in the pantry of their Berlin home from January 1943 until the war's end, two years later. They also arranged safe places for the doctor's wife and sister-in-law.[25]

Turning to employer-employee relationships that evolved into a deep friendship, we continue with the Arndt family and the role of Anni Schulz in their rescue. Prior to Nazi rule, she worked as a governess of the Arndt family's two children. In 1942, the now-married Anni and husband intermittently sheltered Dr. Arndt's mother-in-law, usually for a few weeks or months at a time, in their Berlin suburb home, on top of storing many of the Arndts' household valuables in their backyard. This included a trunkful of medical instruments belonging to Dr. Arndt.[26] Likewise for Maria Meier, who, before the Nazi period and her marriage, served as a governess with the Bernauer family in Troisdorf, in the Cologne region, resulting in a deep friendship on both sides. Many years later, in September 1944, after the married Maria had already left the Bernauer household, Erwin and Nanny Bernauer and daughter Karola were interned in a Cologne transit camp for deportation to Theresienstadt camp. Karola managed to flee, and arriving late at night at Maria's home, she was immediately admitted. But what could be done for Karola's parents, she frantically asked? Maria's daughter Katharina volunteered to undertake this dangerous mission. The following morning, she left to fetch some food for Karola's parents in the Müngersdorf transit camp. Arriving at the camp gate, Katharina struck up a conversation with the SS guards (she was blond, beautiful, and looked the Nordic type). Karola had earlier told her that only non-Jews were assigned kitchen work, so Katharina blandly told the guards she was waiting for her supposedly non-Jewish parents to finish their kitchen shift. As time passed and Katharina's fictional parents did not show up, Katharina was given permission to fetch them. She immediately went to see the Bernauers, who were elsewhere in that camp, not the kitchen. Hurrying back to the gate, she told the guards that her parents were on the way. "I started to flirt and promised to return the same evening." As her "parents" did not show up (as she had prearranged with them), she was again allowed to go inside the camp to fetch them. This was the opportune moment Katharina had waited to spirit the Bernauers out. Turning her coat over to Nanny Bernauer, to cover her Yellow Star, she instructed Nanny's husband to wrap a shawl around his shoulder, for the same purpose. The guards did not stop the three as they left the camp, and they arrived safely at Katharina's home (her father was at the time away in the army). Mother and daughter sheltered the three Bernauers for over four months. They were then moved (with the help of Katharina's husband who was home on leave from the army) to a farm owned by the Ludwig and Elisabeth Weeg family, friends of the Meiers. The Bernauers were registered as refugees from city air bombings. Later Karola's sister Erna joined them as well. All four survived.[27]

d) Business-Client Connection

Some rescue stories were born as a result of an earlier strictly business-client relationship. Siegmund Spiegel, of Ahlen, a decorated World War One soldier, was a cattle merchant and counted many regional farmers as his clients. As anti-Jewish measures mounted, some of his clients from the Münster region promised to help, should the need arise. One of these former clients, Hubert Pentrop, counseled Siegmund: "If they want to send you to Poland, don't go. The news from there is not good. Come to me and I will hide you." In February 1943, Siegmund (who in the meantime had been forced to move to a specially designated Jewish section in Dortmund, where he shared a flat with six Jewish families and was doing forced labor) received the dreaded deportation summons for "resettlement" in the East for his family, which included his wife Marga and daughter Karin. The time had come to take up his former clients at their word. As they surreptitiously boarded a local train, they noticed the remaining town's Jews waiting on the platform for their deportation train. "Not one of them returned," Marga noted. "Out of thirty-seven families, not a single one survived." For the next two and a half years, the Spiegels were continuously on the run, being ushered by one farming family to another, beginning with Heinrich Aschoff's farmstead (also a former client), a man described by Marga as a "sincere straightforward man, the typical Münsterland farmer," and his wife, "with a heart full of generosity and love." Only the two eldest daughters of the Aschoff's eight children were entrusted with the secret of the Spiegels' true origin. For most of the time, the Spiegels split up to better ensure their survival, with Marga appearing as the wife of a soldier fighting Germany's wars. Siegmund was admitted by Pentrop (true to his word) in spite of his wife's hospitalization, where she awaited her seventh child. After a nine-month stay, his presence was inadvertently uncovered, so Siegmund had to move on. During a temporary stay on one farmstead, he was given the room of the two sons who were away in the army.

Siegmund and Marga occasionally met for a few fleeting moments. Constantly on the alert, and occasionally having to flee at a moment's notice, Marga reflected on Goethe's words (learned at school): "Whosoever has never eaten his bread with tears; whosoever never sat weeping on his bed during forlorn evenings – he knows you not, celestial powers." Reminiscing years later, Marga was still astonished at the humanity shown her by these farming families. "These acts of kindness can never be repaid. I came to these courageous people, who didn't even know me [on a personal basis], ate with them and was received as though I belonged with them. . . . What powerful bravery and deep conviction must have been possessed by the people there, who would extend an immediate welcome to my husband, who came to them looking like a leper and knew not where to hide." Siegmund recalled the words told him by some of these compassionate farmers: "We will not let you perish." It had all started as a salesman-client relationship.[28]

A similar gripping rescue story originating in a business relationship involving stage actress Dorothea Neff, originally from Munich, and her dress designer, Lilli Wolff. The business relationship between both women was cemented into an enduring friendship in Cologne where Dorothea performed in the theater. Later, Dorothea moved to Vienna where she was invited to appear at the prestigious Volksteater. In 1940 Lilli, fleeing from Cologne, appeared at Dorothea's fashionable center-city apartment and asked for help. She had mistakenly thought that life for persecuted Jews would be more tolerable in traditional carefree Vienna. As a Jew, Lilli had to move into the restricted Jewish quarter of the city, to where Dorothea occasionally visited her, taking along needed medicaments. Then, in October 1941, Lilli was summoned to appear at the train station for "resettlement" in Poland. Concerned not to cram her valise with more than the allowable weight, she decided to do the packing in Dorothea's home, where a weight scale was available. As the two women crouched on the floor, carefully weighing each item, Dorothea suddenly exclaimed: "Let's stop this. You are not going anywhere. I will hide you." Years later, Dorothea related that Lilli's helpless pale-grey face, during the packing scene, is what triggered her instinctive decision to prevent Lilli's departure to an unknown fate. "I'll never forget the expression on her face. The tear-filled eyes and trembling lips. We got up from the floor, and I put her in my guest bed, where she soon fell asleep. But I didn't sleep that night. I knew what I was risking, and it took me time to come to terms with my decision." Lilli was to remain hidden in Dorothea's apartment for over three years, while Dorothea pursued her professional career as a stage actress, interpreting leading dramatic roles such as Lady Macbeth, Iphigenie (Goethe), and Mary Stuart. When Dorothea entertained guests after an evening opening at the theater, none of those present suspected a Jewish woman was hiding in a back room. Dorothea confided the secret to only one trusty woman, fellow aspiring actress Eva Zilcher. Years later, Lilli wrote: "God chose Dorothea Neff to save my life. . . . When she was born, the world became more bountiful, and part of that bounty was bestowed on me."[29]

Further north, in Munich, a similar business-client relationship led to a rescue operation. Prior to the Nazi regime, Fritz Bach had sold various household goods to local villagers. After Kristallnacht, he managed to leave the country, but the war trapped his Christian-born wife Lotte and their daughter Hannelore. In late 1940, Lotte visited a former client in the village Niederroth to fetch a goose for the approaching Christmas, and voiced her worries about her daughter's safety (considered a half-Jew by Nazi definition). Leonhard Gailer, a farmer and mayor of the village, immediately offered to shelter the nine-year old Hannelore with his family, which included six children. "Everyone in the village knew of me," Hannelore stated in her deposition, "as many had been customers of my father. Relatives of the family in the surrounding villages also knew. I can honestly say that I was never harassed nor called any names. There were no financial re-imbursements from my mother all the time I lived there. . . . There were Nazi party members around, but not one word about me was said to anyone." During the last months of the war, Hannelore's mother also joined her in Gailer's home.[30]

In Ernsbach, Hessen province, Heinrich List, a goodhearted farmer, gave shelter to a Jewish fugitive, a former business associate, when in November 1941 he admitted Ferdinand Strauss (from Michelstadt) into his home. However, in March 1942, after an altercation between List and a Polish farmhand, the latter informed the police of Strauss's presence, which led to the arrest of Heinrich List. The following interrogation of List, from the Darmstadt police blotter, tells the rest of the tragic story:

Question: For what reasons did you admit the Jew Ferdinand Strauss and give him shelter?

Answer: Because we knew each other well since childhood, and he was now all alone.

Question: Why did you not report him to the police?

Answer: I was not aware that I had to report him to the police. It is quite out of the question that I hid him because of any possible hatred toward the regime.

Only because we knew each other well, and previously we entertained good business relations. So I took pity on him and gave him shelter.

List's answers did not satisfy his interrogators. Showing compassion to a Jew was a serious offense in Nazi Germany. In the words of a police investigator: "He must without any doubt be considered a friend of the Jews. I arrive at this conclusion, based on the fact that it was otherwise impossible to hide a Jew in a village of 298 inhabitants [without the others knowing of it]. I therefore take the position that he knew perfectly well what he was doing and what this implied. In my opinion, he impeded [the Jew's] official apprehension and detention in full conscience and foreknowledge of the deed's implications." After several weeks' detention in Darmstadt, the sixty-year-old defendant was sent to Dachau camp on July 17, 1942, where he succumbed (or was murdered) in October of the same year, only three months after his arrival there. List's son Jakob was at the time a soldier on the front, and in 1944 was reported missing in action. As for the sheltered Jew, Ferdinand Strauss, he had made good his escape on the eve of his rescuer's arrest. Today, a street bearing Heinrich List's name appears in his hometown of Erbach (to which the village of Ernsbach has been incorporated).[31]

In Berlin, Wanda Feuerherm sheltered in her home Gerda Weiss, a former business associate, starting in the summer of 1944. Wanda lived in a wooden house on the outskirts of Lichtenberg. To friends, Gerda was introduced as a distant relative from a bombed-out house. At first, when Wanda's husband, Willi, appeared home on leave from the army, Gerda would disappear. He later consented to her presence. In early 1944, when the Gestapo came to investigate, Gerda hid in the cellar. She left the following day, moving to different hiding places in the sprawling city, and at times staying with her mother, who was hiding elsewhere. It was later learned that Willi had himself tipped off the Gestapo, due to his jealousy of his wife's devotion to Gerda. After the war, Willi and Wanda separated.[32]

Finally, in Vienna, Christa Beran (then, Denner) at first sheltered Edith Hahn in her home, after she had been summoned by the Gestapo in 1942 to report for deportation, after Edith's mother had already been deported. Many years earlier, the Jewish Edith had coached the then four-teen-year old Christa with school lessons, and this evolved into a friend-ship. To facilitate Edith's further safety, Christa gave her own identity card, certificate of baptism, and ration card to Edith while simultaneously falsely reporting to the police that she had accidentally lost these precious documents during a boat outing on the Danube River. With these documents on her person, Edith left for a place near Munich, where she worked for the Red Cross, and then moved on to other locations and different job as-signments, armed with Christa Denner's non-Jewish credentials, and thus survived without the authorities detecting her Jewish origin. Her mother, however, was not so lucky, as she did not return from deportation.[33]

E) ROMANTIC AND DEEP EMOTIONAL LINKS

Some rescue stories were fueled by strong emotional links, based either on a romantic tie, filial obligation, or other special close relationship. When dealing with a romantic link between Jew and non-Jew, the rescue operation was not necessarily restricted to the two persons themselves, but may have extended to other threatened Jews. As the reader will recall, romantic links between Jew and non-Jew were strictly forbidden by the 1935 Nuremberg Laws, for those not yet married; hence, those intimately involved in such a re-lationship risked serious punishment. Edith Berlow stated that she sheltered many Jews in her Grunewald-Berlin apartment out of love for her future Jewish husband. In 1936, she met and fell in love with the Jewish medical doctor Kurt Hirschfeldt, but could not marry him because of the Nuremberg Laws. Her love for Kurt led Edith to begin sheltering staff personnel from the Jewish hospital where Kurt worked, while Kurt hid elsewhere. One of Kurt's friends helped by Edith was Walter Frankenstein, an engineer by profession, assigned forced construction duties with the Gestapo. In 1941, he married Leonie, and a child was born to them in January 1943. At first, they hid separately in various places, with Walter occasionally staying over at Edith's home where he noticed other Jews there being cared for. At Walter's and Leonie's other hiding places, Edith provided them with money and other necessities. In spite of their difficult situation, another child was born to Leonie in February 1944, who was at the time staying in a village. When suspicions mounted, she moved back to Berlin with Walter, where they hid in bombed-out houses and, on occasions, at Edith's place. After the war, Edith and Kurt were able to marry – their love for each other had not diminished a bit since they met nineteen years earlier.[34]

A romantic link to a fleeing Jew deepened another woman's resolve to help Nazi victims. Maria von Maltzan was the scion of a noble Swedish family that had settled in Germany in the eighteenth century, and the family owned an estate in Silesia. Her father, Count Andreas von Maltzan, entertained liberal viewpoints, while her mother Elisabeth, by contrast, was fiercely nationalistic and openly antisemitic. Maria's sister Alix was married to the pro-Nazi Field Marshal Walther von Reichenau (known for the infamous antisemitic military Order of Day that he issued to his troops), who died from a stroke during the Russian campaign in 1942, and a soldier brother fell during the invasion of France in 1940. In 1940, Maria was studying veterinary medicine when she met the Jewish Hans Hirschl, who had once edited an avant-garde literary journal, and the two fell in love. His father had been a judge in Breslau, and his mother was eventually deported to Theresienstadt where she perished. In February 1942, Hans moved into Maria's flat in the Wilmersdorf section of Berlin. The romance produced a child, born prematurely in September 1942 in a hospital operated by nuns of the Order of St. Vincent. To cover up for Hans, a homosexual friend of Maria claimed paternity of the child. Placed in an incubator, the child died of a power shortage during an air raid. Maria had a profound dislike of the Nazis. "At the age of 14, I read *Mein Kampf*," she stated. "I knew what the man was talking about. I considered him an evil and cruel man." Maria had already, previous to her meeting Hans, been involved in anti-Nazi activities. Since 1934, she was trailed by the Gestapo because of her help to Nazi victims, some of whom she helped flee the country, and in 1938, during a grueling Gestapo interrogation, her lower jaw was fractured.

In 1939, evidently before she became romantically linked with Hans Hirschl, Maria von Maltzan had begun working with the Swedish church in Berlin, which included helping Jews flee the country via Lübeck harbor in the north, as well as doing many errands to secure the safe passage of the fleeing persons, with the complicity of bribed train conductors. As a cover for her activities, she found temporary jobs in several government ministries, including Josef Goebbels's Propaganda Ministry, and relayed important information to underground circles. She was nevertheless constantly under Gestapo surveillance, but somehow managed to outwit them and simultaneously provide temporary shelter in her home to many persons (the list is too long to narrate), other than Hans whom she hid intermittently for three years.

During one Gestapo raid of her home, the heavy living room couch aroused their suspicion, and they were about to shoot in that direction. Hans Hirschl was at that very moment crouching tensely in an empty space inside the couch. To save him and herself, Maria instinctively decided on a ruse, and exploding in an uncontrollable rage, shouted at the Gestapo agents. "Look here, whoever you are, I'm not going to stand for this. My father was the Count von Maltzan and an officer under the Kaiser. My mother was a well-known antisemite. I am a good German. What makes you think I would have anything to do with Jews?" To clinch her act, she threatened to sue the Gestapo for damages if they pumped bullets into her antique couch. The two agents were taken aback by Maria's "chutzpah," and they quickly left. When the Russians occupied her section of Berlin in April 1945, ten persons were found hiding in Maria's home. After the war, Maria and Hans married, divorced, and remarried. Asked many years later by an Israeli journalist whether her help to Jews was prompted by her love for Hans, she self-effacingly replied: "No; I did not believe then, and still do not today, that anyone had a right to kill persons in the name of an ideology." Many persons, other than Hans, owe their lives to this fiercely individualistic person.[35]

Also in Berlin, Elisabeth Wust, a mother of four sons with a husband in the army, met and fell in love with Felicia Schragenheim, a professional swimmer. When she learned that her lover was Jewish, she immediately offered her shelter in her home. The lesbian relationship lasted for a while, until both were denounced to the Gestapo, who promptly arrested them. Elisabeth was released due to her husband's army service and her previous decoration by the State for producing four sons for the Reich. Felicia was sent to Theresienstadt, then to Gross Rosen and Auschwitz, where she perished. While still in Theresienstadt, Felicia received letters from Elisabeth. Later, Elisabeth sheltered two other Jewish women in her home. After the war, she desperately sought news of Felicia's whereabouts, hoping that perhaps she had survived the horrors of Auschwitz, but to no avail.[36]

In Vienna, Edeltrud Becher's love for Walter Posiles led her to succor other members of his family. The two met in 1937, but a year later, after the Nazi takeover of Vienna, Walter as a Czech citizen fled to Prague. Edeltrud visited him on occasions. Trailed by the police, Edeltrud herself fled to Budapest, where she stayed with relatives of Walter. Informed that the police were no longer interested in her case, she returned to Vienna where Walter visited her secretly. When, in July 1942, Walter and his two brothers, in Prague, were summoned to Theresienstadt camp, they clandestinely fled to Edeltrud's home in Vienna, where Walter was hidden in various places including the atelier apartment of a relative of Edeltrud who was away in the army. Walter's two brothers were also sheltered with friends of Edeltrud. After the war Walter and Edeltrud finally were able to marry.[37]

Filial relationships could also lead to rescue operations. The Puetz family, in Niederkassel-Rheidt, Cologne region, adopted Karola from an orphanage and raised her together with their natural-born daughter Adele. In 1938, when Karola was thirteen, her school principal made inquiries about her background and learned that she was born Jewish. Her foster and already married sister Adele interceded with her husband who, as a police officer and a member of the Nazi party, tried to squash the story. In the meantime, Karola's adoptive parents stopped receiving support from the city, but nothing further happened until 1944, when Karola was arrested at the Puetz home and taken to Köln-Müngersdorf camp. Karola managed to escape, and first headed to a friend in Dortmund. She then moved to different locations. When danger mounted, Karola fled back to her adoptive parents; then she proceeded to Silesia where she stayed with friends of Adele, with the help of fabricated identity papers. The end of the war found her in Czechoslovakia.[38]

A special, strong link between rescuer and rescued could be sustained by a memorable event in the not-too-distant past. Heinz Guttman's father, Franz, was a comrade-in-arms to Johanna Eck's husband during World War One. When Johanna's husband was mortally wounded, he literally died in the arms of Franz. When his son, the Jewish Heinz, was threatened for deportation, Johanna felt obligated to prevent it, and she sheltered him for a long time in her Berlin home; then she arranged for him other hiding places. In one such place, Johanna met Elfriede Guttman (no relation to Heinz) – better known as Mia, who needed a different hiding place. Johanna took the forlorn young woman under her personal care. As for Franz – Heinz's father, and a four-year front-line veteran of the previous war – he died in Auschwitz for the sin of being born Jewish. Asked after the war the reasons for her help, Johanna Eck gave the following philosophical explanation. "Nothing in particular. Basically, I think as follows. If my neighbor needs help and I can do something, then it is my inescapable duty and obligation [to help]. If I forego this help, I fail to carry out the task which life – or perhaps God – has entrusted me. All people, I feel, constitute a single whole, and anyone who mistreats another person is slapping himself and everyone else in the face. This is what motivates me."[39]

Josef Cammerer's help to Gertrud Froehlich was, similarly, linked to a World War One encounter. In 1917, Josef was sent to a Munich military hospital, where Gertrud served as a nurse, to recuperate from a serious wound sustained on the Russian front. Gertrud's care for the wounded soldier resulted in a deep and long-lasting friendship between the two that did not diminish with the passing years. Released and returned to the front in 1918, this time in France, Cammerer kept up the correspondence with Froehlich. No romance evolved; it was simply a long-lasting friendship, and both sides married other spouses. After the war, Josef held various university positions in the field of engineering and published scientific books and papers, one of which (*Der Warme und Kalteschutz in die Industrie*) became a standard textbook. In 1933, he opened a scientific laboratory outside Munich, and in 1938 he moved his laboratory to Tutzing, near a forest. In the meantime, Gertrud met and married Walter Lustig. He was arrested during Kristallnacht and spent a brief spell in Dachau. The brutal treatment inflicted on him permanently undermined his health. Cammerer was then doing research work for the army on food storage and food substitutes. Leasing an apartment in Munich, Cammerer was able to host the Lustigs and keep them there for most hours of the day. In the evening, he accompanied them to their government-assigned crowded Jewish home. When Walter died in 1941 after a long illness, Cammerer moved Gertrud to his Tutzing lab, to protect her from deportation. There, she died in February 1942. Gertrud's parents in Munich had committed suicide a month earlier without her knowledge. Josef at first buried Gertrud secretly in the lab garden. A year later, he contacted Karl Schoerghofer, the non-Jewish caretaker of the Jewish cemetery in Munich, and he helped remove Gertrud's body secretly and bury her alongside her husband. Deeply affected by events of the Nazi period, Cammerer turned to theology after the war. In this he was also influenced by the philosophical and religious discussions he had previously held with Gertrud. At first, he was denied the priesthood since he was a divorced man, but was later admitted in the Benedictine Order at St. Ottilien, and in 1961, he was finally ordained a priest. He then published a book on the relationship between science and theology. In 1978, he wrote that his wounding on the front (a bullet through his shoulder, which almost killed him) was divinely ordained, so that he would later meet Gertrud in a military hospital.[40]

A stranger-than-fiction story, and still not fully explainable, is the more-than-professional relationship, which may or may not have included a romantic interlude, between Ludwig Clauss and Margarete Landé. Clauss was a professor in psychology, ethnology, and Germanic and Semitic languages, and the Jewish Margarete served as his assistant. Before the Nazi period, they visited Bedouin tribesmen in Palestine to study their customs and living habits. Clauss then joined the Nazi party and wrote widely on the superiority of the Aryan race and disparagingly on the inferiority of the Jews. In 1941, he was suddenly arraigned before a Nazi disciplinary court for keeping a Jewish woman (Margarete) in his home instead of reporting her to the authorities, and her present whereabouts were unknown. To protect his Nazi credentials, including his university position, he fervently upheld his antisemitic stance, and claimed that he had kept Margarete solely as a laboratory specimen, so he could observe at close range the struggle taking place between her Aryan and Jewish blood (he falsely claimed that she had disclosed to him that she was a *Mischling*, the product of a Jewish mother and a non-Jewish father). The ruse did not work, and in 1943, he was expelled from the Nazi party and his works were banned.

In the meantime, the police search for Margarete Landé continued, but oblivious of the police she had gone in hiding nowhere else but in Clauss's own Ruentnick forest home, outside Berlin, where she hid in a small alcove above the chicken coop. Then, for additional protection (for the house was frequently searched), he built for her a bunker on forest land that belonged to him, behind his house. There, Margarete spent two winters and a summer. At nights Josef, his future wife, and his twenty-year old son from a previous marriage secretly brought food and provisions to Margarete. Thanks to their selfless aid, Magarete Landé survived the Nazi period. At the same time, incredible as it may sound, Clauss kept up his struggle to have himself reinstated in the good graces of the Nazis, and through friends, he went so far as appealing directly to SS head Himmler – who finally consented in 1944 for Clauss to be enrolled in a Waffen-SS unit for the purpose of continuing his study of racial questions, utilizing Russian and Yugoslav prisoners of war for that purpose. All this did not prevent him from paradoxically going to great lengths, including harm to his career, to save a person who mattered much to him – a Jewish woman, an "inferior" being according to his own theories. Margarete Landé, in her postwar testimony, praised him as a great humanitarian – a claim that, in light of the man's full record, one finds hard to accept. This case represents the exception to the rule – a rescuer who did not hide his animosity toward Jews and helped the Nazis with pseudo-scientific legitimization of their inhumane measures against the Jewish people, while at the same going to great lengths, including personal risks, to save one Jewish woman due to a collegial relationship in his anthropology work, and perhaps also peppered with an episodic romantic interlude.[41]

f) IDEOLOGICAL LINKS

Organizational and religious links could, in some cases, also spur rescue operations. Jews affiliated with movements with a strong ideological content, such as the communist party, stood a better chance of finding help from fellow comrades. The same is true for Jews who had freely converted to Christianity or were born into the Church but were still in jeopardy because of their Jewish parentage, of which we shall speak further in a later chapter. Many of these persons were helped by their separate churches in various ways. Even small organizations, not numbering more than several dozen members, but pursuing an idealistic narrative, could if they wanted protect their Jewish members from persecution. Such was the case of *Der Bund – Gemeinschaft für Sozialistisches Leben*, a club-like association created in 1923 by Artur Jacobs, a non-Jew, with about 70–80 members, mostly teachers and educators. Mainly active in the Ruhr region (between Essen and Düsseldorf), it championed the creation of a society based on socialistic and egalitarian ideals. It refrained from political involvement and took no stand on religious matters. The fact that it was not officially registered as a society, and its adherents did not carry membership cards, made its surveillance more difficult by the Gestapo. Members, of which Jews constituted a minority, met in private and discussed how best to pursue their goals. The Bund arranged sheltering places for over a dozen of its Jewish members, such as Marianne Ellenbogen (born Strauss), who was moved to ten different homes, never staying in one place for more than three months. She survived, as did other Jews affiliated with this small and closely-knit ideological group.

As recounted by her, one Monday morning in August 1943, at ten, the two most-feared leading Essen Gestapo officials entered her house with an order for the Jewish inhabitants to be prepared in two hours for "transport to the East." Previous to that, from 1941 to 1943, Marianne Strauss worked in different jobs for the permanently shrinking Jewish community in Essen – in the kindergarten, as a teacher, and as a nurse, voluntarily and without payment – while keeping in constant touch with her friends, Jews and non-Jews alike in the Bund. Presently, as Marianne and her family were busy packing under the watchful eyes of the two Gestapo agents, Marianne picked an opportune moment to flee, when the two agents rushed to the cellar to pick for themselves some of the household things stored there. So, "without any opportunity to say good-bye to my parents, my brother and my relatives, I followed the impulse of this only moment of not being observed and ran out of the house, just as I was, in my skiing dress, with a few hundred Mark bills, which my father had slipped into my hand a few minutes ago and which I had hidden in the pocket of the trousers. I ran for my life, aware that at every moment someone would shoot me down. . . . No shot, however, no running behind me, no order, no shouting. Thus I ran about in the neighborhood, through silent sideways, to get at any rate rid of my persecutors. I ran to a non-Jewish lady I was acquainted with, who took me in until nightfall." That person was Sonja Schreiber, a colleague in the Bund fellowship. During her frequent visits and conversations with Bund leader Artur Jacobs, he had earlier urged her to head to Sonja's house for shelter when in an emergency rather than his own house since he was married to Doris, a Jewish woman. Marianne remained hidden at Sonja Schreiber's flat for several weeks, stepping out only after nightfall for short errands, for Marianne was well known in Essen and could easily be identified. In Sonja's home she took over the kitchen work, "cooking for the first time in life."

As for the rest of her family – her parents Siegmund and Regina, sixteen-year old brother, Richard, grandmother Anna Rosenberg, her father's twin brother, Alfred Strauss, and wife Lore and mother-in-law Else Dahl, all eight persons who had been living together – they were kept in jail for almost three weeks, hoping that Marianne too would be apprehended, so all could be deported together to whatever fate awaited them. Marianne was declared a "wanted person" by the police. After three weeks, on September 9, 1943, all her relatives were deported; first to Theresienstadt, thence to Auschwitz – never to return.

One evening, Sonja Schreiber's home was damaged during an air raid. Marianne realized it was best for herself and her host to seek another hiding place. "Now my restless wandering began." Her Bund friends referred her to Bund member Karin Morgenstern, who lived in Braunschweig with two small daughters and whose husband was away in the army. During the next autumn and winter months of late 1943, Marianne commuted from Karin's home to another Bund colleague – Hedwig Gehrke, in Göttingen – sharing her house with Hedwig's little son and her mother-in law, while her husband was away fighting on the Russian front. Then, during intervals, Marianne moved to Beversted, near Bremen, to a distant cousin of her grandmother who had not yet been deported due to her marriage to a non-Jewish husband – but only for a three-week stay in order not to arouse suspicion by curious neighbors.

From there, she moved to various locations in the Düsseldorf, Remscheid, Wuppertal, and Mühlheim regions, such as with Bund members Maria and Fritz Briel, in Remscheid: "With them I felt welcome and secure. Their magnanimity and courage, appearing so self-evident every time they sheltered me again, gave me the feeling of confidence, so necessary for surviving. It is like a miracle that during this time of permanent fear there was again and again a network to hold you; that people you had never seen before were willing to endanger themselves for you, or what is still more important, for a human right." In Burscheid, Marianne stayed with Aenne Schmitz and her sister – both of whose husbands were away in the German army.

From time to time, Marianne could also hide for a few days with Jewish friends who were in a mixed marriage situation and therefore temporarily exempt from deportation, such as Grete Menningen, in Barmen. But, when in summer 1944 Grete faced deportation, Marianne arranged for Else Bramesfeld, also a Bund member, to find a hiding place for Grete. Marianne could also stay for a few days in the house of Emilie Busch, a former housekeeper of Marianne's aunt. The bombings by day and night made frequent changes of hiding places necessary. Marianne was worried that without any forged identity papers on her person, in case of injury or evacuation to a hospital she would be in danger of detection. As she stated, "It would have been impossible to look for medical help in my situation; that would have increased the possibility of being discovered and arrested and thus having endangered all those who helped me and hid me."

Travelling became more and more difficult and finally was almost impossible, as the railway system had almost completely broken down. Marianne found herself hopping from place to place, mostly by the still operating tramway system. The Bund main center (the Blockhaus) in Essen-Stadtwald, where Sonja Schreiber had once lived (she had in the meantime been evacuated to another region), continued to serve as a base for Marianne during her peregrinations, "a resting place during the restless flight. To know that there was this refuge, when others were not available or could not be reached or would be too much endangered, gave me the feeling of security, to which I mainly owe (in the widest sense) my surviving." However, being on the Gestapo Wanted List, "I could never be sure that one of those frightening tyrants in their leather coats would recognize me or become suspicious." Luckily for her, she witnessed liberation unharmed when the US Army entered Düsseldorf in April 1945. "A world had broken down. I was waiting and hoping, but no one came back. I had to build up quite slowly another, new life." Marianne Strauss ends her lengthy testimony by expressing gratitude to all those in the Bund fellowship and a few others who lent a hand in saving her: Artur and Dore Jacobs, Sonja Schreiber, Grete Stroeter, Mathilde und Gustav Zenker, Hermann Schmalstieg, Karin und Carlos Morgenstern, Hedwig Gehrke, Meta Steinmann, Aenne Schmitz, Maria and Fritz Briel, Greta Dreibholz, and Hanni Ganzer. [42] It took close to two dozen rescuers to guarantee the survival of Marianne Strauss (later Ellenbogen) – in this rare, uncommon, and dramatic epic of a lone person's determined and courageous willpower not to fall prey to her Nazi pursuers.

g) In Neighboring Countries

Finally, in this chapter, mention must also be made of ethnic Germans residing in neighboring countries who extended aid to Jews in distress, persons with whom they entertained friendly relations or knew casually as neighbors.

In Katowice, Poland, which had been annexed to Germany in 1939 (and renamed Kattowitz), Ernst-Otto Motzko sheltered the sister and mother of the Jewish Martin Dzialoszynski. During World War One, Martin had treated Ernst for wounds sustained in the head, thereby saving his life. Later, before leaving for Bolivia in 1939, Martin exacted a promise from Ernst to look after his family, and Ernst stood by his word. During the massive roundup of Katowice Jews, in August 1942, Ernst, who was then with a civil defense unit, was able to snatch Martin's sister, Hildegard, from a column of marching Jews; he covered her with his army coat and led her back to her home in the Srodula ghetto. The following year, on the eve of the ghetto's final liquidation, he sheltered her and two other Jews in an unused storage room, while at the same times placing Martin's mother in a hospital, and visiting her occasionally. In January 1945, when his unit was ordered to move toward the Czech border, Motzko, refusing to abandon his wards, went into hiding with them until the city's liberation at the end of the month.[43]

In Bratislava, Slovakia, Paul Kerner, a painter and high school teacher, lived next door to Zoltan Lichtenstein, who worked for the Skoda and Fiat industrial firms. When the Germans entered Slovakia in September 1944, Zoltan and his family fled and temporarily hid in a cemetery. At this point Kerner arranged a hiding place for the Lichtenstein family with a farmer in the outlying village of Dubravka and supplied them with food (they would meet halfway in prearranged secret locations) until the area's liberation in April 1945. In nearby Hungary, Dr. Leo Tschoell, originally from Graz, Austria, gave shelter to several Jewish friends in the patent office that he operated in Budapest. They were members of a Zionist cell, and since March 1944, when Germany occupied Hungary, Tschoell's friends used his office to secretly manufacture false credentials. As told by Robert Offner, "We made out credentials for all Beitar members [a Zionist youth organization] in our group, and also for some who were in the ghettos Szombathely and Sopron." Robert's confederates also stored weapons in Tschoell's office. When the place was discovered by the Hungarian police in December 1944, Tschoell, forewarned, went into hiding until the city's liberation in February 1945.[44] In Budapest equally, the German national Helmut Bittner was a consultant to several industrial and financial firms, including a textile factory where Zoltán Reich was employed, and the two became friends. Bittner obtained for Reich false credentials under a non-Jewish identity, which allowed him to continue working in that factory. When, in May 1944, Reich's wife and son were locked up in the Újpest ghetto and about to be deported, Zoltán Reich accompanied Helmut Bittner at the helm of a driven car bearing a German

license plate, and with forged papers in his hands, Bittner effected the release of Zoltán's wife and son. It was just in time, as the other ghetto Jews
were deported to Auschwitz. Bittner then tried to arrange the flight of his
Jewish friend and family to Turkey, but this proved unsuccessful. The Reich
trio nevertheless made it safely to the end of the war, and the two remained
friends in the postwar period.[45]

In Prague, former actress and opera singer Marianne Golz-Goldlust, a
refugee from Vienna because of her known anti-Nazi views (and her marriage
to the Jewish journalist Hans Goldlust), joined a secret Czech organization
that helped people sought by the Gestapo (mostly Jews) to flee the country.
She and her companions were arrested in November 1942. The presiding
judge had accused her of "having been fully spiritually Judaized" (*"selbst geis-
tigt vollständig verjudet ist"*). He added: "She mingled with great zeal among
Jewish circles, and gave much support to her Jewish and half-Jewish friends.
As already emphasized, she acted not as a result of compulsion but out of inner conviction. Her effort to please her Jewish friends is in accordance with
her hostile attitude toward the National Socialist State." She was sentenced to
death and executed the following year.[46] Finally, in Marseille, France, former
German socialist party activist Fritz Heine helped hundreds of German socialist refugees leave the country. They were in jeopardy of being turned over
by the French Vichy government to the Gestapo, as provided by article 19 of
the Franco-German armistice agreement of June 1940.[47]

✳ ✳ ✳

The previous stories – a fraction of a larger number of authenticated stories of
German rescuers recorded at Yad Vashem, under the category of friendship
or acquaintance between both parties – is no proof that all former friendly
links and other forms of acquaintanceship necessarily led to rescue operations
by the non-Jewish side. Most such relationships stopped short of producing
any help. However, a certain number in this category did result in assistance
to Jews. While it is difficult to probe one's heart and mind and identify the
reasons for non-help – whether it was due to fear, lack of courage, or indifference, or perhaps because the Jewish side refrained, for whatever reason,
from turning for help to his/her non-Jewish friend or work colleague – it is of
interest that persons from all walks of life, even Nazi party members, were to

be found who sought to help Jewish friends and acquaintances at great risks to themselves – including persons who sheltered Jews in their homes while their loved ones were away fighting in the German army. Whatever the ultimate explanations, one can safely submit that proximity with the victimized Jewish person, when fostered by years of friendship or other types of close association, played an important role in triggering aid to helpless Jews (to only a fraction of them, one should add) in the intense antisemitic atmosphere of the Nazi regime – in Germany and in countries occupied by her.

CHAPTER 3

Help Through Third Parties

* * *

MANY PERSONS WERE FORTUNATE TO meet their rescuers, not through direct contact, at home or workplace, but mainly via third parties such as friends, acquaintances, and family connections who arranged these relationships. Fewer rescue stories originated this way than through direct contact with the rescuer; at the same time, not a few Jews on the run found temporary or permanent refuge through third-party connections – as in the following stories.

Liselotte Pereles, a kindergarten teacher, only became conscious of her Jewish origin in 1933 when, as a born Jewess, she was peremptorily dismissed from her teaching position. She had until then been fully assimilated into German life. Presently, to support herself she found employment in a Jewish kindergarten. When this too was closed in December 1942, Liselotte began a clandestine existence. She was at first helped by Elisabeth Abegg, a Quaker and former teacher, who arranged for her temporary hiding places, and through which she met Lydia Forsstroem, whom she did not know before. She stayed in Lydia's home for over a year that coincided with the end of the war. Lydia belonged to a student evangelical movement, which was also active in helping Jewish converts to Christianity who were still considered by the Nazis as "full" Jews because of their Jewish lineage. In a letter to Yad Vashem, Lydia wrote: "Yad Vashem is for me a shattering symbol, which painfully and distressingly reminds us how much more one should have done. This is the more disturbing, because of what one omitted from doing as against what one actually did. . . . As for myself, I only did what I deemed the right thing at the time. I was not at all 'noble' or something similar, but the others around me were obstinate, mean, indifferent, and basically without imagination." This was her explanation of her motivation and why she differed from those who did not help.[1]

Third-party connections also came in handy at the eleventh hour for Kurt and Ursula Reich, in Berlin. Kurt married Ursula in May 1942, while doing forced labor for the Nazis, and a daughter, named Monica, was born to them in December of that year, a most unpropitious moment for a Jewish child to make its appearance in Nazi Germany. The doctor who helped with the birth was later deported. That month the three Reichs started a life on the run, moving and transferring to ten different places within the space of eight months. After running out of additional hiding options, at the end of August 1943, they decided to turn themselves in but without their child. Through a third party they learned that a certain couple, by the name of Schroedter, was prepared to help with the little one. Meeting Hedwig Schroedter at her house's doorstep, Ursula Reich told her that she was willing to part with her baby on condition that it be returned to her at the end of the war if, of course, she survived. After Ursula bid a tearful goodbye and turned to leave, Hedwig Schroedter casually mentioned that there was an additional bed in the house that the child's parents could use so as to be with their child. Taken back by this generous gesture, the Reichs babbled that they would of course be prepared to pay. At that point, Ursula wrote in her deposition, "the Schroedters turned us down, since we had offered payments. If we would never mention money again, we could all stay. And so began the most important 19 months in our 3 lives at the Schroedters' one-family home." During that long period, rescuers and rescued withstood many dangers to themselves, including one frightening episode of attempted blackmail (on which occasion, the Reichs were hurriedly moved to another temporary shelter). The Schroedters' son Herbert, who was away in the army, came home on leave one day earlier than expected, in February 1944, and found the hidden persons there (who had planned to be away during his visit). He surprised everyone by insisting that they stay. Not content with the three fugitive Jewish persons in their home, the Schroedters took in another Jewish family for hiding: Robert and wife Eva, and her sixty-three-year-old mother Johanna Hirsch. The elderly Johanna died in April 1944. Late at night, the body was removed and buried in the backyard. The three Reichs spent a full nineteen months in the care of Hedwig and Otto Schroedter, people they had been referred to and had not known before.[2]

In February 1942, Erna Segal, a social worker with the Jewish community in Berlin, was on her way to see a needy person. As she stepped off the bus, a soldier began to follow her. He stopped her and asked her to momentarily cover her Yellow Star marking, for he had something important to tell her – did she know what they did to Jews deported to the East? Not knowing what he was up to and trying to shake him off, Erna said they were probably being taken to work. He countered that this was not true, as terrible things were taking place there, and he urged her to try contacting foreign embassies in Berlin that knew the truth. In the meantime, she should try passing as an Aryan, and having said that the anonymous soldier turned around and took off. Taking this advice to heart, Erna, with the help of friends, was able to make contact with a certain medical doctor named Fritz Aub, who first took Erna in his care and later added her husband Aaron as well. When Aaron was severely wounded during an air raid, which also damaged Aub's home, he first treated Aaron for his wounds, then arranged with a nun working as a nurse at a hospital for Aaron to be admitted for surgery. Aub also arranged other temporary hiding places for Erna and her family (four persons) – never asking for any remuneration.[3]

An unusually touching story in this context, of a random meeting that evolved into something more than a rescue story, is that involving Konrad Latte. In March 1943, he clandestinely came to Berlin from Breslau with his parents to start a life on the run. They first approached a distant relative who was married to a non-Jewish woman and was temporarily exempt from deportation, and this person referred them to Ursula Meissner, a young actress, who immediately consented to shelter them. In Konrad's words: "She did it although she did not know us, and thereby knowingly risked her life. The three of us lived with her for many weeks, in spite of constant bombing alarms that required everyone to go to the shelter, where our presence undoubtedly aroused the suspicion of two military-aged persons." The three Lattes then found different and separate hiding places. Konrad was later arrested while walking the streets, but he managed to flee and was helped by Pastor Harald Poelchau with temporary employment as a replacement organist in churches and at funerals. At night, he slept in attics and cellars of abandoned and bombed-out houses. We shall meet Konrad Latte later in another encounter with his eventual rescuer: a lifelong companion and, eventually, a spouse.[4]

Similar third-party encounters also facilitated the survival of Jews in other regions of Germany. Eva Schmalenbach, whose mother was Jewish and her father non-Jewish, was living in Mainz in 1942 when she suddenly began receiving packages from a certain Anastasia Gerschuetz, a total stranger to her, who lived in nearby Stadtlauringen. Anastasia explained to the surprised Eva that her distant Jewish friends in Schweinfurt (some 20 kilometers from Stadlauringen), on the eve of their deportation to Poland, had left some parcels in Anastasia's care for delivery to Eva. Some months later, Eva's mother inquired of Anastasia whether they knew a farmer who could be trusted to take her in with daughter Eva for hiding. After consulting her family, Anastasia responded that they were prepared to shelter the two women in their own home. In May 1943, mother and daughter left for Stadlauringen (Eva's non-Jewish father had in the meantime died, so his wife and daughter feared they were subject for deportation) and were warmly welcomed by the Gerschuetz family. To outsiders, Eva's mother was presented as a refugee from the big city, fleeing the bombings. A rumor was purposely cultivated that Eva was betrothed to Arthur, Anastasia Gerschuetz's eldest son, and nothing was, of course, done to dispel this rumor. In October 1943, to avoid a population census, which required out-of-town people to also register, Eva's mother left for Munich, where arrangements had been made for her temporary shelter. Mother and daughter (Eva had joined her) then headed for the Swiss border, but they were apprehended, and Eva's mother was deported to Auschwitz, where she evidently perished. A bit luckier, Eva made good her flight from jail on Christmas eve of 1943 and returned to Stadtlauringen, where she was again hidden by the Gerschuetz family for several months. Then, accompanied by Arthur (on his way to rejoin his military unit), she left for Munich. Much later, Eva was arrested a second time, this time by the railway police, and taken to Munich. From a note on her, the Munich police learned of the Stadtlauringen connection, and they began questioning the 1,000 inhabitants of the town about the identity of the person who had helped Eva. The townspeople kept their silence, and Eva was deported to Ravensbrück camp, which she luckily survived. Of the Gerschuetz's two soldier sons: the eldest Arthur disappeared as a prisoner-of-war with the Russians; the other fell prisoner to the English and was freed soon after the war's end.[5]

In the German-occupied countries, third-party encounters also sometimes led to help by German nationals. The Jewish Anna Schein had met Herbert Vogt in Kraków, Poland, through some acquaintances. Vogt, originally from Silesia region, worked as a senior official in the railroads. He provided Anna with false credentials with which she was able to live outside the ghetto (the so-called Aryan side of the city). When Anna felt threatened, in the latter part of 1943, Vogt took her to her sister's hiding place in a nearby village, where she remained for three months. At a later time, he provided her with another set of false documents that made possible her travel to Vienna for a labor assignment, where she remained until the end of the war. He gave her a letter of reference addressed to his friends, who helped her pass as a non-Jew in that distant city. Moving on to Warsaw, we have the story of Ewald Kleisinger, a German military officer, who joined arms with Danuta Czaplinska, his Polish girlfriend, in making their common apartment available to three Jewish women, friends of Danuta, who had fled from the burning Warsaw ghetto in April 1943. He then obtained documents allowing the three women to proceed to Vienna under the guise of Polish agricultural workers, and alerted his parents there to help them – thus assuring their further safety.[6]

In Lublin, Poland, Irena Scipiacky met her future rescuer at the Lublin state theater, which was under German management. The German Eva Gaebler was employed there as a dress designer, and Irena was responsible for the actors' wardrobe. A friendship developed between the two women. When Eva left for Warsaw, she left word with Irena to contact her in Warsaw if she needed help. When the first roundups of Jews began in Lublin, in mid-1942, Irena was able to flee to Warsaw under a false identity and was admitted into Eva's home; then, she shared a room with an actress roommate who was partly paralyzed and whose son was living with his grandmother in Berlin. This woman offered Irena a job tutoring the child in Berlin. However, upon arrival there, the authorities refused to allow a Pole (for thus Eva appeared) to be a governess of a German boy, and she was instead taken to a labor camp with other Polish workers, where conditions were bad. Eva Gaebler's mother, Gaby, brought Irena food and cigarettes and was instrumental in freeing her for Sunday stay-overs in her home. There Irena washed and rested. Gaby's son, in the *Hitlerjugend* (Hitler Youth – Nazi Boy Scouts), and the actor Walter Stoll, Eva's boyfriend, both knew Irena was Jewish, but kept the secret to themselves and accompanied her during evening strolls. Thus, an acquaintance that started in a Lublin theater led to Irena spending the war years, from 1942 onward, in Berlin under a false identity and the constant care of a German benefactor family.[7]

In Bendin, southwestern Poland, Sara Schlanger and her family managed to flee a Nazi raid on the ghetto's inhabitants. Together with her
ten-year old daughter, she wandered and hid in many places. Arriving in
Bielsko-Biala (Bielitz), she was able to make contacts with some Poles, who
referred her to the David family. Originally from Vienna, German citizen
Paul David operated a car repair firm (*Autowerkstatt*), servicing German
army vehicles of all types, including tanks. David's known friendly attitude
toward Poles gained him their trust, and this made it possible for Sara to
be referred to him. David's daughter Margit, who worked as a telephone
operator for the German Ministry of Labor, helped obtain a work permit
for Sara under a new identity, and thus for two years, Sara and her daughter
remained in the care of the David family. She was even invited to spend
Sundays with the Davids, to allay suspicions by neighbors concerning her
true origin. The Davids also warned Sara of anticipated raids in the car
repair workshop, at which time she was told not to leave the house. At
David's place, Sara saw three or four additional sheltered Jews in the basement, and at another time, in the potato storage hole underneath his home,
a group of twelve Jews also found shelter. Concerning her motivations in
helping so many persons, Margit David stated: "It was as though they were
all our children. They had only us, and their life was as important as ours.
How would we have continued living if the Nazis had killed them?" Quite
an extraordinary statement, when contrasted with the behavior of many of
her countrymen who at the same time in occupied Poland were carrying
out a government-orchestrated extermination of all Jews.[8]

Finally, in Brest-Litovsk (today in Belarus), Leah Kirschner fled the
ghetto during a Nazi liquidation raid in 1942 and reached the home of a
Polish family whom she knew. They contacted her with a German civilian
who came one evening and ordered her to follow him into his home, which
on that day he shared with an SS soldier. He told her to act as if she were
on intimate terms with him. This man, Willi Friedrichs, worked as an auto
mechanic for the Todt organization, building fortifications for the war effort. As it turned out, all told, he sheltered six Jewish persons in his home.
He employed a Jewish woman as his house governess and later organized
her transfer to Germany for labor assignments under a different name. Two
other persons, a dermatologist and his sixteen-year-old daughter were hidden under the house stairway. When danger of detection threatened, Willi
Friedrichs moved Leah Kirschner in his car to an abandoned cottage, where

she remained hidden. After he provided her with a new identification under a false name, he was able to move her to Kobryn, where she worked as a house governess in a building owned by the Todt organization. From there, she was sent to Munich as a Polish Christian for household work in the home of an engineer, and thus she survived the horrors of the Nazi period.[9]

Help could also come from the side of non-Jews married to Jewish spouses; who although severely deprived of their rights, were at least initially not immediately threatened with deportation – as further explained in a later chapter – as in the following stories.

The Jewish Ilse Gruen met and befriended Elisabeth Bornstein, through Ilse's former Jewish seamstress. Elisabeth was married to Ludwig, a Jew, which momentarily protected him from deportation. When in January 1943 Ilse learned that she was on the deportation list, she and husband Hans were invited to move in with Elisabeth in their tiny one-room apartment, where they stayed intermittently for a year and a half – hiding in other places but returning to the Bornsteins from time to time. Ilse and Hans braved many dangers, including several arrest attempts by the authorities, but they managed with luck to extricate themselves. In one dramatic incident, Ilse jumped from a train heading to Auschwitz while passing near Breslau, and made her way back to Berlin. Her husband Hans was not as fortunate. Arrested later, together with Ilse, in October 1944, in the flat of Hans Luma, one of the couple's non-Jewish benefactors, he was sent to Oranienburg-Sachsenhausen camp, where he was shot in March 1945. Ilse was held imprisoned in a Berlin jail, on Iranienburgerstrasse, until the end of the war, and luckily survived.[10]

The Jewish Ernst Ehrlich met Franz Schuerholz through a Jewish neighbor who was temporarily protected from deportation thanks to his marriage to a non-Jewess. On February 26, 1943, Ehrlich visited Schuerholz at his home in the Charlottenburg section of Berlin, to inquire on the possibility of shelter for himself and his mother. The following day, the Nazis sprang the large Factory Action, netting Ernst's mother at her workplace. She, along with many others was deported to Auschwitz. Ernst, in possession of a doctor's work release permit due to a work-sustained injury, was able to elude the raid. He immediately went to Schuerholz and was sheltered in his office at Lindenstrasse (southwest Berlin). There he remained for several months while Schuerholz arranged for Ernst an alternate hiding place with a friend in Berlin, where Ernst remained for a time until he managed to flee to Switzerland the same year.[11]

In another story involving assistance via a mixed-marriage couple –
when Margot Bloch escaped a Nazi raid in Berlin, in November 1942, she
at first stayed in the home of Herbert Patzschke, a foreman in the Flohr lift
company, where she also worked. She then contacted Lina Cremer, a Jewish
woman married to a Christian, who invited her to come live in Hannover.
Mrs. Cremer also arranged for her a new identity under the name of Margot
Fischer, whose husband was supposedly away in the army. Through another third party, Margot met Gertrud Kochanowski, a mother of two
children, whose husband was in the army. Invited to move in with her in
May 1943, Margot was again passed off as the wife of a soldier. Through
Gertrud Kochanowski, Margot also met the Heuer family. Albert Heuer
was previously in a concentration camp because of his socialist connection.
Margot stayed with them intermittently, serving as a nursemaid to their
children. At a later period, to elude the constant air raids over Hannover,
Margot was invited to join the Kochanowskis in Freiheit/Osterode, in the
Harz mountains, where their parents lived. Margot stayed there intermit-
tently, moving back and forth to Hannover, where she stayed with the
Heuers, and the Kochanowski home in the Harz mountains – this, until
the end of the war.[12]

In a similar rescue operation, facilitated through a mixed marriage
couple, Ilse and husband Werner Rewald's hide-and-seek game with the
authorities reads like a surrealistic story. Hiding separately, and surreptitiously meeting on brief occasions, they were constantly on the lookout for
danger and not infrequently forced to flee at a moment's notice in order to
avoid entrapment. In 1944, at her wits' end, Ilse looked up an old Jewish
friend, a former cellist. He was married to a non-Jewish music student,
but being Jewish, he was now forced to perform heavy labor, cleaning trol-
leys late at night. This man referred Ilse and his wife to a friend of his –
Hanning Schroeder, who lived in a one-family home on the outskirts of
the city. He was a known music composer, as was his wife, Cornelia, who
reportedly was born Jewish but was baptized at a young age. The Rewalds
were given the room of Hanning's daughter, who was sent off to a Bavarian
village because of the air bombings of Berlin. In the same house, a room
was leased to a Nazi party official, who was told that the new arrivals had
lost their previous house in a recent air raid; hence their sudden appearance
in this somewhat uncomfortable house. The two Rewalds remained intermittently in the Schroeder home until the city's capture by the Russians.[13]

During the last year of Nazi rule, being married to a non-Jewish spouse no longer proved protection from deportation. In February 1945, Karl Herzberg, in Mannheim, who was married to a non-Jewess, received a deportation summons. He met Wilhelm Buerger on the street, a former business associate, who arranged for the Herzbergs and their two children to stay with the Hammer family. Karl's wife's coughing problem made their further stay there dangerous. Again, it was Buerger who arranged for them to move in with Frieda Mueller; years before she had been a housekeeper in the Herzberg home.[14] The same situation prevailed for Clara von Mettenheim, who was protected from deportation thanks to her marriage to the non-Jewish professor Heinrich von Mettenheim. When Heinrich was killed in January 1944 during an air raid over Frankfurt am Main, Clara feared the worst for herself. Indeed, two months later, her premonition proved right, as she received her deportation summons. Through a friend of her late husband, who learned of her predicament, Clara's son was at first hired as a farmhand in Silmersdorf village (Ostpriegnitz), which was adjacent to another farm belonging to Sibylle Dierke. Learning of Clara's predicament, Dierke sheltered Clara and daughter Emilie in her home, in the same village, until the end of the war.[15]

In a similar story in Essen, the Jewish Gertrud was married to Gottlieb Kerklies, born an Evangelical Lutheran. Due to his marriage to a Jewish woman, he was dismissed from the Essen police force. The Kerklies family counted eight children and lived in an apartment house, where they befriended a Mrs. Henrichs, whose sister was Maria Mueller. When Mrs. Henrichs's husband left for the army, her sister Maria and husband Gerhard Mueller moved in with her. In the meantime, the non-Jewish Gottlieb Kerklies was sent to Mulhouse, Alsace province, for work in a Krupp firm. Then, in September 1944, his wife Gertrud and her five elderly children were rounded up and held incommunicado, in preparation for their deportation. The Muellers, thereupon, took the remaining three children in their home. When a month later the authorities wanted to take these children away, Mr. Mueller was able to effect the postponement of the summons; he then arranged for the children to be moved elsewhere. Luckily for them, all the Kerklies family members survived, including Gertrud who was released from Theresienstadt camp at the end of war. However, most of her brothers and sisters, deported to Poland, were never heard from again.[16]

Theodor Görner, whose Jewish wife was momentarily not on the deportation list, was also of help to the Jewish Inge Deutschkron, whom we met earlier in the Walter Rieck story. Before Rieck's involvement, she met Görner, one of a series of her rescuers, through a Jewish acquaintance. Learning of her predicament, Görner arranged work for Inge's mother, Ella, in his printing shop. When the Gestapo arrested Görner for protesting his adopted son's eviction from school (he was half-Jewish), and his shop was closed, Inge's mother moved elsewhere. Inge herself stayed in various places in the Berlin metropolitan area. Through another Jewish acquaintance, she met Lisa Holländer, who was married to a Jewish man, and Inge and her mother occasionally stayed in Lisa's Potsdam flat. On another occasion, Inge was working in a bakery owned by Klara Grüger. When Klara later learned of Inge's true identity, she decided, in Inge's words, "there and then that from now on she would look after my mother and myself with all she could spare." Klara then disclosed to the surprised Inge that she was hiding in her flat a Jewish man (and future husband) in an annex of the bakery. Klara supplied Inge regularly with bakery products. She also forged a certain signature so that Inge and her mother could rent a room under an assumed name. After the war Klara married her ward, the Jewish attorney Hans Münzer, whom she earlier hid for two and a half years.[17]

In February 1943, nineteen-year-old Hanni Weissenberg managed to elude her captors during the giant Factory Action in Berlin. Her parents were no longer alive, and an eighty-year old grandmother was earlier deported to Theresienstadt where she died. Hanni ran out on the street and, with her Jewish star still on her overcoat, headed to a Jewish acquaintance who referred her to a non-Jewish family. They, in turn, connected her with the sisters Elfriede and Grete Most, who lived in the Charlottenburg section of the city. Hanni recalled: "They took me in, without even knowing me, without money and documents." She stayed with them until November of that year and was treated as one of the family. "I have remained for them their 'child,' for whom they cared at the risk of their own lives," Hanni Weissenberg stated. "They never asked for the slightest thanks." When Hanni felt she had better move on, she confided her secret to Viktoria Kolzer, whom she met in the Most sisters' home. She had previously overheard Viktoria making disparaging remarks about the regime. "She knew absolutely nothing about me and my situation, until the moment when I confided to her. I also had no idea how she would react. But she reacted immediately." Viktoria, who was married to a much older man (who died soon thereafter) and had a son, invited Hanni to move in with her. Hanni came to her without papers and money, so the two had to share Viktoria's wartime rations. To supplement her income, Viktoria gave up her job as a cashier at the cinema and found work in a factory. To neighbors, Hanni was introduced as a distant relative come to live with Kolzer after her husband's death. She stayed with Viktoria until the war's end.[18]

Leo Witkowski and wife Liselotte, whom we earlier met in the Gustav Zubeil story, also found succor through the intercession of a third-party Jewish person. When life on Zubeil's boat-home proved too precarious, the Witkowskis approached Hertha Mueller, whom they had earlier learned from a Jewish friend was willing to help. She consented "without a moment's hesitation," in Leo's words. Curious neighbors were told that the Witkowskis were distant relatives whose house had been damaged in an air raid. Another story occasionally used was that Leo was a severely wounded soldier, discharged from the army (he was able to acquire a war-injury certificate). Hertha Mueller, mother to a four-year old boy, cared for the Witkowskis from mid-1943 to May 1945 (as well as for other Jews on the run), while her husband was most of the time away in the army.[19]

We continue with the story of Bruno Gumpel, who was told of Ursula Treptow by a former Jewish schoolmate at the Jewish High School in Berlin who was on friendly terms with Ursula. In April 1943, when Bruno's hiding place no longer proved safe, he headed to Ursula family's home. Bruno and a friend were sheltered in the storage basement of Ursula father's scrap and recycling business. There Bruno stayed until the house was destroyed in an air raid in May 1944 (his friend had previously been picked up while roaming the streets). He then moved with the Treptows to their one-room cottage in a Berlin suburb, where he stayed for a certain time.[20]

In Frankfurt am Main in October 1941, when the Gestapo suddenly appeared in the home of Maria Johanna Fulda and told her to start packing for deportation, she suddenly felt stiff in one leg, which momentarily became immobilized. The Gestapo left, but not before ordering her to vacate the apartment within a few days, that she shared with a non-Jewish woman. Previous to this incident, through a Jewish friend, Maria met Irene Block, a lawyer and financial consultant, who presently advised Maria to contrive a leg paralysis as a means to further postpone her deportation summons; she also simultaneously arranged for a surgeon to commit her to the still existent Jewish hospital for further treatment. In May 1942, Maria Fulda received her third deportation summons, and again Irene Block arranged

another Gestapo medical postponement certificate due to Fulda's ostensible walking disability. Such tactics still prevailed only in Germany, not in
the German-occupied countries, especially in the east, where deportation
of Jews took no account of a person's medical condition. Finally, a day before the anticipated final raid of Frankfurt's remaining Jews in September
1942, Irene Block appeared in Fulda's apartment, told her to remove her
Yellow Star and follow her. The benumbed Maria walked behind Irene to
the train station, and then rode to a small place in the Kassel region, where
Block had rented a cottage with a farmer. There, Maria Fulda stayed for
eight days. In the meantime, Irene Block returned to Frankfurt and concocted a suicide letter, supposedly signed by Fulda. She then secretly moved
Fulda back to Frankfurt, into her own apartment, which seconded as an
office. There, Maria stayed for one and a half years, with Irene feeding her
from her own ration card, looking after her medical needs, and carefully
taking her out for occasional nightly walks. When her home was bombed
in March 1944, Irene Block took Maria with her to a small town unex-
posed to air raids, where both remained until the war's end. Altogether,
Mrs. Fulda was cared for a full two and a half years by Irene Block, a
woman she had only met through the intercession of a Jewish friend.[21]

Some Jewish survivors were introduced to their rescuers via religious
organizations and churches, such as members of the Protestant Confessing
Church, who initially sheltered Christian-converted Jews, then extended
their aid to regular Jews. We have also already noted earlier, in the story
of von Maltzan, the role of the Swedish church in Berlin in helping many
Jews elude capture. Under the stewardship of Pastors Erik Perwe and Erik
Myrgren, Jews there were either hidden in the church compound or referred
to outside helpers, such as Maria von Maltzan, who arranged their further
sheltering or flight to Sweden.[22] The earlier-mentioned Andrea Wolffenstein,
the daughter of a Jewish architect who had built synagogues in Dessau,
Posen, and Berlin, although she herself had passed into the Christian faith,
was provided with a new false identity by the circle of Pastor Niemöller in
Dahlem. She was then admitted into the home of Pastor Karl Reimer in
Nasebaud, near Baerwalde, in Pomerania province. When Reimer was called
up for active military service, Pastor Carl and wife Julie Strecker, from nearby Wusterhause, took over the care of Andrea. She stayed with them for a full
year. "I paid not even a penny," Andrea stated. She was presented as a refugee from Berlin air raids. Previous to this, Andrea, professionally a talented

pianist and music teacher, had been assigned forced labor in the Zeiss-Ikon-Goerz factory, cleaning toilets with other Jewish women. She then was reassigned to peeling potatoes for long hours in the factory canteen. Injured one day while on her way to work (she slipped and fell off the stairs at an elevated S-Bahn station), she was reassigned to an armaments plant. In January 1943, Andrea and her sister Valerie contacted a man who promised them a false Nazi Labor Front card in return for a substantial payment. He turned out to be a swindler, and the money paid to him was lost. The two sisters separated and moved from place to place, including a stay for Andrea with chemistry professor Fritz Strassman. As for Valerie, her incessant peregrinations (eighteen different places) finally landed her in the Munich region, where with the help of Esther Seidel (as already earlier related), she found several sheltering places. In the meantime, due to the mobilization of women in Pomerania to help dig trenches in the effort to stem the Russian advance in the summer of 1944, it was felt safer for Valeria's sister Andrea to return to Berlin. There she was reintroduced to Mrs. Donata Helmrich (they had been childhood playmates), whose husband, army Major Eberhard Helmrich, stationed in distant Drohobych (Poland, today Ukraine) was also involved in aiding Jews (as further mentioned in chapter 8). Wife Donata facilitated Andrea's registration with the police under a different name as Charlotte Maly, a refugee from Poland. Mrs. Helmrich later helped arranged Andrea's travel to Württemberg, where the Confessing Church was active in helping Jews. At a later date, Andrea and sister Valerie were reunited in Esther Seidel's home, outside Munich, where both stayed (though not in the same place) until the war's end.[23]

In another, even more dramatic account, immediately after the war, Max and Ines Krakauer gave a searing account of their peregrinations to over forty places, mostly in the Württemburg area, through the intercession of pastors of the Confessing Church. Reverend Otto Mörike, who lived with his wife and six children in the village of Flacht, seemed to have played a principal role in keeping the Krakauers one step ahead of the authorities by arranging for them short stays with friendly pastors. They stayed in his home for only four weeks (the time permitted for out-of-town persons to stay without registering at the police), before moving on to other places. One of these was the home of Elisabeth Goes, the wife of Pastor Albrecht Goes, who was away in the army as a chaplain. Upon the urging of Pastor Mörike, Elisabeth Goes, who lived in Gebersheim village with her three children (aged five, eight, and nineteen), sheltered the Krakauers for five weeks in the fall of 1944. From there the Krakauers moved to Heimerdingen where further sheltering places had been prepared for them. Mrs. Goes accompanied them, crossing a forest, to their new place. After that Mrs. Goes took in two more Jewish women, one after the other. It was the turn of Reverend Richard and Hildegard Goelz to shelter the Krakauer couple in their Wankheim home, near Tübingen, for four weeks. After sheltering another Jewish person, Goelz was betrayed to the authorities, arrested, and imprisoned in Welzheim labor camp from late December 1944 to April 1945. Reverend Alfred and Luise Dilger are also part of the Protestant clergy team that sheltered the Krakauers. Arriving in October 1943 at the Dilger home, in Stuttgart-Bad Cannstatt, under an assumed name, the Kraukauers remained there for five weeks.

In his postwar memoirs, Dilger wrote that he was originally approached by members of the Confessing Church with a request to help Jews threatened with deportation. When the Krakauers arrived, "we went together toward the main door, and immediately knew what sort of visit it was. We greeted her as warmly as possible, with 'Good Evening, Most Welcome!' This way, she could immediately realize in what kind of a house she had arrived." Dilger added that the fifty-six-year old Max and wife Ines had typically Jewish appearances. "Her Jewish origin was clearly evident by her looks." They came without money and ration cards, and the "Brotherhood" provided for the upkeep. The household children, however, were not told of the secret. The new arrivals were presented as Berliners who had lost all their possessions in an air raid. The Kraukauers shared the family's dinner table and attended Lutheran church services regularly to mix better with the surroundings. Max made himself useful in the garden; Ines tried to help out with household chores. When Prelate Karl Hartenstein arrived for an inspection tour from Stuttgart, he told Dilger point-blank he knew precisely the true identity of his guests and admonished him that in case of trouble, Dilger should expect no help from him. Dilger calmly responded that he felt himself under the protection of a higher power than the church authorities. After a short stay in the Dilger home, the Krakauers parted ways and moved on for short stays in different locations – all told, over forty places. After liberation, the Krakauers immediately wrote of their peregrinations in a special booklet, entitled *Lichter um Dunkel* (Lights in Darkness).[24]

Not to be overlooked is the woman pastor Reverend Ruth Wendland. Having studied theology before the war, she then joined the Confessing

Church. During 1936–1938, she attended the lectures of theologian Karl Barth in Basel and came under his influence. She was ordained in October 1943. That same year, her family gave refuge to a Jewish brother and sister: Ralph and Rita Neumann. The Neumanns had earlier hidden in various places. Ralph had stayed for a time with a farmer, and Rita did household chores elsewhere. Returning to Berlin, and not knowing where to turn, the seventeen-year-old Ralph mixed with crowds on the S-Bahn, and at night slept in outdoor places – and was occasionally helped by another hiding Jew. At this juncture, Rita was introduced to Ruth Wendland who, seconded by her mother Agnes, offered shelter to her brother Ralph in their home at Gethsemane Street, and set aside for him a small room. When danger threatened, Ruth secured for Ralph a temporary hiding place in a vacant house, to where she brought him food. During daylight hours, Ralph would leave his room, as though going to work, and then spend many hours in the home of the previously mentioned Elisabeth Abegg – also a major rescuer of Jews on the run, as already told.

Then, in February 1945, Ralph Neumann was arrested by a military patrol while seeing a relative off on a train. He was turned over to the Gestapo who, in turn, arrested Agnes Wendland. To spare her mother, Ruth turned herself in and Agnes was released. Ralph also met his sister in jail and was brutally beaten. When all seemed lost for the two, a stroke of good luck came in the form of a heavy air raid, which made it possible for the two to make good their escape, though wounded by the falling bricks. They found shelter with the previously mentioned Reverend Harald Poelchau (whom they met earlier at Wendland's home, and who at the time promised his help). Poelchau, together with his wife Dorothee, tended the wounds of the two, and Ralph and Rita stayed with them until the end of the war. Before the war, Poelchau studied theology under Paul Tillich and was influenced by his theology of religious socialism. During the Nazi period, he was linked to the Kreisau circle, one of the anti-Nazi underground networks. As chaplain of the Berlin Tegel prison, he was present during the execution of the July 20th plotters on Hitler's life and attended to their last religious rites.[25]

On the Catholic side, the foremost rescuer of note is undoubtedly Gertrud Luckner. With a doctorate in theology, she was active in the Catholic Caritas center, in Freiburg, which included aid to baptized Jews and, later, to regular Jews as well. Her activities included sending packages to those deported to Łódź ghetto and smuggling persons across the Swiss border (reachable not too far from Freiburg). One of her beneficiaries, Ruth von Schulze-Gaevernitz, wrote: "on the third morning, before the evening of my flight, you traveled for my sake to Schwarzwald-Autobus, to a very convenient resort place. And from the post office of that village, you cabled by telegram to my friend Bela in France (St. Otilienberg), informing her that I would arrive, with God's help, with the local train from Strasbourg to this or that Alsace village, at this or other hour, approximately at noon." On March 24, 1943, Luckner was arrested on a train with 5,000 marks in her possession bound for distribution to needy Jews in Berlin. She underwent an intensive nine-week interrogation. Questioned who her bosses were, she replied, "My Christian conscience." She asked to be taken to Theresienstadt (to be together with her friend Rabbi Leo Baeck, who had already been sent there). Instead, the Gestapo officer told her: "For you, lover of Jews, we have something better" ("*Für Sie, Judenfreundin, haben wir was Besseres*"), and she was sent to the infamous women's Ravensbrück camp, which she luckily survived. After the war, she edited the annual *Freiburger Rundbrief* to promote a greater Jewish-Christian dialogue.[26]

Finally, in this section, one should note the help extended by many Quakers to Jews in distress. Foremost among them is the aforementioned Elisabeth Abegg, a history teacher at a girls' school, who was dismissed in 1933 by the newly appointed Nazi school director for her pronounced anti-Nazi views. In 1942, although quite advanced in age – she was then 60 – and charged with caring for her bedridden eighty-six-year old mother and elderly ill sister, she nevertheless made her home in the Tempelhof section of Berlin available as a temporary way station for many Jews, especially her former pupils. Creating a rescue network made up of Quaker friends, friendly pastors, and former school students, Elisabeth Abegg helped dozens of Jews escape deportation and deprivation for close to three years. This included sheltering Jews in her own home for several nights (in a building that housed several known Nazi-party members), or in adjoining, temporarily emptied apartments in her care, or other distant locations (such as in Alsace and East Prussia), as well as helping others make their escape across the Swiss border, an undertaking she helped finance by selling her jewelry and other valuables.

In a booklet dedicated to her 75th birthday in 1957, entitled *Und ein Licht leuchtet in der Finsternis* (And a Light Shone in the Darkness), her former charges praised Elisabeth Abegg for her dedication, care, and humanity. Liselotte Pereles wrote: "In my mortal fear, I listened to your good words, which you imparted to me on my dangerous trip [to seek shelter among friends]: 'I will allow nothing to happen to you.'" Hertha Long-Goldstein, another of Abegg's beneficiaries, noted: "With Fraulein Dr. Abegg was revealed the truth that a life of love for fellow men, bound with respect for every being, is the most elevated and eternal value." Charlotte Herzfeld, a Jewish woman brought to Abegg's attention in 1943 after her parents committed suicide on the eve of their deportation, was given comfort and care. "You were there, calm, serene, courageous," Charlotte wrote to her years later, "Perhaps one should add 'self-composed.' I regained trust, I sensed warmth, I felt sheltered. You reminded me of the calmness, warmth, and equanimity of my mother, under different circumstances." "She encouraged us not to despair," recalled Yitzhaq Shwersentz, "to believe in a better future through belief in mankind, and I always refer to her as a helping and saving 'angel' amidst this terrible hell. She acted, not for compensation, but out of love for persecuted people."[27]

For other persons in the Quaker category, we note the case of Gerhard and Ilse Schwersensky (respectively, a social worker and kindergarten teacher), to whom was referred the sixteen-year-old Lorraine-Hannelore Jacoby, who stayed in their modest home, sharing food and comfort with the Schwersenskys' three children. Previous to that, in 1942, Jacoby had attempted crossing the German-Swiss border but was almost apprehended by border guards. Eluding capture, she returned to Berlin, where friends in the Quaker church referred her to the Schwersenskys. To neighbors, she was presented as an out-of-town secretary who had won a prize for a special course offered only in Berlin. Similarly, Lottie Katz, an employee at the Jewish community who had been ordered to report for deportation, was given shelter intermittently in the Schwersensky home and cared for with food and necessities in other places of concealment: bombed-out buildings, train stations, and office building basements.[28]

CHAPTER 4

Foremen, Supervisors, and Work Colleagues

* * *

MANY RESCUE STORIES EVOLVED OUT of special work relationships between both sides: German-appointed work supervisors and Jewish forced laborers under their supervision. When these workers were threatened with deportation while performing work in Germany or in the occupied countries, or were on the verge of facing liquidation by Nazi execution squads, some of their supervisors rose to the occasion and went to great lengths to save a fraction or most of their Jewish laborers. We first examine rescue stories initiated by work supervisors on German soil, then move on to similar settings in German-occupied countries, and end with related rescue operations inside concentration and labor camps.

The Nazi plan to murder all of Europe's Jews depended on the scrupulous obedience and efficient execution of all measures by the civilian and military bureaucracies operating both in Germany and in the occupied countries. German military and civilian administrators in positions of command could, if they wanted, exercise their authority to explore loopholes in the Nazi machinery of destruction and find ways and means to stay the executioner's hand and save Jews from death. This was especially true during the war years for persons in managerial positions who depended on Jewish forced labor to meet army and other defense contract deadlines. In general, officials who were willing to exert themselves even slightly to save their Jewish workers, and were astute enough to come up with acceptable excuses (such as claiming that Jewish labor was vital to meet military-related work schedules) and pull strings with persons in high positions, could become authors of rescue operations. Such rescue attempts by German officials did not necessarily imply serious risks to themselves. There were, however, others who were even willing to go beyond the permissible limits and place themselves in some jeopardy vis-a-vis their superiors, in an effort to save their Jewish assigned workers. Some went even further down this road and actually distorted and falsified rules, regulations, and records, so as to divert the SS and other killing units from their murderous designs, or at least postpone the fatal date. In only a few cases were persons prepared to directly challenge Nazi antisemitic measures and bear the consequences for such defiance. We shall have occasion to illustrate these various forms of opposition to the killing of the Jews, as recorded in the Yad Vashem files. The underlying lesson is that even in Nazi Germany, with its stifling totalitarianism, individual acts of humanitarian action were possible. The Nazi dictatorship did not totally paralyze individual rescue endeavors for those prepared to take up the challenge. Unfortunately, such persons were far too few to make a serious dent in the pace of the destruction. Be that as it may, in this chapter, due recognition will be given to those few rescuers in positions of command who dared and saved Jewish lives, or succeeded in postponing the bitter fate awaiting their Jewish workers – within the measure of the authority available to them.

a) Inside Germany and Austria

We begin with a story, which took place in Berlin, of a firm that employed semi- and fully blind Jews and that was owned by a handicapped German. Otto Weidt, who was himself over half blind, operated a workshop in Berlin producing brooms and brushes for the army and employed many blind and other handicapped Jewish workers. He protected his Jews by claiming they were needed to meet contract deadlines with the military. To keep the Gestapo at arm's length, he purposely procrastinated completing work schedules, making sure that production assignments were not honored too quickly – thus justifying the need for his Jewish workers. One day, while away from his workshop, the Gestapo raided the place and carried off all the Jewish workers: the blind, deaf, and dumb. Weidt hurried to the Gestapo detention place at Grosse Hamburgerstrasse and adamantly demanded the release of his workers. The sight of a semi-blind German – an "Aryan" – stoutly demanding the return of his Jewish workers must have touched a chord with the Gestapo, for they released the imprisoned Jews. Then, marching at the head of his blind Jews, who held on to each other's hands, he led them back to his shop. It was an unforgettable sight. At a later date, Weidt's blind Jewish workers were taken away and deported to Auschwitz. Weidt also helped others, and not necessarily invalid Jews, by arranging work for them in his shop. The earlier-mentioned Inge Deutschkron, for instance, was registered under the name of a certain prostitute, replacing a woman who, although also listed as one of Weidt's employees, found the oldest profession a more profitable proposition. When the police arrested that woman, Inge Deutschkron, whose ID card bore that woman's name, had to leave and move on. Alice Licht, another Jewish woman on the run, and her parents were hidden in the firm's storeroom, behind brooms and brushes. When Alice was betrayed and sent to Auschwitz, Weidt decided to try to reach her there with food parcels in his hands. He was able to have himself invited to the Auschwitz camp's offices on the excuse of displaying his new line of brooms and brushes. While there, he learned that Alice had been transferred to Gross Rosen camp, then to Christianstadt am Bober, where she was assigned work in a munitions factory. Although Weidt was not permitted to see her, his food parcels reached her there. During the evacuation of Christianstadt in February 1945, Alice made good her escape during a forced march toward Bergen-Belsen camp, and returning to Berlin, she remained in hiding with the help of Weidt until the city's fall to the Russians.[1]

In the following story, Lola Alexander was doing compulsory labor in a munitions factory, the *Deutsche Hydraulik und Präzisionswerke Alfred Teves* company, in Berlin-Wittenau, when her mother suddenly took her life in 1942 to avoid deportation to the camps. Lola was fortunate that her foreman, Willi Daene, who was also responsible for the other over 100 Jewish women forced laborers in that place, showed kindness and care for his Jewish workers – such as reducing their daily work shift schedule from twelve to a normal eight hours. A spinner by profession, Daene had earlier been active in the socialist party and was twice arrested and released by the Nazi regime in the 1930s. In January 1943, Daene, who was already sheltering a Jewish girl in his home, devised a rescue operation for Lola. She was taken to one of the three lending libraries that he also operated with his wife – the one near the Frankfurt train station, where Lola was presented as Mrs. Schneider, a war widow, who found it necessary to live in the back of the storeroom since her house was supposedly demolished in an air raid. When she felt despondent, the Daenes took her to their family home in Conradshöhe, a different section of Berlin.

During the massive Factory Action of February 27, 1943, Daene was able to temporarily hide several of his Jewish workers. Ursula Finkel, another Jewish woman on the run, was sheltered by the Daenes in their other lending library in the Moabit section. When danger of detection increased, both Lola and Ursula spent the evenings at the Daene home in Conradshöhe. A year later, in August 1944, Ursula was arrested while on the street. Fearing a police raid on the Daene home, Lola Alexander and the other Jewish girl were immediately moved to a different location. Willi Daene was nevertheless arrested, not for sheltering Jews but for his participation in clandestine political activities at the firm, but at his trial he was able to acquit himself of the charges against him and was released in December 1944. In the meantime, Lola Alexander moved from place to place, until at Mrs. Daene's invitation, she moved back to her previous job in the lending library at the Frankfurt station. Lola was lucky to stay safe through the Russian siege of Berlin, and see liberation safe and sound. But not so for her loved ones, as Lola Alexander was the only one of her entire family to survive.[2]

Still in Berlin, Ken Lindenberg did errands for a pharmacy owned by Kurt and Edith Zabel. When they learned that Ken stood in danger of deportation, they offered the cellar of their shop as storage space for Ken's belongings – and also left him their home address. On several occasions, he intermittently stayed with the Zabels, each time for a period of three to ten days, while at the same time planning his escape to Denmark, which he carried out in November 1943. On other occasions, Ken hid in Christa Wrudnitski's home, a worker he met at an electrical appliances factory he Ken was doing compulsory labor. Christa's father, Ludwig, was formerly a train conductor; his wife stole Ludwig's railway-man's hat and gave it to Ken for use during his escape toward the Baltic coast aboard freight trains.[3]

Work-related help was of course not restricted to the Berlin area. Albert Grüneberg, a medical doctor from Cologne who worked for the German railroads, was helped by former railway employees to flee from a detention camp in Köln-Bocklemünd soon after his arrest in October 1943. He and his non-Jewish wife were then hidden in several regional locations.[4] Far to the south, near Gmünd, Austria, Ludwig Knapp operated a farm in Weitra and was assigned two-dozen Jewish laborers from Gmünd. It was the latter part of 1944 when these men and women forced laborers were brought in

from nearby Hungary for various difficult physical assignments. Upon arrival at his farm, they were surprised by the humane treatment of Knapp,
in light of the cruelties visited upon these hapless persons by German work
supervisors in the camps. Four of the women were assigned light household duties; the others, various chores on the farm and at a sawmill several
kilometers away, where Knapp installed for them heating and a kitchen,
and gave them warm winter clothing. During the Jewish Yom Kippur fast,
Ludwig gave them the day off. At other times, some worked only half-days
and were treated with consideration by Knapp, something quite out of the
ordinary for a German supervisor in those inhuman days (for instance, on
Christmas eve, Ludwig and wife Maria handed out gifts to everyone). When
one of the women workers developed a toothache, he took her secretly to his
private physician.

On April 17, 1945, Knapp was ordered to return his Jewish laborers to
the SS authorities for a possible forced march to a different location. Instead,
he provided them with food to last a month and instructed them where to flee
and hide until the imminent approaching liberation. Others remained hidden
in the Knapp home for three weeks, during which time the Knapps took care
of all their needs, including milk for one of the women's child. To cover up his
rescue operation, he left for Vienna and, returning two days later, he reported
that his workers had in the meantime fled, then led the soldiers with hounds
in the wrong direction, toward Linz. In 1970, Ludwig Knapp stated to a journalist that because of his help, he is no longer very popular in his home village
of Weitra. He added that the idea of rescuing people did not originally enter
his mind. When earlier he went to the Labor Department to ask for manual
help, the man behind the desk told him: "You would be doing something good
if you were to take Jewish labor." So he did just that. After all, he needed
additional hands to keep his farm in operation. Slowly but surely, he began
taking a personal interest in the welfare of his Jewish laborers. As they needed
more food to remain work-fit, he rationalized his help in that situation. "One
must after all properly feed one's workers," he stated. Same reasoning when it
came to proper clothing: "One must after all properly clothe one's workers." He
simply wanted his workers to look fit for work, he blandly explained. The full
transformation into a rescuer occurred when they wanted to take his workers
away from him, which he knew meant their death. Here, he was determined
not to let that happen. So, he stated, he saved them! Simple words, to explain a
herculean humanitarian deed! The Knapp story demonstrates the significance

of proximity and eye-to-eye encounters as factors in triggering non-self-described altruists to initiate ever-expanding acts of rescue.[5]

B) IN THE OCCUPIED COUNTRIES

Some of the help extended by German work supervisors in the occupied countries to Jewish labor assigned to them – persons with death constantly staring them in their eyes, especially in east European countries – may have initially seemed minor and matter-of-fact in their own eyes, such as to instill a greater and better production output. However, to the distraught Jewish workers, a friendly disposition, fewer working hours, and an additional slice of bread was to them of crucial importance and a tremendous psychological lift, a boost to their willpower to survive against tremendous odds. Karl Dangelmeier, for instance, was director of the railway station in Nowy Targ, Poland. From the start, he displayed a friendly attitude toward the Jewish laborers assigned to him. When winter approached, he distributed coal to their wives for home heating. On one occasion, learning of a severe fuel shortage, he told one of the workers to fetch his horse thrice a week and load coal for the needy persons in the ghetto. Because of his friendly attitude toward Poles and Jews, he was called back to Germany in late 1941, where he was placed in charge of a small train station. When his Jewish workers learned of his reassignment, they added their signature to a special letter of thanks and appreciation that they handed him on the eve of his departure. The letter, dated November 17, 1941, partly reads:

> Unfortunately, the news is true that you are leaving us. . . . We wish to underline that your leaving this place is a blow to everyone. It is like one's state of health. Only when one loses it, does one realize what one had, and what you meant to us. . . . We cannot specify here all your good deeds, Herr Director, the list would indeed be quite long. In addition to the material and financial help, which we appreciate much, we wish to underline your spiritual and moral assistance. At a time when our humiliation knew no bounds, you made us feel true human beings. Your sensitive and friendly behavior, your courageous and fatherly attitude toward us, in order to prevent anything evil from happening to us, and foremost toward your Jewish

workers, has restored our belief in man and humanity as a whole. . . .
We are therefore filled with concern and fear at what can and may
happen to us without the presence of your shining personality. . . .
We can only wish you, Herr Director, to obtain a position where you
will be able to fulfill your ideals, both for the good of your people
and for humanity as a whole..."[6]

Some German work supervisors facilitated the escape of their Jewish laborers
when their lives were in jeopardy – even helping with the arrangements, as in
the following two stories of supervisors for the German government's sponsored Todt engineering and construction organization. Konrad Schweser, a
civilian engineer from Sulzfeld am Main, was in charge of a road building
project in Teplik, near Uman, Ukraine, which used Jewish labor from a camp
near Kransnopolka. The conditions for the Jewish laborers, under constant
watch by SS and Ukrainian collaborationist troops, were extremely harsh,
and they were kept on a starvation diet. From time to time, the SS carried out selections where the sick and those considered unfit were taken out
and shot. When Schweser learned of an SS-planned raid in the fall of 1942,
he alerted the camp inmates to either report to work, thus avoiding being
netted at their camp base, or make other hiding arrangements for the day.
In June 1943, he smuggled out a group of persons in a hay-covered wagon
and had them moved to the Czernowitz area, which was then administered
by the Romanians who at that particular time had dispensed with treat-
ing harshly the Jewish inhabitants of that city. He reportedly also smuggled
medicaments into the Jewish labor camp to contain the spread of typhus
and thus avoid an SS-planned liquidation of the camp, and had a Jewish
physician smuggled into the camp to help falsify the records and report the
typhus epidemic as simply a severe flu infection that could be contained.
He also helped several women to escape and reach the Bug River to reach
the Romanian side. It is told that he used his personal van for that purpose.
In another life-saving action, he hid a group of 60 children in a safe place
under the stage floor of a building inside the camp that formerly served as a
theater, after he learned of an SS-planned raid to nab the reported children
who in SS eyes were of no "productive" value. On another similar occasion,
he concealed six children in a loaded cart that he kept hidden in a construction storehouse until he arranged with a certain Ukrainian, who in return
for payment agreed to ferry them across the Bug River to an orphanage in

Berschad, then under Romanian control. For his help to Jewish fugitives, Schweser was tried by a German court in Vinnitsa, Ukraine, but the charges could not be sustained. He then came down with typhus, was hospitalized in Uman, and then sent home on leave. The camp itself was liberated by the Russians in March 1944.[7]

Willi Ahrem, an ethnic German from Bukovina province (then part of Romania, an ally of Nazi Germany), was in Nemirov, Ukraine, with the Todt organization in 1941. One of his tasks was keeping the streets clean with the help of Jewish labor. In November 1941, Ahrem alerted Yehoshua Mencer, one of the workers, of an approaching raid against the town's Jews, and the latter passed the word around to others, who then fled to the surrounding forests and villages. 2,500 Jews were killed during this action, while Ahrem arranged for provisions to reach those who fled into the forest. In July 1942, Ahrem again warned his Jewish workers of an impending raid, and he led a group of Jews to his home for temporary shelter. He then took Yehoshua Mencer, his wife, and son, and another woman (whose family perished in a previous raid), and moved them to Transnistria, which was under Romanian control, bribing Romanian soldiers on the way to ensure the safety of the passage. In 1943, Ahrem was reassigned to another region.[8] In a similar story, Hans Sürkl, a foreman for the Todt organization on a road construction project in the Uman region, freed a group of Jewish women laborers who had fled the camp in late 1943 when they sensed that they were about to be shot. Recaptured, they were brought to Sürkl for identification before being liquidated. At this crucial point, Sürkl told the guards: "The Ukrainian women are not able to fix my beautiful socks as well as the Jewish women. Leave them with me, and after they will have finished washing and mending, I will finish them off personally." He then fed the women and told them how to reach the Russian lines. Previous to this incident, Sürkl was known for the good treatment of his Jewish laborers (such as extra bread and less harsh work conditions).[9]

In Rakow, near Częstochowa, Poland, Fritz Mühlhof was responsible for the security of a Hasag firm (armaments production network) that employed Jewish labor, among whom were members of a Jewish underground. During the liquidation of the Częstochowa ghetto, Mühlhof took with him a group of laborers into the burning ghetto to help spirit out surviving Jews and bring them to the factory, as well as to fetch furniture, equipment, and medications left over by those killed during the raid. In the Hasag firm,

Mühlhof helped acquire additional vital necessities for his charges, especially food to supplement the meager rations for his starving workers. When
word of his magnanimous treatment of the workers reached the authorities,
Mühlhof was removed and sent to the front for combat duty. He fell into
Russian captivity, but was released at the end of the war.[10]

There are several more accounts of German civilian entrepreneurs and
administrators of economic enterprises in the occupied territories of Eastern
Europe who stood up with much effrontery and courage in the attempt to
save the Jewish laborers under their care when these were faced with deportation or immediate execution. In Lublin, Poland, Bernhard Falkenberg, a
civilian contractor assigned to drying marshes, employed Jewish labor from
the Włodawa camp near Lublin (and close to the Sobibór death camp),
and took special care of them. During one Nazi liquidation raid in 1942,
Falkenberg was given the choice of liberating 30 persons from those assembled in the square. Falkenberg insisted he needed more. The SS refused
and led the people to the train station. Falkenberg rushed to call a German
official in Lublin, who immediately arrived on the scene and ordered the
local SS commander (Richard Nitzke) to release the people needed by
Falkenberg. A bitter argument ensued; in the end 500 were released to him.
By the summer of 1943, the SS had decided on the final liquidation of that
labor camp. Falkenberg kept his workers late, so as to postpone their return to their quarters; he then urged them to escape in the forest and make
contact with the partisans. He bribed the Ukrainian guards with drinks in
order to give the remaining camp inmates time to flee to the nearby woods
to link up with the partisans there. He was arrested after a letter was found
on a partisan, addressed to him, asking for some supplies. As punishment,
he eventually landed in the notorious Mauthausen camp, which he luckily
survived.[11]

As noted in the previous stories, some work supervisors occasionally
went so far as to shelter their Jewish laborers during Nazi raids, with all the
risks attending them for such a personal involvement in help to Jews. Otto
Busse went even further. By profession a painter, he arrived in Białystok,
Poland, in 1943, where he set up a paint and pictures shop and worked as a
contractor for the German army and police. Many of his workers were Jewish
laborers from the nearby ghetto. After the liquidation of the ghetto, five
Jewish girls who acted as couriers for the Jewish underground and lived on
the Aryan side of the city worked in Busse's shop disguised as Poles. Hassia

Bornstein related she was terrified and feared a trip she was about to undertake when Busse told her he believed she was Jewish, but immediately calmed her fears by saying that he would help her and her friends. Paradoxically, the other Germans trusted him because of his Nazi party membership. True to his word, Busse then placed his apartment at the disposal of the young women, where weapons were occasionally stored. He also supplied them with vital information of weapon placements in the city. In this he was helped by two other Germans, both still professing communists and therefore strenuously opposed to the Nazis. As a believing Christian, Busse often quoted from the Bible, including the special mission of the Jewish people in the divine dispensation. When the Russians appeared, he was taken prisoner and did hard labor for five years in the Kiev region before being released.[12]

In the same city of Białystok, the German Artur Schade was placed in charge of a large requisitioned textile firm, which was converted into producing uniforms for the German army and which employed many Poles and some Jews from the nearby ghetto. Schade impressed those who first met him as a typical German overlord of those days: disciplinarian and tyrannical, and not beyond striking a worker in the face when the latter was shirking his work assignment. All feared him, especially the Jewish workers, who noted the Nazi party emblem that Schade wore proudly on his coat lapel. Only much later did they learn that the man was a sworn socialist and pacifist and had joined the Nazi party in 1939 simply as a cover for his radical anti-Nazi viewpoint. With the start of Nazi liquidation raids in the Białystok ghetto, Schade personally spirited some of his Jewish workers out of the ghetto, hid them in his home attic, and attended to their needs. One of the Jewish workers he hired as his personal secretary. When the SS action was over, Schade smuggled them back into the ghetto. This he repeated on several occasions. To Chaika Grossman, a Jewish underground operative and later a noted Israeli parliamentarian, he gave a work certificate upon her request, to facilitate her movement on the Aryan side of the city and her ongoing contacts with Jewish partisans operating in the nearby forests. When the ghetto was liquidated in August 1943, Schade helped a group of survivors, some of whom had earlier worked in his firm, to flee to the forests and supplied them with vital necessities. In 1944, as the front reached Białystok, Schade himself joined the Jewish partisan forces in the forests. The stern-looking Nazi member work manager – a man of few words and a stickler for rules who was feared by his workers – turned out to be a staunch anti-Nazi who eventually joined forces with those fighting Nazi tyranny. Several dozen Jews owe their lives to this unusual, and at first unpredictable, humanitarian.[13]

In a different setting, Karl Laabs, professionally an architect, had served as a front soldier during World War One. A member of the socialist party before the advent of the Nazis, in 1935 he ran afoul of the Nazis because of his criticism of the Hitler Youth, and his name was stricken from the list of teachers of architecture. Conscripted into the *Luftwaffe* (German Air Force), with the rank of sergeant, and sent to Krenau (today Chrzanow, Poland) in Upper Silesia, he was assigned various construction assignments for the military with the help of Jewish labor from the nearby Sosnowiec ghetto. According to them, he allowed Jews threatened with deportation to be found on his construction project, while in reality not doing any work, and cared for their sustenance. On the eve of the last great raid of the area's Jews, on February 18, 1943, he hid a group of Jews in his home; he then took them in his van to a safe location, where they could make good their escape.[14]

Of even greater magnitude is the rescue operation of Hermann Graebe. Born in 1900, and by training an engineer, he was successively head of a construction firm and an architecture and engineering business before joining the Josef Jung concern, which had railway contracts with the Todt organization in occupied Lwów, Poland (today Lviv, Ukraine). Years before that, he had been an early member of the Nazi party but left it, disenchanted with the Nazi regime's treatment of Jews. Up to 1941, he participated as a civilian contractor of military fortifications in occupied France. Appointed as the company's representative in Ukraine, Graebe was sent to Zdolbunov to supervise the building of locomotive sheds, warehouses, and ancillary railway projects. He gradually increased the number of Jewish workers to meet the growing work schedules of the military. By November 1941, close to 5,000 persons worked for his company in several branches in the Rovno region. While there, he witnessed several SS killing raids in which thousands of Jewish men, women, and children were shot. Constantly confronting SS officers, he adamantly insisted to defer some of the raids or, at the very least, spare his workers, which he claimed were professional construction workers and absolutely needed to meet work schedules set for him by Berlin chancelleries. In addition, he kept a Jewish woman, which he passed off as a Pole, as his private secretary.

On July 13, 1942, Graebe learned of another planned Nazi raid taking place in nearby Rovno (although he was assured that it would not take place) that also targeted his workers. Hurrying there, he walked up to SS commander Dr. Puetz, in charge of the killing operation, who stood with a revolver in one hand and a dog whip in the other. Facing the SS officer, Graebe recalled saying: "Dr. Puetz (I deliberately stressed his title), I want to remind you of what you told me yesterday. Exactly the opposite has happened. Why the lies? I repeat once again, I need my workers and I must get them back!" Puetz coolly replied: "Nobody gets out of here." Graebe repeated his request, and Puetz cautioned him to lower his voice. This altercation took place in front of some Jews who were squatting on the ground, and it went on for some time until Puetz relented and allowed Graebe to take his people out, with the exception of those already assembled in the square. Graebe asked Puetz to assign an SS officer to assure no harm would befall him on his way out of the carnage site. Graebe assembled his Jewish workers, and with a pistol in his hand kept the Ukrainian militia at bay. He then led them out of the city (150 people, according to Yad Vashem records), "with my automatic pistol at the head" while the Ukrainians were shooting at every Jew in sight.

In the final liquidation raid three months later, on October 13, 1942, Graebe could no longer save his Jewish workers, who were among the victims – shot in a nearby ravine. Graebe was, however, able to save some more Jewish laborers in a related rescue operation, when he transported them in stages, in his own car, to the far-flung company branch in Poltava, hundreds of miles to the east, a place that was at the time safer for the Jews. The Poltava branch was pure fiction: Graebe had set it up and maintained it at his own expense for the sole purpose of providing shelter for his Jewish workers. Had Graebe's car been stopped at one of the numerous German roadblocks on the way, both rescuer and rescued would have faced serious risks to their lives.

After the war Graebe was one of the first Germans to testify at the Nuremberg trials against some of the SS officers who presided over the aforementioned killing raids, which made him quite unpopular in his own country. After receiving anonymous threats, and feeling increasingly isolated from friends and acquaintances, he left for a new life in the United States. Years after the war, he attributed his wartime behavior to his mother's influence. "From my earliest youth, my mother taught me one principle, which, of course, she did not know came from the great philosopher and teacher Hillel who lived in Jerusalem 2,000 years ago: 'Do not do to others what you would not have done to yourself.' I often heard that saying from her, when I tortured an animal or pulled a leg off a fly or did any such other things that children so often do. And as I grew older I heard my mother's voice transmitted in other forms."[15]

As one may infer from the previous stories and the other unmentioned records on hand, incidents of help by Germans supervisors in various industrial installations were more prevalent in the occupied lands, where Jewish labor was more extensively used in various defense-related vital projects (before they were herded off to be killed). Many of these supervisors acted as trustees (commonly termed *Treuhänder*), who were officially appointed as managers and administrators of these industrial and labor projects and received their pay from the German occupation authorities. This is especially true for Poland, where thousands of Jews were initially conscripted in various German controlled industrial shops. Many erroneously believed that the vital work they were freely performing protected them from further physical harm and death. But as soon as the "non-productive" Jews were eliminated, the Germans turned their attention to those considered "productive" and began to eliminate them as well. While work in German-controlled shops was no assurance that even a kindly disposed work manager could prevent the bitter fate awaiting the Jewish workers, the extra valuable time momentarily gained made possible the taking of preventive measures and escape-hatch plans, at times in collusion with German appointed work managers, as illustrated above as well as in the following examples.

In Będzin-Zaglębie, annexed to Germany during the war (and returned to Poland after the war), the German appointed *Treuhander* Johann Pscheidt tried to save his Jewish workers. An ethnic German originally from the Czernowitz region (now Chernivtsi, in Ukraine), he was a building contractor before the war and entertained good business relations with local Jews, some of whom he employed in his firm. Repatriated to Germany in 1940, after Czernowitz was handed over to the Russians (under the August 1939 Nazi-Soviet non-aggression treaty), he appeared in Będzin-Zaglębie in 1941 as an administrator on behalf of the occupation authorities of a confiscated Jewish soap firm. He was also given to manage a large Polish-confiscated shoe firm. During the Nazi killing raid of July 1943, Pscheidt hid some 80 Jews in his firm, arranged for their feeding and other necessities, and facilitated their contacts with Jewish underground operatives in the vicinity. From the roof of his firm, many made their escape; Pscheidt provided them with money, gold, food, clothing, and encouragement. In addition, he allowed his private office to be used as a workshop for the manufacture of false credentials, seals, etc. He also contacted his sister in Vienna (whose husband was in the army) to help some of the Jews who were sent there for labor assignments, and her home also served as refuge for a group of clandestine Jews in Vienna, who were without food and credentials. Pscheidt would occasionally visit them, bringing along clothing and money.[16]

Still in Będzin-Zagłębie, Alfred Rossner, as a paid work administrator for the SS, operated an even larger firm than Pscheidt's, producing uniforms and other clothing items. Before the war, Rossner worked in a textile firm in Berlin whose Jewish owner was later expelled to Będzin. It is told that he and other Jewish businessmen asked Alfred Rossner to come there and assume control as a German-appointed trustee of one of the Jewish expropriated firms, in the hope that this would assure the survival of the ghettoized Jews. A natural impediment (he limped on one leg) and chronic sickness exempted him from active military service. Before the Nazi rise to power, he was active in the socialist youth movement, and it is therefore still a mystery why the Nazis agreed to use his services.

One of the first workshops supervised by Rossner employed thousands of Jews. Another workshop produced and repaired shoes and boots for the army. By 1942, there were an estimated 10,000 workers in both shops – quite an astounding figure when compared with Jewish labor in other German-controlled workshops. In Rossner's shops, Jewish section leaders worked side by side with him. Some of them were also involved in racketeering: they accepted bribes by Jews wishing to be listed as his workers. Rossner took exceptional care of his workers; in some cases, he was able to free persons already selected for deportation – sometimes in collusion with the SS, on other occasions by circumventing them. At times, he threw caution to the wind in the attempt to save Jews. During one Nazi raid, he rode into the ghetto in a horse-driven buggy, screaming in Yiddish (which he learned from one of his section heads): "Jews, don't be fools. Don't go when you're called." Carola Baum related that after hiding in a coal cellar for a week to avoid deportation, she wandered aimlessly ("without shoes, without money") in the streets. She then decided to head directly to Rossner's home. "I looked terrible; dirty, with wounds on my feet, and frightened." Rossner took her in. She washed herself and was properly fed. The following day, he took her into his shop. Yocheved Gelili also related how Rossner took her out from a column of marching Jews in summer 1943, on its way to the deportation train. "He approached an SS man, and said I was vital for his shop. I grabbed my sister's hand, and she grabbed my cousin's hand, and three more held on to her. Then a heated discussion ensued between Rossner and the SS man, who consented only for me to leave. I refused to leave without at least my sister. The five in the chain held on to me like a life vest. . . . There followed turmoil, beatings, pushing, and shots during which all the six managed to escape. Until today, I do not understand how it happened. Some of Rossner's German aides covered our flight, and we were quickly hidden in the shop's offices." Other witnesses testify how Rossner admitted many fleeing Jews for hiding in a bunker in his shoemaking shop.

Rossner's Jewish workforce was gradually reduced as the Germans launched one raid after another, with the victims deported to Auschwitz camp. During the August 1943 raid, Rossner was livid with rage at the SS betrayal of their promise not to further touch his Jews. In the words of Henrietta Altman, one of his wards: "On Rossner's orders several open trucks were sent into the ghetto, under the pretext of bringing clothes for the people. . . . Under the layers of clothing, people hidden in the bunkers were smuggled" into one of Rossner's workshops. Edward Retman, another witness, stated: "We all knew it for a fact that he financed the Jewish underground in our town. It was his money that sent the illegal transports to Hungary and Romania via Vienna. This was a big secret, and none of us knew any details except that he was involved."

At the end of 1943, he was arrested by the Gestapo and executed in January 1944. It is not known what the precise charges were: corruption or help to Jews to avoid their deportation, or both. One day, Rossner's aunt appeared in one of the shops, now down to 50 workers, and spilled out the news: "They hanged him, because he helped Jews. I saw his body." It is said that the Gestapo found 90 gold watches hidden in his home (some accuse him of having enriched himself at the expense of his Jewish workers); others claim that his intervention on behalf of his Jews and his other clandestine activities caused his downfall. In the eyes of Henrietta Altman, one of those helped by him, Rossner remains a hero. She described him as "a man who endeavored to save Jews from the *Judenrat* and from the Final Solution. It is not a story of spectacular rescues and achievements, but of desperate attempts. He paid with his life and the few whose lives he touched want his story to be told and his name to be properly honored." He is, indeed, on Yad Vashem's list of the Righteous.[17]

Further to the east, in Boryslaw, from whose soil oil had been extracted and refined for decades, Berthold Beitz headed the important *Beskiden*

Ölgesellschaft, which in October 1942 was renamed *Karpatenöl A.G.*, and which controlled all oil firms in the city. In that capacity, he employed up to 1,500 Jews from the city's ghetto and looked after their needs. He was also able to free some from deportation, and when the need arose to save others, he helped by suggesting hiding places to them, which sometimes led to sheltering one person in his home during a Nazi raid. Oil production was understandably crucial to the German war effort, and Beitz used this to the best advantage when it came to saving his Jewish workers. During the large August 1942 raid on the city's Jews, when hundreds were shot on the streets and thousands were deported to the death camps, Beitz rushed to the train station and was able to release his workers. He continued protecting his Jewish workers from further raids until the spring of 1944, as Russian forces edged closer to Boryslaw. In one incident, he drove up to a column of Jews heading toward the forest (where all were to be shot) and asked for the release of a certain Lea Altbach, who did cleaning assignments in his firm. He claimed she was his personal secretary. The SS commander on the spot asked for Lea's secretarial credential, and Beitz replied that he had accidentally left it in the office. The ruse worked, and Lea was released and saved. At times, Beitz went beyond saving people simply because he needed them for his oil work. Marian Estreicher, who testified to having been saved from the Ukrainian police, who were about to shoot him after they found him in hiding; due to Beitz's on-the-spot intervention, he and his family were freed. In Estreicher's words, "I was then 12, and could therefore not be considered an oil expert."

It is interesting that many, if not most, of his laborers could hardly be considered proficient oil industry workers. Before the war, many could be counted as tailors, shoemakers, barbers, and housewives, as well as cleaning persons, laundrywomen, and merchants. In addition, on occasions he also saved persons who were not even employed by him, claiming they were his workers. When his plant was closed in early summer of 1944 because of the approaching Russian army (Beitz had by then already been discharged several weeks earlier), some Jews managed to flee; others were taken to Płaszów camp, outside Kraków. After the war, Beitz served as chairman of the board of directors of the Krupp works, and Vice-President of the International Olympic Committee.[18]

In occupied Kraków, Poland, Julius Madritsch was at first a German-appointed trustee over two formerly Jewish sewing workshops, which he then purchased. He eventually employed some 800 Jewish workers each in his Kraków and Tarnów affiliates. Only about a fraction of the workforce was really qualified for this type of work. They had previously mostly been tradesmen and members of the free professions. In order to justify an increase in his Jewish workforce, Madritsch solicited large orders of goods in factories under SS supervision in Tarnów and Bochnia, and thus created a demand for 200 more laborers. Learning that an "action" was about to take place, he moved women and children out of the Kraków ghetto to the area of his factory, and for this purpose the small children were put to sleep with the help of sleeping tablets and hidden inside bags. In March 1943, on the eve of the ghetto's liquidation, several hundred Jews were smuggled out (with the complicity of the German policeman Oswald Bosko), and into Madritsch's factory, which was just outside the ghetto walls. From there they were moved to his Tarnów factory, ostensibly to accelerate production quotas for the war effort, but in reality, it was a ploy to enable some 230 Jews to escape to nearby Slovakia with the help of Raimund Titsch, the factory operating director, who accompanied the group to Tarnów. Madritsch was the outside man, negotiating with Gestapo and SS officers; Titsch, the inside man, ran the company's operations and supervising the workers. Titsch also kept in contact with Poles in the city with whom Jews had left their valuables. He fetched these and bought extra provisions that he smuggled inside the nearby Płaszów camp, where all Jewish workers were eventually moved. He also secretly photographed inside the camp from a hidden camera; the photos were eventually smuggled out of the country. The pictures show men and women at work and the brutal camp commander Amon Göth in various poses. Oswald Bosko, the policeman in charge of the ghetto, helped Jews who remained hidden in makeshift shelters to escape after the final liquidation raid of March 1943. When the Gestapo suspected his involvement, he escaped in a priest's robe, but was caught, arrested, and executed.

Madritsch took especial care of his workers, even setting up two kitchens in his factory, one "fully Kosher," the other "partly Kosher." His factory inside Płaszów camp spread over five barracks. When the camp was ordered closed in August 1944 due to the advancing Russians, Oskar Schindler (whom we will meet below) agreed to take 100 of Madritsch's workers with him to his new facility in Brünnlitz, in the Czech region. The remaining workers were distributed to various other camps. After the war, Madritsch wrote on the moral qualms he had in his efforts to save his Jewish workers. "Help us!. . . Don't abandon us!. . . This was the call which I heard from the screams of thousands of persons, who had committed no other crime than being born as Poles or Jews, that at a moment of greatest emergency and despair considered me their last life-saving rescuer, and therefore they gave me the strength to try to save them. It was a battle for life and death! Since my fight was against the system, my behavior did not always seem to be fair. Some disliked me, but I could not do otherwise! I had to carry on my struggle with shaded eyeglasses, fighting not only people with whom I was on friendly terms and who also looked at me as a friend, but also against criminals – whose friendship and goodwill I had to cultivate like a whore!" Madritsch, together with Tisch and Bosko, is on Yad Vashem's roster of the Righteous.[19]

One of the most, if not the most, celebrated rescue stories to emerge from the Holocaust, of a factory administrator responsible for a large number of Jewish forced laborers, is undoubtedly that involving Oskar Schindler. He was born in 1908 in Zwittau (today, Svitavy), Moravia, which, as part of the Sudeten region, was detached from Czechoslovakia and ceded to Nazi Germany during the Munich conference of September 1938. Before the war, he was an agent of the Abwehr, the German military intelligence, and a Nazi party member. Arriving in Kraków in late 1939, on the heels of the German invasion of Poland, he took over two previously Jewish-owned firms dealing with the manufacture and wholesale as well as retail distribution of enamel kitchenware products, one of which he operated as a paid trustee (*Treuhänder*). Eventually purchasing these two firms, the main manufacturing one located in the Zablocie section near the Kraków ghetto, Schindler employed mainly Jewish workers from the ghetto, thereby protecting them from deportations.

When the Nazis began liquidating the Kraków ghetto in early 1943 and transferred many Jews to the newly created nearby Płaszów labor camp, noted for the brutality of its commander Amon Göth, Schindler used his good offices with high German officials in the Armaments Administration and other government agencies to allow him to set up a branch of the Płaszów camp on his own factory premises, for the ostensible purpose of promoting production. In reality, the some 800 Jewish workers in his expanded factory in 1943 included persons unfit and unqualified for the labor specifications of the enamel firm and its production needs. He had earlier built special barracks for his Płaszów inmate workers on his company grounds, so as to dispense with the need of having them return to the camp and its horrors at the end of the day's work. In late 1943, he travelled to Budapest to meet with Dr. Rudolf Kasztner, of the Jewish Rescue Committee, and report to him on the liquidation of the Polish Jewry – he also agreed to serve as a funnel for the distribution of money to Płaszów camp inmates and for pictures of the camp to be smuggled out to Hungary. In October 1944, with the war front close by, he was able to save many of his workers, plus several hundred Płaszów camp inmates, through the ruse of ostensibly restructuring his now defunct enamel firm into an armaments factory in Brünnlitz (Moravia). In an operation unique in the annals of Nazi-occupied Europe, he succeeded in transferring to Brünnlitz some 700–800 Jewish men via the Gross Rosen concentration camp, and some 300 Jewish women via the Auschwitz camp. In Brünnlitz, the 1,100 Jews were given the most humane treatment possible under the circumstances (food, medical care, and consideration of religious needs). Informed that a train with evacuated Jewish detainees from the Auschwitz-affiliate Golleschau camp was aimlessly stranded at nearby Zwittau, he asked and was granted permission to remove the 100 frozen and skeletal-looking Jewish men and women from the ice-sealed wagons. They were swiftly carried to his Brünnlitz factory and nursed back to life, an undertaking to which his wife Emilie lent herself with much devotion. Those too late to be saved were buried with proper Jewish rites in a section of a local cemetery – also specially arranged by Schindler.

Schindler was noted for the humane treatment of his Jewish workers and his care for their physical and even psychological needs. One survivor noted: "He was the first German since the beginning of the war whose presence did not instill fear in me." This was in sharp contrast to many of the other German-appointed trustees and civilian carpetbaggers who supervised Jewish forced labor in Nazi-occupied Poland. Schindler also knew how to pull the wool over the eyes of those from whom he needed favors. The tactics used were a combination of good connections with the Abwehr and friends in high positions, coupled with an irresistible personality laced with charm and joviality, and an earthy fondness for wine, women, and the good life. These he used to the best advantage to befriend and ingratiate himself with high-ranking SS commanders in Poland and to extract highly prized favors, such as ameliorating the work and living conditions of his workers and mitigating punishments for work-related accidental damages, which in other instances would have resulted in death for the innocent offender. His genuine camaraderie, coupled with the judicious distribution of exquisite gifts (liquor, jewelry, and money) to the right persons, made it possible for him to save the large number of Jews under his care. These bribes and his black market dealings landed him in jail several times, as the Gestapo accused him of corruption – but he was soon released upon the intervention of his connections in Berlin ministries.

What is remarkable about the Schindler story is that he was a man who, by his own admission, arrived in Poland in order to enrich himself, hoping to exploit the huge and reliable cheap Jewish labor available there under German rule in order to make fast profits; he did not favorably impress the Jews who met him in Kraków in 1939, who saw him as no different than the other carpetbaggers in the occupied country. Yet this man underwent such a dramatic transformation as to become the single greatest German rescuer of Jews, constantly risking his life and safety for the sake of "his" Jews. For a man previously noted for the hedonistic pursuit of his own pleasures and material gains with very little thought to the needs of others, he ended the war penniless and in the care of his erstwhile Jewish charges. Perhaps the clue to this metamorphosis was his profound horror at the immensity of the Final Solution, the brutality of which he was a constant witness, and the convulsing effect this had on him. In his words: "I hated the brutality, the sadism, and the insanity of Nazism. I just couldn't stand by and see people destroyed. I did what I could, what I had to do, what my conscience told me I must do. That's all there is to it. Really, nothing more." The man's true character is still a mystery to his many beneficiaries. Whatever the motivations, the feat of single-handedly saving 1,200 Jews in Nazi-controlled territory, over a relatively long period and in broad daylight, has earned Schindler an honorable place among history's humanitarians. Schindler played for high stakes, constantly risking his own safety in the superhuman effort to save, not a few or most, but all of his Jews – and he won big! Of all German supervisors of Jewish labor, there was none like him for the courage, audacity, and care displayed, for the sole purpose (if not at the start of his wartime career, then ultimately) of saving innocent lives.[20]

c) The Military

We have seen in earlier chapters that not a few rescuers had sons, brothers, or fathers serving in the German military while they simultaneously were sheltering Jews. There are also on record some German military men who themselves extended aid to Jewish laborers under their supervision, with or without the knowledge of their families back home. This is important in light of the official antisemitic propaganda constantly drummed into the minds of not only those in the SS, but also regular army soldiers. In 1939, for instance, the German military high command called the just begun war a "struggle against World Judaism," which had to be fought like a "poisonous parasite," since Jews "are the embodiment of a satanic and insane hatred against the whole of noble humanity." In 1942, officers were instructed not to differentiate between "so-called decent Jews and others," since the Jews were to blame for the current war.[21] Field Marshal Walther von Reichenau (brother-in-law to Maria von Maltzan, who rescued many Jews back in Berlin), who led a German army in the invasion of Russia in an Order of the Day to his troops, declared, "The most important objective of this campaign against the Jewish-Bolshevik system is the complete destruction of its sources of power and the extermination of the Asiatic influence in European civilization. . . . For this reason the soldier must learn fully to appreciate the necessity for the severe but just retribution that must be meted out to the subhuman species of Jewry."[22] The few Wehrmacht officers and soldiers who withstood this poisonous propaganda and were willing to help Jews under their supervision to survive are therefore of special merit.

Of particular interest are the stories of two German army sergeants who helped Jews escape execution in their respective regions. In 1942 Master Sergeant Hugo Armann was responsible for arranging reservations for German soldiers on leave, on trains leaving Baranowice (today Baranovici, Belarus) for Germany. In this capacity, he had access to all military camps in the area. In the city, the Gestapo employed specialized Jewish labor, which they fetched from the city's ghetto, and marched them to a special camp for the day's work (carpentry, mechanics, tailoring). During calls to the German military in that particular camp, Armann made contact with the Jewish workers and occasionally smuggled in food and other provisions. Learning of an approaching Nazi raid, he urged the camp workers not to return to the ghetto after the day's work but to stay put. One woman he hid in his home attic. On the eve of the third and final liquidation raid, he urged them to flee to the forest to join up with the partisans. On the appointed day, in November 1943, he led them himself to a rendezvous with a Pole, Eduard Chacze, who continued with them into the forest. In Jerusalem, in 1986, in a ceremony in his honor, Armann stated: "I only did a little. However, I cannot escape the thought that if many more people had each done their little, the

Holocaust would not have happened." The son of a baker, after the war he resumed his prewar profession of a schoolteacher.[23]

In Vilnius, Lithuania, Sergeant Anton Schmid, originally from Vienna, was responsible for a unit (*Versprengten Sammelstelle* – Straggler Collection Point) collecting straggling German soldiers near the railway station, many of whom were returning from home leave, and reassigning them to new units. In this capacity, he employed many Jewish laborers from the Vilnius ghetto for various immediate work-related assignments: upholstery, tailoring, locksmith, room furnishing, heating, and shoe mending. He also had several homes at his disposition, and this afforded him much latitude and freedom of movement. In late 1941, after witnessing the nearby Ponary forest massacres of thousands of Jews, he began to aid Jews in various ways. At first, he sheltered some in several houses in Vilnius during Nazi raids. Making contact with Jewish underground leaders, such as Mordechai Tennenbaum-Tamaroff, he facilitated their movement to Warsaw and Białystok so they could report to their brethren on the Ponary killings and warn them of the Nazi intention to exterminate all Jews, everywhere. He actually rode with them in his military van and allowed some of them to meet and plan operations in his home. He helped other Jews to move to relatively safer places, again transporting them in his van to places like Voronova, Lida, and Grodno. The Gestapo eventually uncovered Schmid's collusion and had him arrested. He was sentenced to death by a military tribunal and executed on April 13, 1942, for high treason. In his farewell letter to his wife and daughter in Vienna, he wrote: "I have come to terms with this and fate also wills it. Our dear God has so decreed and that cannot be altered. I am today so calm as to find it difficult to believe it. God has so willed it and has made me strong. I have only acted as a human being and desired doing harm to no one." His widow suffered harassment by local Nazis, who broke into her home and vandalized the place. To many Jews in the Vilnius ghetto, Schmid remained a legendary figure and a source of courage and hope.[24]

We continue with the story of army Major Eberhard Helmrich, who headed an agricultural farm station in the Hyrawka labor camp, outside Drohobycz, Poland (today Drohobych, Ukraine) and whose task was to supply the German army with farm products. On this farm, he employed Jewish labor from the Drohobycz ghetto, who comprised over half of his close to 300 labor force – most of whom had no previous farming experience. He protected them from deportation roundups, hiding some in his home and helping to release others already arrested with the excuse that they were need-ed for the proper functioning of the farm. When it became evident that all the Jews were to be liquidated, Helmrich helped disperse his Jewish workers wherever possible, including some to German administrator Berthold Beitz's oil firm in nearby Boryslaw. For a select small group of girls Helmrich ar-ranged – together with his wife Donata who visited him from Berlin – to spirit them out of Poland and send them, armed with false credentials, to Germany as Ukrainian or Polish domestics with German families. In Berlin, wife Donata looked after her Jewish charges, making sure they were not placed in proximity to other non-Jewish, Eastern European female laborers to lessen the chances of exposure. According to one estimate, over 20 Jewish girls were thus saved.

Tall and blond, Eberhard Helmrich looked the typical German Aryan illustrated in Nazi propaganda journals. Susi Altmann (later Bezalel) related how Helmrich suddenly appeared at her place in Lwów. Born in Vienna, Susi's family moved to Drohobych before the war. There, they met Helmrich when the German authorities assigned their home to him, on which occasion Sebastjan Altmann asked the German officer for a personal favor – to bring his daughter Susi, who was in another city. Susi had left earlier to Lwów, when it was under Russian control, to attend school. Soon after the German take-over, the bell rang at Susi's front door. "A tall German stood there; my heart stopped beating. He saw my fear and said very quickly: 'Pack up, your father asked me to bring you home.'" It was highly unusual for a German military officer to make a special trip to another city, at the request of a Jewish person, in order to bring back a close family member. For a few months, Susi worked as a housekeeper in Helmrich's home; later, she joined her parents on the Hyrawka farm. Eberhard Helmrich then arranged Ukrainian papers for her and her younger sister Hansi, and when Eberhard's wife Donata came for a visit, she took with her Susi (her sister joined her later), properly dressed with a Ukrainian embroidered blouse, on a train trip to Berlin armed with false credentials. In Berlin, Donata Helmrich arranged additional false credentials for the two sisters and work as domestics in an elegant neighborhood. As for Susi's parents – Helmrich arranged for her mother work as a domestic, under a bogus name, with a German. Unfortunately, both parents did not survive.

Earlier in Berlin, during the 1930s, Harvey Samo knew the Eberhards through his former governess, Hedda Rathsack, who had to leave her employ-ment due to the Nuremberg Laws that forbade German female domestics under the age of 45 in Jewish households. The Helmrich family, who had four young children, then hired her. In the words of Samo: "We used to visit our 'Fraulein Hedda' every now and then, and thus became acquainted with the Helmrichs." Harvey learned of the Helmrichs' anti-Nazi views and of their many trips to England on which they took along children of Jewish friends. During the Kristallnacht pogrom in November 1938, Samo's parents were invited to stay with the Helmrichs for about ten days; they were then able to leave Germany in time. After the war Harvey learned of the Helmrichs' extensive help to Jews in Poland.

Asked how they justified risking their lives and the possibility of their children becoming orphans, the Helmrichs replied: "We were fully aware of the risks and the clash of responsibilities; after about a week's discussion of this difficult problem, we decided that it would be better for our children to have dead parents than cowards as parents. After that decision, it was comparatively easy; we figured that after we had saved two people, we'd be even with Hitler if we were caught, and with every person saved beyond that, we were ahead." The Helmrichs did not keep their anti-Nazi views secret from their four children, and kept them out under various excuses from Nazi youth movements, such as the *Hitlerjugend* for the Helmrichs' son and the BDM (*Bund der Deutschen Mädchen*) for their daughters. Donata's father, Ernst Hardt, suffered repercussions to his literary career due to his outspoken anti-Nazi views. Fortunately for Eberhard and Donata Helmrich, they were able to sidestep any Nazi retaliatory acts for their outspoken anti-Nazi ideological views.[25]

An abrasive standoff to ward off a Nazi killing raid involved two army officers: Major Max Liedtke and Lieutenant Albert Battel. Liedtke was the area military commander (*Ortskommandant*) in Przemyśl, Poland, and Battel his aide. On July 26, 1942, both prevented the SS from staging a roundup of some 80–100 Jewish workers, who were at the time assigned labor duties with the Wehrmacht. Liedtke placed troops on a bridge spanning the San River leading into the ghetto, with orders to shoot if the SS tried to force their way through. The audacity of a German military officer using German troops to block – by force, if necessary – the SS from carrying out an "action" reverberated up to the highest military and SS echelons in the region, and was eventually referred to SS chief Heinrich Himmler and Hitler's adjutant Martin Bormann. Himmler, in a letter to Bormann, stated he intended to arrest Battel (whom he considered the leading spirit in this undertaking) after the end of the war, and also to ask for him to be stricken from party ranks (Battel was a member of the Nazi party). Before the war, Battel practiced law in Breslau. In World War One, he was decorated with the Iron Cross 1st class for bravery. As for Liedtke, he was reassigned to the Caucasian front. At the end of the war, he fell into Soviet captivity and died in a Siberian camp. Battel survived the war unharmed and resumed his law practice.[26]

Not as extensive, and a bit less heroic than the previous stories, the following accounts of help by German military personnel also deserve mention. Oskar Schönbrunner was assigned to the Vilnius military headquarters as chief purser (*Oberzahlmeister*). He also somehow doubled as manager in charge of several workshops employing over 100 Jews from the ghetto (according to witnesses, this was at the invitation of some Jews for their own protection), which produced army uniforms. When some of his workers were rounded up and taken to the infamous Lokishki prison, he somehow effected their release.[27] To the south of Vilnius, Fritz Müller served in the army as a gardener on a military farm, to provide agricultural products for the army. There, most of the workers were Russian prisoners-of-war with the exception of one Jew, Ignacy Bucholc, an agricultural surveyor, who was assigned to draw up plans for the enlargement of the vegetable garden and who succeeded in hiding his Jewish ancestry. After one year on that farm, during which Müller and Bucholc had become friends, in February 1944, the German farm commander was shocked to learn of Bucholc's Jewish origin and ordered his arrest. When Müller was informed that the Gestapo was on the way to pick up Bucholc, he went to fetch him and hide him in the garden house attic; he told the Gestapo that "unfortunately" the man had fled to join up with the partisans. The following day, the dog in front of the garden house broke loose and began to bark in the direction of where Ignacy was hiding. Müller had no choice but to shoot the dog. Ignacy remained hidden for another week, with Müller looking after his nourishment. Then Müller moved him in his own car to Białystok, where Ignacy knew some people who would take him into hiding. He had saved the man's life, while taking no mean risks upon himself.[28]

Similarly, in Białystok, German soldier Herbert Coehn arranged for Paula Stein and her family to be sheltered at the home of his Polish woman friend, Stefania Dobrowolska, who was married and had a little child. Paula had met Coehn while working as a telephone operator for the Todt organization, and a friendship developed. She referred to him as the man "who later became my saving angel." While at work with the Todt organization, Coehn passed on letters to her from her husband, Meier Stein, who was in Warsaw. A bit later, Coehn also arranged for Paula's own child to join her at her hiding place. After a short interlude in the Białystok ghetto, the three Steins returned to hide for an additional eleven months in Stefania's home. In the meantime, Coehn was reassigned to frontline duty.[29] In Warsaw, Captain Wilm Hosenfeld accidentally ran into the Jewish musician and pianist Władysław Szpylman in his hiding place in the Warsaw ruins after the suppression of the Polish uprising of late 1944. Hosenfeld provided Szpilman with food and provisions in the closing days of the German occupation of Warsaw, thus assuring the man's survival. Hosenfeld later died while in Russian captivity.[30] Finally, Herbert Haardt, an engineer by profession, was during the war a military officer assigned to the Kaunas municipality, in occupied Lithuania. In his home, he at first employed Adina Segal as a housekeeper until this was disallowed due to her Jewishness, and she had to leave. Trying to save Adina's mother, Haardt thought of a ruse: he would place an ad in the newspaper for new household help, and Adina's mother, armed with a false ID, would apply and be accepted. She indeed stayed there for seven months. Later, Haardt also sheltered in his home Adina and her husband Shmuel for a short time, days before the city's fall to the Russians. Haardt had, in the meantime, been evacuated from Kaunas together with the German personnel. He had saved three Jewish lives in a city that had otherwise lost most of its Jewish inhabitants to the Final Solution.[31]

d) Labor and Concentration Camps

One cannot truly appreciate Nazi tyranny without a consideration of the vast array of concentration and labor camps of various sizes and time periods, and other forced labor facilities (running into an estimated several thousand), of which over 900 especially designated for Jews were to be found on Polish soil alone.[32] The camp system was Nazi Germany's most outstanding institutional innovation, whose presence could not be overlooked by the German populace. The Berlin region, for instance, claimed 645 camps for forced laborers, and the small Hessen state 606 camps.[33] In the latter part of the war, tens of thousands of Jews were spared immediate death in Poland and Hungary by being instead shipped to Germany for the most difficult and meanest physical assignments (such as excavating huge underground bunkers where the German military was experimenting on secret weapons). The death toll at these places was frightfully high, though not as terrible as before 1944, when Germany's military fortunes were sky high. To illustrate, during 1942–1943, Jewish labor attrition levels reached a 100% level in Mauthausen camp, compared with 1 to 3% for Poles, 1 to 4% for Soviet prisoners, and 1 to 3% for political prisoners.[34] Foreign non-Jewish workers also had certain privileges denied to Jews, such as writing home to loved-ones, vacations, even fraternizing with local Germans.[35] Jewish labor was expendable, the aim being the full liquidation of Jewish labor "through natural wastage," in the words of Reinhard Heydrich at the Wannsee Conference of January 20, 1942; in other words, in the quickest way possible.

Only a few of the thousands of Jews, transferred to camps on German soil or assigned labor in various installations, were fortunate to benefit from good treatment, and in some isolated cases they received even more: help by ethnic Germans they met at work. Erna Roth and five other Jewish women inmates were such fortunate persons. Brought from Auschwitz camp to a Krupp company industrial installation in Essen (as an affiliate of the Buchenwald camp), they were promised aid by Gerhardt Marquardt, a German camp worker. Making their escape from the camp site during an air raid in February 1945, they at first hid in an abandoned building in the local Jewish cemetery. Gerhardt then brought three of the women to his home. The women then split up – one was sheltered by Karl Schneider, a foreman at the Krupp company who had previously shared his lunch with some of the workers. The other girls found shelter in the home of Fritz Niermann, in Essen as well, where they stayed until the area's liberation several months later.[36]

In Dessau-Kapen camp, near Halle, Judy Finkelstein was working in a munitions factory under a non-Jewish identity. She had arrived from Poland, as a non-Jewish Pole with a group of fellow Poles for forced labor duties. There she met Heinz Scheidling, the head architect, who took a special interest in her. After her recovery from a bout of scarlet fever, he suggested she work in his family home, in the Wannsee section of Berlin, to where he commuted on weekends. There, she was well treated and shared a room with one of the maids. After a while, Scheidling was forced to return Judy to the camp (Poles were generally not permitted to leave the camp area). When Scheidling learned that the Gestapo suspected Judy of being Jewish and had begun to interrogate her to try to force her to disclose the presence of other possible Jewish women workers, he began to plan her escape – especially after Judy admitted to him the truth. At first he suggested that she hide in his mother's home, but Judy refused to jeopardize his family. An alternative plan was devised whereby Judy would flee the camp at the end of the week, accompany Scheidling on foot to the train station, and from there travel to Posen, where Scheidling's friends on a farm had been alerted to take her in. Each day of the week preceding the escape, Scheidling moved some of her clothes and belongings to his room where they were temporarily stored. On the escape day, in May 1943, Scheidling picked her up on the road in his car (after she successfully eluded the camp guards) and, boarding a train, they headed for Berlin, where he packed her belongings along with toiletries provided by his wife and returned to meet her at the train station. He again urged her to come with him to his mother's place, but Judy declined. He then bought her a train ticket, gave her ration cards and money, and bid her good luck. As it turned out, she was unable to get off the train in Posen because the place was heavily guarded. Instead she continued to Poland and found work on a Polish farm until the arrival of the Russians in January 1945.[37]

The Scheidling story illustrates how Germans in positions of authority (even minor) inside labor camps could, in some instances, be of invaluable help. The following stories highlight this point further. Walter Groos, a civil engineer with a company doing construction work in the Kaufering camp, a subsidiary of the larger Dachau camp, came on inspection tours two or three times a week in Kaufering, where a group of about 1,000 Jews were put to work laying railway tracks and building bunkers. Work was done by hand, without the use of any tools and implements necessary for such arduous labor, and under the watchful eyes of merciless SS guards. Moved by the inhuman conditions in the camp, Groos, who lived in nearby Augsburg, provided additional food and medicaments, gloves, and warm clothing to the workers. His family participated in buying the additional necessities in various places in Augsburg and the surrounding region. Asked what prompted him to tend after the needs of the camp prisoners, Walter reportedly responded: "Here I stand – I cannot act otherwise" (*Hier stehe ich and kann nicht anders*).[38] Far to the south, in Gmünd, Austria, Dr. Artur Lanc, the local regional doctor, in late 1944 learned from Dr. Fisch, a Jewish medical doctor from a nearby labor camp, that a certain injection was needed for a man suffering from a heart stroke. Lanc supplied him with the necessary medicine plus additional medicaments and suggested for the Jewish doctor to try and come to see him at his home every Friday. On such visits, Lanc and wife handed Fisch a bountiful amount of medicaments and food for distribution to the starved Jewish camp laborers. When these prisoners were later slated for deportation to Theresienstadt camp, Lanc was able to spirit out several of the laborers (including Dr. Fisch) and lead them to a forest hideout, where they remained until liberated by the Russians.[39]

In Buchenwald camp, German prisoner Willi Bleicher headed an underground cell of mostly communist political prisoners. In 1944, Stefan-Jerzy Zweig (Cyliak at the time), a three-year-old Jewish boy, was smuggled inside the camp, hidden in a rucksack, when he arrived with his father, Zacharias, in a transport from Poland, and was immediately hidden inside the clothing storeroom (*Effektenkammer*). "Senta," the terrifying watchdog guarding the storeroom, took a liking to the youthful Stefan – even allowing him to ride her back. Other prisoners looked after the child's needs. In September 1944, Stefan's father was told that his son would be deported to Auschwitz. Zacharias Zweig, whose wife and daughter had earlier fallen victims to the Nazis in Poland, pleaded with Bleicher to save his son, and Bleicher arranged for Jerzy to be given a typhus injection, which according to camp regulations required his quarantine in a special section of the camp, which was off-limits to SS personnel. A bit later, Bleicher thought it best to arrange the boy's escape from the camp; this, especially after Bleicher began to be interrogated and tortured by his SS overlords to reveal the names of underground members in the camp.[40]

In the same camp, Wilhelm Hammann, also a political prisoner (a past and still professing communist), was charged by the camp underground to teach a large group of Jewish children, evacuated from Eastern Europe camps, enough German to make it possible for them to understand orders by camp guards, and to give them courses in construction, so as to make them handy for war-related camp work and thereby save their lives. The children were quartered in Block 8, and their ages were falsified to make them appear older than the danger age for camp inmates. Of the 148 children, 27 were in truth below 15 years. In April 1945, the SS planned to liquidate the camp's inmates, to forestall their liberation by the advancing US Army. Sensing the danger to the children, Hammann rehearsed with them how to scrupulously hide their Jewish origins. When questioned whether they were

Jewish ("*Wer ist Jude?*"), they were to promptly respond that they were Poles, Czechs, Russians, Hungarians, etc. – anything but Jewish.

Several days before the camp's liberation on April 11, the SS lined up the children and ordered all Jewish children to step forward. None responded. A while later, the SS came back, and repeated the order: "*Wer Jude ist, vortreten!* (Whoever is Jewish, step forward)." Hammann replied that the children did not understand German and asked for a translator. No translator could be found in the camp at that particular moment. Again the order, "Jews, step forward." Only one child complied. Hammann immediately went over to him and berated him for stepping out of line, as he was not Jewish. The SS left to consult among themselves. Soon thereafter the alarm sounded as American tanks were sighted in the vicinity, and the SS took fright and left to take cover. That evening passed without incident. The following day, April 11, American troops liberated the camp and found that it was already under control by the camp underground. Hammann's self-held motto was: "I would rather die than be implicated in the murder of Jewish children."[41]

Another remarkable story, of a German political prisoner who exploited to the full his limited (but vital, in the harsh conditions of Auschwitz) authority to help fellow prisoners, mostly Jews, is that of Ludwig Wörl. Born in Munich 1906, he was by profession a carpenter but was also active in sports (such as kayaking). Before the Nazi rise to power, he was a medical orderly for the Red Cross, helping injured alpine climbers. Arrested in 1934 for his socialist activity, he was at first sent to Dachau camp. There he was in isolation for the first nine months to force him to disclose names of friends. He was then moved to the Dachau camp infirmary where he specialized in x-rays. In August 1942, he was transferred to Auschwitz, together with a group of prisoner medical orderlies, and placed in charge of Block 19, in the Birkenau section. At that time, SS policy was to appoint only criminal prisoners as Kapos (work supervisors) and other control positions. These supervisors were generally known for their brutality and sadism. Wörl began by appointing Jewish doctors in charge of the prisoner medical facility in spite of opposition from other non-Jewish physicians, and these Jewish doctors were exempt from labor. He also improved conditions in the sick ward and took care not to have more than the allotted number in the infirmary, forcing the less sick to return to work, thus saving them from selection to the gas chambers. On several occasions he beat up Kapos who unnecessarily brutalized Jewish workers. When five workers were caught trying to escape, he was given the dubious honor of hanging them. He refused, was lashed by an SS officer, and then placed in the *Stehbunker* (a narrow cell with only standing space), which upon his release left him fully exhausted and almost blind.

After his release, he was placed in charge of laborers as camp head (*Lagerälteste*) in Günthergrube, an Auschwitz-affiliate camp, where 600 Jews were employed in coal mining. Here too, he cared for his workers, providing more food and rest periods and forbidding physical punishment. Many non-Jewish laborers were not too happy with his preferential treatment of Jews, to which he would respond: "Jews have no one to help them." Asked by a former camp inmate why he never tried to escape all these years he was interned, he responded: "Perhaps, I could have succeeded to escape and hide. Then I would have rescued only myself. Here I have the feeling that I can also help others."[42] Wörl and the others listed above represent the few good persons among the supervisors who, while others in the camps gave full vent to their aggressive instincts, preserved their humanity and tried to help within their limited means in these unprecedented, ferocious precincts of the Nazi kingdom of hell.

CHAPTER 5

Random Meetings and Sudden Encounters

∗ ∗ ∗

AS ALREADY AMPLY SPELLED OUT, many rescue stories originated with people who knew their rescuers from before, either through a long-standing friendship and camaraderie, or through a business and work relationship. At the same time, not a few rescue operations were prompted by random meetings and sudden encounters between people who hardly knew each other, and very close to the time of the fugitive Jew's flight from the Nazi authorities – even at the time of flight itself. These do not constitute the majority of cases, but they still represent a significant enough share of rescue operations to justify our attention, as in the following examples.

Before the start of deportations, Sophie Mayer, a Jewish medical doctor in Munich, accidentally met Maria Letnar when they crossed each other in a Munich park and struck up a conversation. As the conversation turned to thoughts on the Nazi regime, Sophie learned of Maria's disagreement with the regime's persecution of Jews. From that moment, the two formed a long-lasting friendship. When Sophie was threatened with deportation to Poland in 1942, she decided to approach Maria for help. Maria immediately left for Lenggries (near Toelz) to ask her sister, Rosa Mayer, to help the distraught Jewish woman. Without consulting her husband Paul Mayer (no relation to Sophie Mayer), a police inspector, Rosa immediately consented to her sister's plea. Rosa kept Sophie's presence hidden from her husband for several weeks (she was closeted off in a separate room). When he was finally told, he at first wished to place her with a village farmer, but the plan was dropped because of the risks of this undertaking, and Sophie stayed on in the Paul Mayer home. The danger for the Mayers was especially acute, in spite of Paul's membership in the Nazi party, as there was a police station in the same house and SS personnel frequently dropped in to visit. Sophie remained sheltered in the Mayer home for almost three years, from July 1942 and until the war's end (probably disguised as non-Jewish), paying a nominal three marks per day as her share in the additional expenses.[1]

Up until February 1943, Henry Lax did forced labor, loading and unloading merchandise at the Berlin railroad yards. Escaping a Gestapo raid that month, he approached many friends for help but was rebuffed. At his wit's end, Lax suddenly remembered Otto Noerenberg, the furniture moving man, who had removed his belongings when his apartment was ordered vacated by the Gestapo. In the words of Henry: "I contacted him as a last resort, not expecting anything, but only because at the time of the move, he had made a few anti-Nazi remarks and vague offers of help in case things got really tough." Otto's on-the-spot reaction was first to give Henry proper clothing. He then arranged for Henry to be reunited with his brother Wolfgang, who had also escaped the recent Gestapo raid. Otto then enlarged an empty underground cavern on his property, which was full of trash and which was accessible through a hatch. Inside, he placed two cots, a night pot, and some blankets. An unused van was placed over the hatch to camouflage the secret entrance. In that hole, Henry Lax remained hidden throughout the rest of Nazi rule in Berlin. With Henry secure in the improvised shelter, Otto acquired for Wolfgang a false certificate and employed him in his business with a salary (in addition to providing him with clothing and food), to beef up the man's morale. "Words are completely inadequate to describe what Mr. Noerenberg and his family did for us," Henry Lax recalls. "It was not my own cleverness that saved me but only Mr. Noerenberg. Without Otto Noerenberg I would have been a dead duck. Although food was rationed and extremely scarce, he scrounged around for us and shared with us his own meager ration coupons." Henry's mother and stepfather were earlier deported to Theresienstadt. Henry Lax and Otto Noerenberg had only accidentally met when the authorities had ordered Henry to vacate his apartment, and Otto was picked to do the job.[2]

Still in Berlin, at the end of 1942, the Reichs left their apartment unannounced and began an underground existence. They stayed in various temporary places, at times together and other times separated, in the eastern part of Berlin until August 1943. Then Ismar Reich was caught by the Gestapo and placed on a train to Auschwitz. On the way he was able to cut a hole in the side of the cattle wagon and escape a few hours before the train's arrival at Auschwitz. Shortly before his arrest, he had met Erika Friedrich in an apartment where black market items were exchanged, and both took a liking to each other. After his arrest, Ismar's mother hurriedly contacted Erika, who took her to her parents' cottage. The recently escapee Ismar joined his mother several weeks later, where they both stayed until the end of the war. The Reichs shared a cottage dwelling with Erika's elderly parents and her sister. A double wall was constructed in the nearby rabbit hutch for hiding, in case of sudden visits by strangers. Neighbors were unaware of the Reichs' presence.[3]

Moving onto other sudden encounters, an unusually touching story in this regard is that of Konrad Latte and his rescuer, Ellen Brockmann. The story, as recounted in chapter 3, begins in Berlin in early 1944. While on the Berlin elevated S-Bahn, Konrad ran into a warden of the prison where Konrad was previously incarcerated, but this man, instead of turning him in, suggested that he apply to the Hessian Volkstheater, which was looking for a musician. Arriving there, Konrad told the band leader that he lost his papers in a bombing raid and promised to register for a new one. (The tactic used by Konrad was to mail an unfilled carbon copy of an application form, and attach the postal receipt to a real printed copy. The original was discarded. Konrad repeated that ploy every fourteen days. The printed carbon copy with the postal certified mail receipt served for inspection purposes.) Meeting the band, he was introduced to Ellen Brockmann, a twenty-four-year-old singer to whom he eventually became romantically linked. After he disclosed to her his true origins, she helped him ward off suspicious glances and questions by others in the band. When theaters were closed in September 1944 due to the deteriorating war situation, Pastor Poelchau arranged for a telegram to be sent in which the Berlin state opera asked for Konrad's transfer to Homburg vor de Höhe, where Ellen kept an apartment. There, Ellen looked after Konrad's everyday needs until the end of the war, presenting him as her fiancé. Again, as in former Berlin days, he performed as a pianist at ceremonies, even acting as director of a church choir. In November 1945, the couple's child was born; they had married earlier on April 28, 1945, days after their city's liberation. In 1977, Konrad Latte served as director of the Berlin Baroque Orchestra until his retirement.[4]

In most rescue stories, the initiative was usually taken by the fleeing person, who took the first step in approaching the potential rescuer – but this was not necessarily so in all cases. On rare occasions, it was rather the rescuer, or someone close to a rescuer, who made the first move, when he or she suddenly approached a fugitive Jew. Regarding all the stories recounted up until now, it is hard to evaluate them according to the depth of their human courage. But the following one certainly ranks among those at the top of the list. In Berlin, during the Factory Action of February 1943 in Berlin, Rachela Schipper and her fifteen-year-old daughter Jenny were, by a stroke of luck, not at their workplace and thus were spared arrest, as unfortunately happened to the father and eldest daughter of the family, Hermann and Paula. Not knowing what to do next, mother and daughter stood in the street in front of a synagogue, when they were suddenly approached by a lady who, noticing the yellow stars on their coats, suggested they try to hide someplace. When told that they had nowhere to go, she scribbled a note on a piece of paper, which was the address of a woman in the Biesdorf sector of Berlin. This unknown lady was married to a Jew. Mrs. Schipper was still not sure whether to follow up this lead. But the following day, after Mrs. Schipper attempted to end her life, her daughter Jenny made her take off the star patch and head to this unknown lady, known only as Mrs. Ledetsch. When they arrived at her home, the Schippers had no identification papers, no ration cards, and no money on themselves.

At first, headmistress Elsa Ledetsch agreed to admit only one person (in a house already occupied by a grown-up son, a twelve-year-old granddaughter, and an elderly boarder), and she chose this to be Jenny. But since Jenny would not part with her mother and began to weep bitterly, Mrs. Schipper called over her daughter Gisela to help out with a solution. At the time, Gisela was living nearby with her new husband, an ethnic German from Romania, in a tiny one-room apartment. They agreed for the elderly Rachela Ledetsch to be added to their household, while Jenny stayed with Elsa Ledetsch. Soon thereafter, Gisela took in another Jewish couple, Gustav and Irma Compart. The four persons had to make do in that small place. Later, Gisela helped find a place for Mrs. Schipper at the home of a friend, Mrs. Hilda Koch, in another Berlin suburb. Meanwhile, back at her mother's home, Jenny had to share a bed with Gisela's twelve-year-old daughter from an earlier marriage, who was staying with her grandmother. Fortunately for Jenny, Mrs. Ledetsch's elderly non-Jewish sub-tenant was an anti-Nazi, and he constructed a hideout behind a movable back wall of a wardrobe, where Jenny could hide in the event of unexpected visitors. At night, when everyone was fast asleep, Jenny would quietly slip out to visit her mother at Gisela's home, then quickly return to her own hiding place. The Ledetsches were total strangers to Rachela and daughter Jenny, two Jews on the run, when they stood facing each other on a day when the major part of the last Jews in Berlin were being rounded up, in the capital city of Nazi Germany.[5]

Another very touching story, of a rescuer making the first move, is that of Maria Nickel's help to Ruth Abraham. In 1942, Ruth was doing forced labor in a pharmaceutical firm in Berlin that produced medicaments for the German army. She was also at the time in her eighth month of pregnancy. One day she noticed a woman trailing her. As told by Ruth: "I asked her to stop following me so as not to endanger me. She, nevertheless, continued following me, and one day brought me food in the factory. She assured me not to fear anything, and that she wanted only to help. Several days later, she appeared again, and proposed to save me. As I told of this to my husband, he refused to believe it. But, as he himself came to know this woman, he realized that she was serious." Several days before Christmas, Maria returned with a basket of food. She told Ruth: "I couldn't eat my Christmas dinner knowing that you are hungry." She then provided Ruth with false papers to make it possible for her to start an illegal existence, refusing any payment in return. Ruth gave birth to baby girl, Reha, in a home occupied by other Jews, at a time when other Berlin Jews were being deported. In January 1943, Ruth and husband Walter decided to go underground, but only after Maria agreed to care for the baby. Reha was deposited at Maria's door in a blanket and was adopted by the Nickels, who had two children of their own. Maria's care for their baby allowed the Abrahams to move from place to place with greater ease, and thereby survive the Holocaust.[6]

Also in Berlin, Martin Moses was told one day by the Gestapo to report to the employment office for Jewish forced laborers. When one of the officials learned that Martin was a custom tailor and designer, he wrote an address on a slip of paper and told Martin in a subdued voice to go there immediately. It was the home of Willi and Aenne Otto, who lived in northern Berlin and had a tailoring store, stacked with English materials and trimmings, which catered to high Nazi officials. By bribing them with tailor-made gifts, Willi Otto was able to exact favors from them. This included at first postponing the deportation of the Moses parents, and later, when such urgings no longer produced the desired effect, diverting the destination from Auschwitz to Theresienstadt. Otto also hired Martin's wife, Regina, in his clothing atelier as a seamstress. Up to February 1944, Martin continued working in Otto's shop, even while already forced to spend the evenings in a camp where he and his wife were incarcerated in 1943. But, when that camp was shut down by the authorities, the two Moseses stood in danger of immediate deportation. As he equally did for Martin's parents, Otto was able to help redirect the couple's destination to Theresienstadt, where chances of survival were somewhat better than Auschwitz.[7]

In Gelsenkirchen, Dr. Rudolf Bertram was a physician in the St. Joseph Catholic Hospital and the Marian Hospital – both in the Gelsenkirchen area, and both close to a Buchenwald satellite camp, where in 1944 thousands of Hungarian Jewish women were interned as forced laborers for the Krupp armament plant. During a massive Allied air raid in September, many of the Jewish women were killed or severely wounded. Dr. Bertram took it upon himself to treat the wounded women with precious doses of penicillin, which were otherwise not allowed for Jewish patients. One of the Jewish women, whose leg needed to be amputated, was kept by Bertram for a longer period, in spite of German demands to release her into their hands; he arranged for her to be hidden in one of the hospital's storerooms. She survived. Previous to this involvement with Jewish women prisoners, Bertram had a run-in with the Gestapo when he was denounced for making anti-Nazi remarks, but the charges could not be substantiated and the case was dropped.[8]

In countries occupied by the Germans, in some cases random encounters between German nationals, military or civilian, and Jews threatened with deportation evolved into rescue operations. Following are several such stories involving German military personnel.

Austrian-born army Lieutenant Roman Erich Petsche was with the German invasion force, which occupied Novi Sad in Yugoslavia, in March 1944, which up to then was under direct Hungarian control. He and a fellow officer were billeted in a home belonging to the Jewish Tibor family. A month later, on April 15, 1944, Petsche learned that all remaining Jews were to be deported on the following day. He quickly rushed home and informed his hosts (Mrs. Tibor and her twin daughters) of the grave news, but calmed their fears and promised to help. Taking the two daughters with him, as well as their nursemaid, he boarded a Budapest-bound train (some 260 kilometers to the north), presenting the nursemaid on the train as his wife and the two girls as his children. In Budapest, he confided the girls into the hands of a convent's Mother Superior for the duration of the war. Returning late that evening to Novi Sad, he told the children's mother and an aunt to board the train as ordered, then jump off at a certain rail junction inside Austria and proceed on foot to his home in Vienna, where his wife had already been alerted to hide them. He then personally arranged for the children's grandmother to be admitted in the Novi Sad city hospital and continued visiting her from time to time. "A German officer visiting an elderly, lone, and helpless Jewish woman is already a unique and extraordinary thing during that tumultuous period," Hava, one of the daughters, noted in her deposition. As for the children's mother and aunt, they indeed boarded the deportation train as urged by Petsche but hesitated and did not jump off at the prescribed spot; they both landed in Auschwitz. The mother, Mrs. Tibor, did not survive, but the aunt was more fortunate, and she returned to claim the two girls, then thanked the family's benefactor, a former lieutenant in the German army, whom they met when he was billeted in their home and with whom they have since maintained close contact.[9]

Another rescue operation initiated by a Wehrmacht soldier took place in Tunisia, at a time when that country was under direct German control, and involved Sergeant Richard Abel. In December 1942, he was assigned to supervise a group of four Jews who had been caught trying to cross over to the British side and were arrested and accused of espionage. Learning that the SS would soon take charge of the imprisoned people, Sergeant Abel urged them to escape. To gain their confidence, he provided them with a map of the terrain and the minefields to be avoided, and also supplied them with food and a loaded Luger revolver. On the night of the escape, Richard sent the compound sentinel in another direction, and with a pat on their shoulders, sent the four Jewish prisoners off. The escape succeeded. They later learned that Abel had visited one of the men's parents in Tunis and informed them of the successful escape and visited them several times. Abel eventually was captured as a prisoner of war. In 1964, Louis Beretvas, one of the Jewish escapees, met Abel in Geneva. "It was a wonderful reunion, with my whole family."[10] Back in Europe, in the Premyslany-Hanaczow area of eastern Galicia (today in Ukraine), army Lieutenant Walter Rosenkrantz was sent, in May 1944, to interrogate a woman wounded in an engagement between partisans and German troops. Learning that she was Jewish, and intent on saving her life, he reported her as a Polish patriot wounded in a battle with Ukrainian nationalists and gave her a new, non-Jewish name. Rosenkrantz told the bewildered Hanna Hochberg: "There are still Germans who have not lost all semblance of humanity." During the German retreat, Walter took Hanna in his lorry and dropped her off in Strij, with a note stating she was a kitchen worker in his Panzer division. She then moved to the Sudeten region of Czechoslovakia and worked on a horse breeding farm, and survived.[11]

A most fascinating story in this context (but not meant to demean the other fascinating rescue stories), of a random encounter with a German soldier that evolved into an extended rescue story, is that of Sergeant Kurt Reinhardt and the Jewish Thum-Scharf families, which began soon after the German invasion of Poland. Kurt, a photo buff, walked in one day in late 1939 into the Eliezer Thum photo shop in Tarnów to buy a roll of film. An extended conversation on photographic matters led to Kurt promising to supply Thum's shop with photo equipment from Vienna, Kurt's hometown. This led Kurt to take a greater interest in the travails of the Thum and related Scharf families, who were facing increased persecution from the occupying Germans. His help included disbursing money to Thum's relatives in other Polish cities (Jews were not allowed the use of public transportation). Kurt was then transferred to France and later to Russia, but he kept in touch with his Jewish photo friends in Tarnów. Around Christmas 1941 Kurt, passing through Poland on his way to the Russian front, again met the Thum-Scharf families and urged them to leave immediately ("You must leave, before it gets 'hot'!"). Sent home later to Vienna to convalesce from an undisclosed illness, Kurt resumed his contact with the Thums.

In the meantime, Hermine Scharf (later Kirschenbaum), born 1920, survived several Nazi killing raids in Tarnów, which liquidated that city's Jewish population. Fleeing to Kraków, she wrote to Kurt's mother in Vienna and received a letter from him with the following message: "See to it that you come here; you need not worry further – I will look after you." Finally, in March 1943, Kurt was able to provide her with a work permit from the Munich Labor Department (*Arbeitsamt*) for work in Germany as a non-Jewish laborer. She left with a transport of Polish workers and arrived in Vienna, where she was met by Kurt's mother. From there, Hermine proceeded to Munich, where Kurt was working as a test pilot for army motorized vehicles. Fearing that the other Polish laborers would detect Hermine's Jewish origins, Kurt devised a plan to get Hermine to work outside the camp, by suggesting she should claim to be an ethnic German (*Volksdeutsche*). With Kurt at her side, Hermine registered at the Association of Foreign Germans (*Verband der Deutschen im Ausland*), where she was asked to provide proof of her German ancestry. While ostensibly waiting for Hermine's German accreditation to arrive from Brody (Hermine's fabricated hometown), she was allowed to work as a governess with a German family. In the meantime, Brody had fallen to the Russians, which saved the day for Hermine. She was finally registered as a *Volksdeutsche* and officially permitted to live outside the laborers' camp. Kurt Reinhardt then arranged a work permit for Hermine's mother, Helene Scharf, at a Munich pension, and a photo lab assistant's job for another relative – both, of course, under assumed names. In the meantime, Kurt married and moved with his newlywed to a different city, whereas Hermine and her mother drifted to Gmünd, Austria, where they witnessed liberation in May 1945. Combining cunning, risk, daring courage, and above all a large dose of humanitarian compassion, a lone German sergeant was able to save several members of a Jewish family from destruction by his own government. Most other family members perished in the Holocaust, including Hermine's father, Jakob Scharf.[12]

In Lwów, occupied Poland, Josef Podoszyn was busy preparing a prescription in the city's largest pharmacy when he overheard a conversation between a lady customer and a Polish pharmacy worker over a medicament that the employee refused to deliver without a proper prescription. Josef intervened and sold her the desired medicine. The lady returned several times thereafter and always approached Josef for prescriptions, which he honored without undue inquiries. She was Imgard Wieth, a German secretary working for the occupation authorities. Sometime later, Imgard suggested that Josef use her apartment as a place of refuge should it ever become necessary. Josef responded by asking whether she would instead admit his wife, who was hiding in a shelter beneath the pharmacy, and Imgard consented, adding, to the surprised Josef, that the thirteen-year-old Jewish girl already staying with her would now have a steady companion.

A year passed, and in May 1943, the Germans liquidated the remaining Jews in the Lwów ghetto. Josef now joined his wife at Imgard's apartment. What was originally intended as a few days' stay (Josef initially hoped to join up with the partisans) stretched into a full year. In Imgard's flat, Josef met the thirteen-year-old girl's mother, and now there were four persons in hiding. Wieth's apartment was located in a prestigious building reserved for high-ranking German officials, including the commander of the Ukrainian militia that collaborated with the Germans in the extermination of Jews, and an SS officer, formerly commander of an internment camp in occupied Belgium, who took a romantic interest in Imgard and was in the habit of popping in unannounced. His sudden calls and the constant danger of detection were a continuous nightmare to Imgard and her wards. When Imgard was out at work, care had to be taken to avoid the slightest noise; walking or using the faucets or flushing the toilets were forbidden, for fear of arousing the suspicion of neighbors. In May 1944, Josef and his wife secretly renewed their contact with friendly priests of the Uniate (Ukrainian Catholic) church, who promised to help them and the two other women in Imgard's apartment. All four slipped out quietly from Imgard's flat and headed to the Uniate church where they were in turn dispersed to various hiding places. This was just in time, for soon thereafter Imgard Wieth was evacuated together with all German personnel on the eve of the city's liberation by the Russians. It had all started with Josef Podoszyn casually helping out a customer who visited his pharmacy in occupied Lwów – a city known for the brutal elimination of the city's 200,000 Jewish inhabitants by the Germans with the large-scale help of Ukrainian collaborators.[13]

Much has been written on the Death Marches, when the Germans emptied outlying concentration camps, mostly in Eastern Europe, during the waning days of the Third Reich and led on foot the surviving prisoners toward the interior of Germany. Most marchers did not make it to their new destination, felled as they were on the way by the cold (especially during the winter marches of January 1945), lack of nourishment, and proper clothing, as well as by fatigue, brutal beatings, and shootings by SS guards. Goldhagen records in considerable detail one such march in southern Germany, near Helmbrechts, during March 1945, where the cruel disposition of the guards showed no signs of waning, even at the approach of U.S. forces, during the twilight days of Nazi Germany. Even when explicitly ordered by higher authorities to cease the killing of Jewish prisoners, they continued shooting them randomly. Passing villagers watched passively in disbelief at these skeletal-looking men and women; some ventured to help out with a morsel of bread, while others even jeered and threw stones at them. The Americans who met the few surviving victims on May 6, 1945, were appalled at the state of these still-surviving marchers and surprised that they were still among the living.[14]

Those lucky to evade the marchers' route and escape were in desperate need of help, if they stood a minimum chance to survive. In these horrific circumstances, there could be no question of rescuers doubting the Jewish identity of their future wards. The encounters were sudden and under the cruelest conditions imaginable, and the response by the rescuers had to be immediate – to help, and thus save, or decline, and thereby doom – as in the following stories.

Such a harrowing tale is that experienced by Frieda Kleinman. On the night of January 31,1945, Frieda and a group of about 10,000 Jewish women were taken from a labor camp near Stutthof, East Prussia (then, Germany), on a death march toward the Baltic Sea coast. The night was bitter cold as the lightly clothed, hungry, and haggard-looking women were driven by SS guards who prodded them forward, felling those who could not keep up with the column, which was marching on roads clogged with snow and ice. "We left many corpses on the road," Frieda recalled. They were told that the sooner they arrived at the Baltic Sea shore, the faster they would be evacuated by boat to the interior of Germany, out of the way of the quickly advancing Russian army. However, when they reached the sea, SS machine guns from the surrounding cliffs suddenly began strafing them with deadly bullets. In a setting taken from Dante's Inferno, flares lit up the sky to illuminate the area so the machine-gunners could take better aim at their victims. Frieda fainted after being hit by two bullets, one of which penetrated her belly, the other her foot. Awakening hours later, just as she was on the point of drowning in the icy seawater, she was surrounded by the eerie deadly silence of bodies floating between chunks of ice. She was without clothes but found a drenched robe with which she covered her nakedness, and wandered into the nearest village of Sorgenau (near Palmnicken), where she knocked on the first door. A woman appeared at the door, and Frieda begged for help. Erna Härtel could not believe her eyes: before her stood a dirty, haggard-looking, wounded, and lightly clad woman. "I looked like a monster," Frieda recalled. With tears in her eyes, this Good Samaritan "quickly swept me in her home, embraced and comforted me. From that moment she cared for me like a mother." Erna, whose husband was away in the German army, burned Frieda's baglike dress, washed and cleaned her hair of lice, and tended her wounds. She then put Frieda to sleep in a bed draped with a mattress-covered white sheet. "Now you are a person like the others," Erna told Frieda. "You shall stay with me until the war's end." And so it was, for the next two and a half months, until the area's liberation.[15]

Celina Manilewitz also formed part of that death march to the Baltic Sea. The macabre scene on the shores of the sea will never leave her memory.

"All around, in that grey-green sea, corpses were floating, half hanging on the ice blocks. The wounded were moaning; some prayed to God to let them die." Satan's hell could not have looked more horrifying. After the shooting subsided and the SS men withdrew, Celina and two fellow women survivors managed to wade ashore and straggled to the nearby village of Sorgenau. After eluding a pro-Nazi inhabitant who had wanted to turn then in, they were admitted into the home of Albert and Loni Harder. They were hidden in the pigsty attic until it was safe for them to circulate in the Harders' home itself. In Celina's words: "It was almost too much. It was like a dream – having a proper bed again, for the first time after long years of concentration camps. . . . Here in the midst of our enemies, the Germans, we three Polish girls – and Jewish, too – had suddenly found a mother." The Harders arranged for them new German identifications, and rehearsed with them a concocted story – of ethnic German refugees in flight from Memel (now named Klaipėda, in Lithuania), already in Russian hands, who had contracted typhus – thus their shaved heads. After sufficiently recovering from their weakened state, for the next two and a half months, they made themselves useful with household chores, until the arrival of the Russians on April 14, 1945. The Harders had cared for them for 105 critical days.[16]

Another similarly harrowing rescue story, which also took place in the closing days of the Third Reich, is that of the rescuer couple Karl and Walburga (Hanna) Zacherl, of Muenzelbach region, near Munich. In April 1945, sixteen-year-old Elisabeth Fischer, sick with typhus, was allowed, with the other marching prisoners, to rest near a highway with other Jews who were being force-marched away from the approaching front under SS guard. The Zacherl couple was just then driving by in their car on the way to Munich and stared at the column of prisoners who were resting on the road between Morenweis and Jesenwang. Their eyes fell on Elisabeth, a pitiable-looking young girl. They asked and received permission to take her in their car in order, as they explained, to place her at the head of the column. Instead, they took the forlorn girl with them. On the way, they were strafed by passing American warplanes. At night, Elisabeth was moved into their cottage home in Luetenhofen. They washed and cleaned her and cared for her until the area's liberation. During daytime hours, she remained hidden in the cellar, and in the care of their housekeeper, who was taken into their confidence, while Karl Zacherl and wife Hanna left for work in a factory. Immediately after liberation, they placed her in a hospital to treat her typhus infection and afterwards brought her home with them until she had fully recovered.[17]

In a related story of a sudden encounter during a forced-march rescue story, this time in Austria in February 1945, Tibor Weiss, his sister, brother, and mother fled from a march leading a group of Jewish laborers from Floridsdorf, near Vienna, in the direction of Mauthausen camp. As they passed the village of Grafenwörth, Maria Grausenburger, a farming woman with three children (her soldier-husband was killed in the war and one son was still away in the army) was watching the procession, when she was accosted by a woman marcher who pleaded for help. "We cannot go on; please have pity on us, dear Frau; please help us." Maria made an on-the-spot decision to shelter the distraught woman and her two sons and daughter in the cellar of her home. The following day, neighboring farmers urged Maria to send away the escaped prisoners, for her own good. She replied: "But I cannot permit the woman and the children to be killed. I lost a husband in the war; this terrible tragedy must once and for all come to an end. My baby boy is on the front, and I want him to come out of it in the same way as the two children of Frau Weiss." The following day, she registered them as escaping Hungarian fascist refugees (the Russians had already occupied most of Hungary). Tibor and his brother found work as farm laborers, and together with their mother and sister stayed in Maria's home until the area's liberation several months later. The danger for Maria was real, as the area was infested with retreating SS troops during these final and chaotic days of Nazi rule.[18]

Jewish prisoners on labor assignments outside the camps stood a better chance of being saved if, of course, they had the good fortune of encountering a civilian German with a humanitarian disposition and the courage to do something about it. The youthful Ilona Katz and her family, a group of young Jews from Debrecen, Hungary, had been taken to the Vienna region in 1944 for various work details, including cleaning up debris after air raids and tidying up cemeteries. While at work, they were permitted to buy food at nearby stores. Some of the forced laborers stopped passersby asking for food, or, not being able to control their hunger, wandered into local bakeries and coffee shops. One Sunday, Ilona ran into Anna Ehn, who was on her way to church, and Ilona begged her for food. Anna gave her the roll and sweets in her purse. From that day on, Anna made it a point to bring food for Ilona at her workplace. When Ilana's sister was wounded during an air raid and taken to a hospital supervised by the SS, Anna succeeded in releasing the girl to her care and nursed her for the next three months, thereby saving her life. Toward the end of the war, the Jewish workers were removed and taken to Mauthausen camp, where Ilona Katz and her sister managed to survive – largely, no doubt, due to the previous good treatment including nourishment at the hands of Anna Ehn, a woman they had accidentally met on a street in Nazified Vienna.[19]

Similarly, in Vienna, it was late 1944 and Anna Deutsch, originally from Hungary, was on assignment with other Jewish forced laborers, clearing bombed-out buildings. A certain woman would pass every day and unnoticeably leave food so that Anna could take it without being noticed. One day this woman left a note with an address, and a brief message: "If you're in danger, come to us." In January 1945, the Jewish prisoners were told to make ready within minutes for a long march toward the prewar German frontier with Austria. Anna hurriedly left the school building where the prisoners were assembled and was able to sneak out through the cellar. Remembering the message, she went straight to that stranger woman's address. Anna Frissnegg and husband Ludwig admitted Anna Deutsch and kept her hidden in the coal cellar, where she stayed until Vienna's liberation several months later. The Frissneggs did not ask for any remuneration, knowing well that Anna had nothing on her to give. After the war, Anna was reunited with her husband Hermann in Budapest, after he survived a German concentration camp.[20]

Further north, in Bremen, Germany, in January and February 1945, the Jewish sisters Ella and Eva Kozlowski were part of a forced-labor gang cleaning up the rubble left from aerial bombardments. Starting on a certain day and continuing on the following days, they were surprised to receive while on their work assignment food from a strange young girl in the form of a bottle with warm milk and flaked oat packed in a plain wooden stocking, so as to avert the curious glances of the suspecting German guards. It turned out that the person responsible for this humanitarian deed was the youngish Erika's mother – Henny Brunken. She was living with her mother and her two children while her husband was away in the navy. Learning of Eva's approaching eighteenth birthday, Henny Brunken presented her with a handmade handkerchief with her initials embroidered on it. Three days later the work gang was moved to another location and contact was lost between both sides. Many years after the war, Henny (whose navy husband died in the war) responded to a notice in a Bremen newspaper by Ella Kozlowski searching for her. Both sides exchanged warm letters, culminating in a visit to Israel by Henny Brunken to be reunited with the two sisters whom she had helped to survive.[21]

Some who escaped, not necessarily from death marches, but from camps or labor locations in the closing days of the war were lucky to be sheltered by kindly disposed private individuals whom they encountered during their flight. In April 1945, two Jewish men (one named Yerucham Apfel) escaped from a work detail from Ganaker camp in the Kaufering region, and began wandering aimlessly until they approached the village of Parnkofen. They spied out an isolated home on a hillock at the edge of the village. When they approached the home, a man of about fifty came toward them. To their plea for shelter, he suggested they use the barn where he provided them with some hay. Later, the man and an aide returned with large slices of bread and milk bottles. "We soon felt that instead of death came deliverance; we fell into the hands of a delivering angel and he would save us." The man, Josef Dinzinger, told them: "You're probably hungry; eat and then you will be able to sleep." The two men asked to be hired for work. He demurred, since he had many visitors on his farm, including a Nazi medical doctor. Instead, he suggested for them to hide in the nearby forest during the day and return to the barn at night, where food would be waiting for them. In the passing days, he managed to register them under different names, with an appropriate cover story, and thus they were able to appear as hired laborers. For the first time in many years, the two men sat at a proper eating table – with the whole Dinzinger family, where plenty of food was served to them. Thus, they stayed on his farm until liberated by the US Army. Dinzinger dimmed their fear of arrest with assurances that the police were too busy with other pressing matters during this twilight period of Nazi rule.[22]

In a similar story, in March 1945, Mania Balsam, Mina Silberfard, and her mother, Rosa, fled from Türkheim, a Dachau ancillary camp, after rumors spread that the SS were about to blow up the camp and shoot all its prisoners. After wandering for hours, and totally exhausted, they stopped a man on a bicycle and pleaded for help. The man, named Wilhelm Seitz, asked them to wait for him for a while inside the forest and returned later to fetch them to his home in a nearby village, where the three fugitive women were warmly welcomed by his wife, Maria. In fact, Maria had Mina's elderly mother, Rosa, put to sleep in her own bed. Wilhelm and Maria Seitz kept them hidden in the attic for five weeks, until the war's end.[23]

In another rescue story of escaped Jewish work prisoners, after the heavy Allied air raid on Dresden in February 1945, a group of Jewish laborers, who were no longer needed for work in the demolished ammunition firm, were marched off to an unknown destination. Three men succeeded in escaping. After some aimless wandering, the three – Roman Halter, Abramek Sztajer, and Josef Szwajcer – reached the farmhouse of Kurt and Herta Fuchs on the outskirts of Dresden. Kurt knew of the men's true identity but admitted them into his household under the pretext they were Polish forced laborers whom he needed for his additional farm chores. There they stayed, doing various household and field work, until the arrival of the Russians in early May. Roman Halter, who left them on the day of liberation, learned that Kurt Fuchs and Josef Szwajcer were shot by a soldier of a Russian unit collaborating with the Germans, led by the renegade Russian general Andrey Vlasov, and come to wreak vengeance on a German who had saved the Jewish Josef Szwajcer. His two other Jewish companions were away elsewhere during that tragic incident.[24]

We close this chapter with another equally gripping story, originating in a random encounter. After surviving the death march following the evacuation of Auschwitz camp in January 1945, Michael Rozenek and brother Yonah were loaded on a train heading to the interior of Germany. While passing through the Erz Mountains, the two brothers, joined by two other prisoners, jumped off the train and walked aimlessly in the forest. Spotting a distant house beyond an open field, two of the men immediately ran toward it while the Rozeneks climbed a tree to survey from a distance. They suddenly saw the two men frantically running away from the house, with shots fired in their direction, which felled them. Returning to the forest, the two Rozeneks slept in a shack where local forest workers kept their tools. The following day, the two brothers, totally exhausted, decided to step out to the nearest highway and give themselves up. As they exited the forest, they ran into Arno Bach, a forester on his way up the mountains to his tree-cutting work. Surprised and taken aback by this sudden encounter, the two ran back uphill. Following them, Bach assured them he meant them no harm. He knew who they were, as he had heard of the many prisoners who had jumped from the train a few days earlier. He then gave them the food he had brought for himself and cautioned them not to leave the place but to hide, since soldiers were combing the area, and assured them he would come back to feed them again. In the meantime, the two built a hiding nest for themselves, covered with leaves. Toward evening, Arno returned and told them that his work group was cutting trees and placing them on the road to block the advance of enemy tanks that were nearby. He also said he was not a Nazi and wanted to help them. He left and returned with cooked food. He then told them of his son who was in the army, and another one who had fallen in combat.

Expressing his sympathy over the fallen son, Michael Rozenek begged to be sheltered in any place with a roof over one's head, even inside a barn or pigsty. Arno replied that he had a wife, a sister, and her husband, and another woman (whose husband fell in combat) with a son – five persons to whose welfare he was committed. To which Michael responded: "Suppose your other son deserted and was looking for a safe place, would you refuse him? This is our situation. But if you help us survive, perhaps fate will decree a similar fate for your son." There was a momentary silence. Then Arno said he was going back home to consult with the other people. He returned that same evening, late at night, and told them to follow him. Michael Rozenek trudged along on his aching wounded foot with much pain ("Tears stream down my face as I write these lines, as I recall our experiences, as I often think this is but a bad dream, and that we never really underwent all this"), together with his brother. Crossing a stream, Arno led the two men to a shack where felled trees were stored. Placing some straw on the hard ground, he then brought them some blankets. In that village shed (Niederschmiedeberg, near the city of Chemnitz), the two remained hidden from April 2 to May 5, 1945. The household women fed the two brothers twice a day, and every evening Arno came to remove the human waste. The two Rozenek brothers survived, thanks to the generosity of a group of German foresters they had accidentally stumbled upon, on their flight to freedom.[25]

CHAPTER 6

Mixed Marriages, *Mischlinge* and Baptized Jews

* * *

THROUGHOUT NAZI RULE, JEWS LIVING in mixed marriages and those classified as half-Jews were not exempted from discriminatory measures. At the same time, they did not, for the most part, fare as badly as those considered "full" Jews by Nazi definition – that is, anyone with at least three Jewish grandparents, irrespective of the person's current faith or lack of it. Moreover, Jewish women married to non-Jewish men, or vice versa, who had children were of a somewhat less risky status within the mixed-marriage category; known as "privileged" mixed marriages, they were accorded preferential treatment. To complicate matters, the 1935 Nuremberg Laws led to the creation of a new race: neither fully Aryan nor fully Jewish, but something in between – *Mischlinge*, in Nazi parlance. While discriminatory measures against this newly established group gradually increased with the passing years, their situation was a bit more secure than that of baptized Jews and certainly that of "full" Jews, and a majority of them survived the Nazi era. As we have earlier noted, the Nazi attempt to arrest and deport Jewish male spouses in mixed marriages, in Berlin, met with a resounding protest by their Aryan wives – the famous Rosenstrasse incident of February/March 1943 – which resulted in the authorities relenting and releasing the Jewish husbands.

In 1933, the number of persons in mixed marriages, in which one person was fully Jewish, was estimated at 35,000. In addition, there were the thousands of racially mixed marriages in which the Jewish spouse had been baptized at birth but was still considered as a full Jew by the Nazis due to the Jewishness of his or her parents or grandparents. It was difficult for the authorities to isolate people in mixed marriages from the non-Jewish popu-lation since many non-Jewish (or Aryan, in the Nazi terminology) relatives were affected. In some cases, family connections extended well into the lead-ing circles of the Nazi Party, the administration, the economic sector and the military. To the Nazis, the morale of the German people was of decisive im-portance, especially as the country slid into war, and they hesitated to tackle this issue drastically. The considerations affecting Nazi decisions in this re-gard were mostly of an opportunistic nature, and they waited for an oppor-tune moment to liquidate the embarrassing (to them) phenomenon of mixed Jewish-Aryan marriages in what the Nazi leadership strived to become – a racially pure society.

At first, the authorities tried to reduce this problem by encouraging the non-Jewish side to dissolve the marriage. At the Wannsee Conference of January 1942 (where the extermination of all of Europe's Jews was discussed), it was suggested that such marriages should be peremptorily dissolved, if pos-sible at the request of the German partner, and failing that, at the request of the public prosecutor, but this idea was dropped in favor of another idea – forced sterilization of the Jewish male spouse. This was considered a possible "humane" alternative to more brutal measures (Himmler wished to enforce sterilization even on "quarter Jews," persons with only one Jewish grandpar-ent). Both these suggestions were never implemented in Germany (but they were, to a certain degree, in nearby Netherlands – the Dutch being considered by the Nazis a pure Germanic tribe), perhaps due to the fear of arousing public resentment at a time when public support for the country's involvement in an ever-larger war was of great importance to the regime.[1]

With the onset of war in September 1939, curfew was imposed on Jewish partners of mixed marriages. They received reduced rations and were given mostly menial, unhealthy, and physically exhausting work as-signments. In April 1940, Hitler ordered persons married to Jews to be excluded from the German army. At the same time, he also ruled that if the husband was non-Jewish and the wife Jewish, the couple was to be allowed to continue living in their present flat, even if they were child-less. If, on the contrary, the husband was Jewish and the wife Aryan – everything depended on whether they had children. If so, for the time being, they were not required to move into special Jewish-designated quarters. Similarly, Jewish husbands with offspring were not required to display in public the Yellow Star on their outer garment, as required for all Jews, as of September 1941, nor did it apply to Jewish women in mixed marriages without children – as long as that marriage remained intact.

When Berlin was declared *Judenrein* ("cleansed of Jews") on May 19, 1943, there were still surprisingly hundreds of married partners living openly in the capital city of Nazi Germany, and many more so in other cities – let alone hundreds, if not more, "full" Jews also living in hiding. The pressure on these persons, however, mounted. In Wiesbaden, for instance, a Jewish wife married to a non-Jew, ordered to appear before the Gestapo, did not return home. She was sent to Auschwitz and died there in August 1943. In October 1943, half-Jews and Aryans married to Jewish wives were forcefully conscripted into the labor battalions of the Todt organization (for road building and fortifications). This was implemented starting the following year. However, as late as 1944, the exclusion of persons in mixed marriages from civilian posts was not yet fully concluded. That year, the regime still felt it necessary to evict from government jobs some non-Jews married to Jews or of mixed descent.

Months before the curtain came down on Nazi Germany in January 1945, the authorities decided to throw previously cautionary considerations to the wind, and ordered all Jews in mixed marriages, including those in the "privileged" category who were fit to work, to be transferred to Theresienstadt camp, whether or not they had German nationality, or to be conscripted to various labor assignments. Most survived, only due to the rapid collapse of the Nazi regime. Those who tried to avoid deportation went into hiding. That these were not isolated cases, especially starting in late 1944, is confirmed by a recent study of persons in hiding in Germany, in which 28% of married Jews in hiding (based on 65 interviews) were persons married to non-Jews. Among the non-Jewish spouses in mixed marriages, even before 1944, many were already involved in various rescue operations, as the following examples will demonstrate; we begin with cases in which the wife was non-Jewish.[2]

A) RESCUERS MARRIED TO JEWS OR TO PERSONS OF JEWISH PARENTAGE

Kurt Grünberg was married to the non-Jewess Marie, so he was shielded from deportation but did forced labor at the Siemens firm. The two were forced to vacate their previous home, and they moved into an outlying wooden cottage home. In March 1943, Kurt's Jewish brother Martin was admitted into their home in the Blankenburg section of Berlin, where he stayed intermittently together with a friend. Several other Jews found temporary refuge in Kurt and Marie's home, including a deserter from the army. Conditions were difficult, as the wooden cottage had no indoor toilet – with all the danger this implied of detection by neighbors – and food was scarce. The house was half an hour walking distance from the nearest store, and Marie had to feed four people (of which two had no ration cards) and fetch extra food in a way that none of the neighbors would suspect that something was amiss in that house. Vegetables were grown in the garden. Tension at times among the four hidden persons in that wooden cottage erupted into heated verbal fights, but Marie's strong character and resoluteness made it possible for all to pull through and survive.[3]

Charlotte Weiler, also in Berlin, was married to a Jewish man who died just before the start of the deportations that began in late 1941. In March 1943, she admitted into her home Hedwig and husband Erich Senger, two persons she knew from before, after their home was hit in an air raid. Hedwig was introduced as a distant aunt, and a hiding place was found elsewhere for Erich. In October, the Sengers were able to acquire false credentials, which made it possible for them to move to Horst, near Kolberg, on the Baltic coast, where they waited out the war until the arrival of the Russians.[4] In Berlin, as well, the non-Jewish Trude Wisten, who was married to the Jewish actor Fritz Wisten, hid a Jewish friend in her Berlin home from summer 1943 to the end of the war. Husband Fritz survived by doing forced labor. When later he and Trude were jailed, Admiral Wilhelm Canaris, head of the powerful Abwehr (German military intelligence), who lived in the neighborhood, arranged their release, and they were never threatened again, even after Canaris's arrest in 1944 by the Nazi regime.[5]

Still in Berlin, the earlier-mentioned Lisa Holländer, who sheltered Inge Deutschkron for a while in her Berlin home, was married to a Jew, who was released from a concentration camp after a brief stay. Elisabeth Bornstein, who hid a Jewish couple in her Berlin home, was also married to a Jew. When her husband Ludwig was taken to Buchenwald camp, Elisabeth wrote to Hermann Göring (the number two man in the Nazi hierarchy), pleading to have him released. Surprisingly and highly unusual, to say the least, after several months Kurt returned home.[6]

In Vienna, Maria Steiner, married to a Jewish man who had left and immigrated in time to Canada, via Shanghai, sheltered a Jewish woman in her home for 35 months. Maria introduced Hedwig Mendelssohn to outsiders as her stepsister and provided her with proper Aryan papers under the name of Hedy Steiner (she continued to use that name in the postwar period). Maria also helped two others Jews acquire Paraguayan visas, thereby facilitating their travel abroad via Italy. Maria Steiner stated that she was motivated by an intense hatred of Hitler and the Nazis, which she felt from the start, and she wanted to be of assistance to someone else who also shared this feeling. When she met Hedwig Mendelssohn at a private gathering and learned of her predicament, she immediately offered her help, and she extended her help to other Jews in need. In the same city, Anna-Maria Haas helped the Jewish Rubin couple, Josef and Sidonie, in various ways – occasional shelter in her home and help with milk to the Rubins' newborn baby. Anna-Maria's husband, Benno Haas, had converted to the Catholic faith when he married her. In 1942, he succeeded in fleeing the country and enlisted in the British army.[7]

Still in Vienna, the earlier-mentioned Marianne Golz, an actress and opera singer, was married to the Jewish journalist Hans Goldlust. In 1933 the couple moved to Prague, and when the Germans marched in, in March 1939, Hans managed to flee to England in time, leaving Marianne behind. She joined a clandestine Czech organization (made up mostly of Jewish members) that helped Nazi victims, Jews, and others to escape to Italy via Vienna. Arrested with them during a Gestapo raid in November 1942, she was sentenced to death in May 1943 with seven of her colleagues. As justification for the harsh sentence, the judges pointed out her Jewish connections and her "judaized" frame of mind, probably also due to her marriage to a Jew.[8] Marie-Luise Hensel, also previously mentioned, who failed in the attempt to smuggle several Jewish friends across the frontier into Switzerland and took her life while in a Gestapo jail, was married to a part-Jewish law professor, who died in 1933 from a stroke after his summary dismissal from a teaching position in a Königsberg university.[9]

Similar rescue stories also originated in which the male partner in the mixed marriage was non-Jewish, or of partly Jewish origin, such as in the following stories.

Werner Krumme, living in Breslau, was married to Ruth, a Jewish woman. At the outbreak of the war, he participated as a soldier in the Polish campaign of September 1939, but was then dismissed from the army because of his refusal to divorce his Jewish wife. Arrested in November 1942 with his wife while accompanying two Jewish sisters (Renata and Anita Lasker) to the train station in Breslau in an attempt to flee the country, the Krumme couple was sent to Auschwitz; he, as a political prisoner; she, as a Jewess. Ruth Krumme was gassed one month after her arrival. He, as a pure blooded "Aryan," was assigned relatively less harsh work in the prisoner labor administration. He used his position to falsify selection lists of those slated for death from among the internees and to assign Jews to work units with less harsh conditions, so as to increase their chances of survival. He too luckily survived.[10]

There are many more stories of Jewish women married to non-Jewish men in Germany, who benefitted from this arrangement to avoid deportation at least momentarily; some were able to evade captivity for quite a lengthy period, and their non-Jewish husbands used that occasion to extend help to other Jews in distress. In Berlin, Carl Strecker, an evangelical pastor, who, as stated in an earlier account, gave shelter to Andrea Wolffenstein, was married to Julie Pfefferkorn – probably of Jewish origin. It also seems that the earlier-mentioned engineer Walter Groos, who aided Jewish prisoners in Kaufering camp, was either married to a Jewess, or his wife was the daughter of a Jewish woman who was sheltered in the Groos home. The documentary material does not make this point too clear. Still in the Berlin area, the earlier-mentioned Hanning Schroeder, a known music composer, was married to Cornelia, a Jewess by birth but baptized at a young age. They sheltered, in their Rostock home, the Jewish couple Ilse and Werner Rewald, who were referred to them by a friend of Hanning, a music student, herself married to a Jew, a cellist by profession. The Rewalds stayed in the Schroeder home from early 1944 until the end of the war. Before arriving at the Schroeder home, the Rewalds were aided by several Jewish-Christian couples.[11]

Similar rescue initiators also included persons who were partly Jewish or stemmed from Jewish ancestors, as in the following stories. Pastor Werner Sylten was an aide to Heinrich Grüber, who headed a self-initiated association to help Jewish converts to Christianity from excessive harm by the Nazi state (officially called *Hilfstelle für evangelische Rasseverfolgte*, in Berlin, but better known as *Büro Pfarrer Grüber*). Grüber's organization also extended assistance to full Jews. When Grüber was arrested in December 1940 and sent to Sachsenhausen camp, Reverend Sylten (who was partly Jewish) replaced him. He was himself arrested in February 1941 and sent to Dachau camp where he died. The *Büro* was closed in February 1941 and all its members dispersed. Before entering the clergy, Sylten had fought in the First World War, then joined a *Freikorps* unit that fought to secure Germany's new frontiers in the east. When his first wife died, leaving him with two children, he was prevented from remarrying, because he was considered a *Mischling*. Also not allowed to practice the ministry in Thuringen, he moved in 1938 to Berlin and was invited by Grüber to join his organization to help racially persecuted, baptized Jews.[12]

The earlier-mentioned Theodor Görner, owner of a Berlin printing shop, was arrested in 1944 for protesting the eviction from school of his adopted daughter, who was half-Jewish (precise details are lacking). The authorities ordered the closing of his firm and he was declared an enemy of the people. Previous to his arrest, Görner helped a number of Jews, including the already-mentioned Inge Deutschkron's mother. In Hannover, Margot Bloch was helped by a Jewish woman, married to a Christian, after Margot fled there from Berlin in late 1942. This woman introduced Margot to friends, with whom Margot found shelter during the war years, such as the earlier-mentioned Kochanowskis.[13]

These are but a few of an estimated larger number of cases in which help was extended to Jews by non-Jews married to Jewish spouses, as recorded at Yad Vashem. Information culled from other sources suggests that the number of such cases is far larger; such as the records kept by the Berlin Senate, in the late 1950's and early 1960s, under its own program of *Unbesungene Helden* (see Appendix B).

B) RESCUED JEWISH PERSONS MARRIED TO NON-JEWISH SPOUSES

As earlier noted, Jewish spouses in mixed marriages were usually exempt from deportation until late 1944, although they too fared badly from discriminatory measures, though not as severely as "full" Jews or as baptized Jews who claimed at least three Jewish grandparents and were therefore considered as plain-and-simple Jews. However, some of the Jews in mixed marriages began to seek shelter for themselves even before their deportation became official policy.

The Jewish Lotte, born Mayer, and married to the non-Jewish literature historian Dr. Ernst Paepcke, from Mecklenburg, at a certain point in her cat-and-mouse game with the authorities, she felt the urgent need to "dive" (*U-Boot*) – to disappear and live as a person on the run, already at the early period of 1942. She first fled to Leipzig, then Freiburg, and eked out a secret existence. After a particularly heavy air raid on the city in November 1944 that she luckily survived, she thought of turning herself in. However, through a friend, she was referred to Father Heinrich Middendorf, head of the Herz-Jezu monastery in nearby Stegen. There she remained mostly hidden (even after several Gestapo visits to verify that no Jews were staying in that religious institution) with her son Peter (a *Mischling* Grade A) in the care of Middendorf, who assigned her gardening chores, until the city's liberation by French troops in April 1945.[14]

In Krefeld, Mrs. Frings, a Jewish woman married to a non-Jew, was sheltered for a while in the home of Pastor Heinrich and Margot Hamer, beginning in early 1944. Later, her three sons, considered "half-Jews" (officially, *Mischlinge* first grade) by the authorities, were also admitted into the Hamer household. They stayed incommunicado during daylight hours; when the six Hamer children were asleep, the Frings were allowed to come up from their cellar hideout and join the Hamers in conversation. Hamer was a member of the Confessing Church.[15] As for Erna Etscheit, in Düsseldorf-Oberkassel, she escaped deportation due to her marriage to a non-Jew. But when her husband died in March 1944, Erna was notified by the Gestapo to make ready for deportation. She was then sheltered in the home of Joseph and Hilde Neyses, where she remained hidden from September 1944 until the entry of the US Army in March 1945. Joseph Neyses, a longtime musician, was at the time an orchestra director. After the war, he headed the Robert Schumann Conservatoire.[16]

In Primasens, Johanna Fronmueller and her sister Gustel Wagner were married to non-Jews, with children. They therefore came under the classification of "privileged mixed marriages" (*privilegierte Mischehen*). In August 1944, sensing the approaching danger of deportation, the two sisters sought shelter with Ernst Pfau, who hid them in a forest shed near Eppental (Bad Dürkheim), where they remained hidden until the end of the war. When the Gestapo came looking for them, their non-Jewish husbands reported that their wives and children had left to an undisclosed location to seek shelter from the constant air raids.[17] In another story, the Jewish Gertrud Beer was married to Eberhard Schnellen in 1912, at which point she converted to the Catholic faith, and gave birth to eight children. The couple lived relatively unharmed in Dortmund-Brachel until late 1944. Gertrud was then hidden with relatives of Maria Hueren, in Hinsbeck-Orlig, near the Dutch border. Her husband simultaneously informed the police that his wife had suddenly disappeared. When he nevertheless received a summons to report to the Gestapo, Eberhard and several of his children were helped by friends to find secure hiding places, including a Franciscan institution in the Mönchengladbach region. Two of the Schnellen sons were imprisoned in a camp in Kassel-Bettenhausen but were able to escape during an air raid in March 1945, and they were then hidden in several places with relatives.[18]

In yet another similar story, Clara Hirschhorn was married in 1918 to university medical professor Heinrich von Mettenheim, a non-Jew, in 1918 and lived with him in Frankfurt am Main. In January 1944, Clara wrote to her eldest daughter, in England (perhaps the letter was mailed via the Red Cross): "Last week, 60 widows and divorced women (many had divorced so as to protect their husbands' livelihood) were deported to Theresienstadt." When Heinrich was killed during an air raid on Frankfurt that same month, Clara's future safety was in jeopardy. Moreover, because she was a born Jewess, Frankfurt University refused to pay her the compensation to which she was entitled as the widow of a tenured professor, although she was a practicing Christian. When she received the dreaded summons in March 1944, she found shelter in the farming household of Sibylle Dierke, in Silmersdorf/Ostpriegnitz. Sybille had not directly known Clara before February 1944, only through a brother-in-law who had been a friend of Clara's husband, and now learned of her distress. Prior to Clara's hiding, she and Dierke had never met.[19] Finally, Gertrud Kerklies, who was married to a non-Jew, gave birth to eight children. In September 1944, Gertrud and five of her children were picked up by the Gestapo in their Essen home and taken to Berlin, and held imprisoned; Gertrud alone was then deported to Theresienstadt. Maria and Gerhard Mueller, neighbors of Gertrud, took in Gertrud's remaining three children. Gertrud's husband was then away in the Mulhouse region, building fortifications for the army.[20]

Conditions were no different in mixed marriages, where the husband instead of the wife was Jewish. Both were definitely in jeopardy by the Nazi state as of late 1944.

Jewish Richard Schreiber was a medical doctor in Bad Godesberg. Until 1944, he was not harmed, due to his marriage to an "Aryan." Then, in collusion with Otto Kessel, the local head of the Criminal Police (*Kripo*), Schreiber went into hiding with two women friends of his wife – Auguste and Katharina Boehm. It had been previously decided that Schreiber's non-Jewish wife would report her husband's absence to Kessel, who would then register him as missing. The Gestapo ordered an investigation but failed to track down the missing man. According to Kessel: "For me, it was a very critical and dangerous situation. If Dr. Schreiber had been uncovered, it would have meant the death penalty for him as well as for me." Schreiber remained in hiding until the arrival of the U.S. Army in March 1945.[21]

In Berlin, Max Mandel's wife was born a Christian woman but converted to Judaism before the advent of the Nazis to power, and was therefore considered Jewish by the Nazis as a *Geltenjude* (rated Jewish in spite of being born Aryan). In 1939, Max's Jewish-converted wife left for Brazil, where she had relatives, in an attempt to get her family out of Germany. Her son, Gert, left behind in Germany, was in the eyes of the authorities a *Mischling* Grade A. The war intervened, but only in 1944 did the authorities learn of her absence. Until then, Max did forced manual labor on the railroads but his marriage to a born Aryan woman protected him from deportation. Presently, fearing the worst, Max contacted his longtime friend Erich Büngener, who together with his wife Erika hid Max and his son in a corner of his furniture store (closed down because of the war), from February 1944 until the end of the war. Also added were Max's sister, Erna Kantorowicz, and husband Kurt, a total of four hidden persons.[22]

In Hamburg, Dr. Berthold Hannes and his non-Jewish wife were sheltered by Elisabeth Flügge, after the Hannes' home was damaged in an air raid in July 1943. The Hannes' two daughters had left for England before the onset of the war, and a son remained with them in Germany. Dr. Hannes lost his post as a medical doctor in a Hamburg city hospital, and in 1935, he was forbidden to treat non-Jewish patients. His rescuer, Mrs. Flügge, a teacher by profession, had stood up for her Jewish students, and this cost her a job at a private school for the wealthy. She then took up a teaching post in one of the poorest schools in the city. Elisabeth Flügge's son, a soldier, fell in battle. This did not diminish her resolve to shelter the Hanneses, who remained in Elisabeth Flügge's home until the end of the war.[23]

c) More on the *Mischlinge*

As mentioned earlier, in the Nazi obsession with a racially pure society, persons not qualifying either as "full" Aryans nor "full" Jews were lumped together into a new racial grouping – the "mixed" or *Mischlinge*. They included persons who claimed one or only two Jewish grandparents (three Jewish grandparents placed the grandchild together with "full" Jews). This group was further subdivided into two: the half-Jews, half-Aryan (two Jewish and two non-Jewish grandparents), or *Mischling* Grade A, and the three-quarters Aryan, one-quarter Jewish (three Aryan and one Jewish grandparent), or *Mischling* Grade B. Judging by the increasing assimilation of Jews into German life and culture in the years preceding the Nazis, there were many tens of thousands of descendants of such "mixed" persons, and the Nazis hesitated, prevaricated, and could not make up their minds on the final disposition of these racially "impure" persons.[24]

In April 1935, the German Ministry of the Interior estimated the number of *Mischlinge* of both categories as 750,000. This, however, is considered a gross overestimate. Four years later, Dr. Bernhard Loesener of the Interior Ministry estimated the total number of *Mischlinge*, Grade A only, as 64,000. The situation of most *Mischlinge* was quite tragic, as they considered themselves full Germans, were overwhelmingly Christian, but were at the same time increasingly shunned by the rest of German society. The fact that many *Mischlinge* were related to families of military officers and university graduates, and included persons who had rendered significant contributions to German life, only exacerbated the ordeal of these persons.

The Nazi indecision on this issue was compounded by Hitler's own ambivalence. He did not consent to the integration of all *Mischlinge* into the German peoplehood, but he was not always consistent about how far to go in the opposite direction – to define the borderline between *Mischlinge* and Jew. It is known that he placed great weight on the facial features of petitioners who sought an upgrade to a higher status – from 1st degree status to 2nd, and thence to full Aryan status. The hope of many Nazi party heads was to eventually absorb all quarter-Jews into the German population (except those with distinctly Semitic features), while at the same time fusing the half-Jews with the Jewish population, and dealing with them accordingly. By the time the war drew to a close, no formal decision had been taken in that regard, although all *Mischlinge* experienced increased persecution at the hands of the authorities.

The Interior Ministry received several thousand petitions by *Mischlinge* for marriage restriction exemptions. In only about a dozen cases were such permissions granted (for persons who had a conspicuous "Nordic" appearance and had a remarkable record of service in the war, the Nazi party, or other vital profession). Hitler reserved for himself the final decision in all cases. By May 1941, 263 positive decisions by Hitler were handed out, out of a total of 9,636 requests, in which half-Jews (*Mischlinge* Grade A) were "promoted" to quarter-Jews (*Mischlinge* Grade B). However, in March 1942, the further processing of these applications was suspended for the duration of the war. [25]

Until 1937, *Mischlinge* were still able to attend German public schools, although a *Numerus Clausus* (a restrictive 2quota admission program based on prejudicial criteria) was introduced for *Mischlinge* in secondary schools. *Mischlinge* children were not permitted to hold teaching jobs of any sort, and they also experienced difficulties in studying pharmacy. They also experienced economic difficulties, as many firms declined jobs to them for fear of being sidestepped in obtaining government work contracts. Paradoxically, in 1939, *Mischlinge* of both categories were still called up for military service. The following year, however, Hitler fumed when told of this situation and ordered that half-Jews and those married to full Jews were to be excluded from the Wehrmacht – a total of 25,000 men. However, by the time the Hitler rule went into effect, the campaign in France had already begun, and several *Mischlinge* were even decorated for bravery on the field of battle. The full exclusion of the *Mischlinge* from the military had not been concluded that year, for in 1942 Hitler returned to the issue. He regretted the numerous exemptions that the army was making in allowing half-Jews to serve in the Wehrmacht. For, as he explained, "experience showed that from these Jewish offspring for four, five, or six generations pure Jews kept 'Mendeling' out (*ausmendeln*)."[26] Finally, in October 1942, Hitler decreed that no further petitions from semi-Jews to enlist or continue serving in the army should be processed.

During the Wannsee Conference of January 20, 1942, to synchronize the various government agencies in the extermination of all Jews on the European continent, the *Mischlinge* issue appears to have dominated to a large extent the discussion, judging from the space it occupied in the typed minutes of the conference. One proposal was to treat *Mischlinge* Grade A as Jews (as the Nazi party demanded) – apart from those already married to German spouses, and others enjoying official exemption – and slate them

for destruction. Those exempted would be offered the choice of sterilization or deportation. *Mischlinge* Grade B were to be treated as full Germans.
Furthermore, in marriages of quarter-Jews with full Jews – both sides, including the children, would be "evacuated" (a euphemism for extermination).
Likewise, for marriages between half- and quarter-Jews. The conference also
decided that marriages between half-Jews and so-called Aryans, where there
were no children, or between full Jews and Aryans, should be dissolved, if
possible at the request of the non-Jewish partner, and, failing that, at the
request of the public prosecutor. A few days after the conference, Wilhelm
Stuckart of the Interior Ministry wrote that he objected that half-Jews be
included in the Final Solution, because it would mean "abandoning that half
of their blood which is German." Later that year, Stuckart continued arguing that deporting half-Jews would involve giving their German genes to
Germany's enemies and thereby provide them with future leaders. He reiterated his advocacy of sterilization as the appropriate solution.

Further discussions produced no final decisions. In November 1942,
Gestapo chief Heinrich Müller ordered the deportation of all Jewish inmates
already found in German concentration camps, including the *Mischlinge*
Grade A, to the extermination camps in Poland. During 1943–1944,
Mischlinge children in welfare institutions were sent to the euthanasia center
at Hadamar, where they were killed by poison injection. In 1943, Göring
decreed that half-Jews, still circulating in the open, were to be conscripted
into labor battalions of the Todt organization, and this was implemented the
following year. However, as late as 1944, it was still necessary to evict 24
Mischlinge from government posts. The following year, as many *Mischlinge*
as could be rounded up were sent to Theresienstadt camp. In Wiesbaden, for
instance, many of the *Mischlinge*, who numbered between 800 and 2,000,
were arrested in 1944.

In the final event, according to one study, the *Mischlinge* owed their
survival in part to the fact that there was a lobby within the ministerial bureaucracy, especially the Ministry of the Interior, which worked to exclude
them from persecution. Pressure in the other direction came primarily from
the Party and SS leadership. According to Noakes: "Above all, however, the
Mischlinge owed their survival to Hitler's own caution and uncertainty which
produced a stream of contradictory and confusing impulses. He was clearly
hostile to the *Mischlinge* but, at the same time, acutely aware of the danger
of provoking unrest among their numerous Aryan relatives."[27] At the same

time, had Germany won the war, it is safe to assume that the *Mischlinge* 1st degree would probably have shared the fate of the Jews, while the *Mischlinge* 2nd degree would have been subjected, at the least, to selective sterilization and further discrimination.

At any rate, it was obvious to most *Mischlinge*, right from the start of the Nazi regime, that their personal security hung in the balance. Although most rescue stories involving the *Mischlinge*, as further illustrated, date from 1944, there were also those who, seeing the handwriting on the wall, began planning their own escape even before that. As most of the *Mischlinge* preferred in the postwar period to resume their integration into German life, they understandably preferred to keep their identity and rescue stories to themselves; hence, fewer such stories are known and made available for study and research. We continue with sample stories of help to *Mischlinge* by regular "Aryan" rescuers, as recorded at Yad Vashem.

Elsa Blochwitz was an air-raid warden in a Berlin house that counted over 30 flats. In this capacity, she had access to many empty apartments and cellars, where she occasionally hid Jews and semi-Jews. One of these "mixed" Jews was Rita Grabowski, who as a *Mischling* was under threat of arrest since mid-1944. She had until then lived in the Czech region (where German laws prevailed), but when *Mischlinge* there were targeted for deportation, she returned to Berlin, where she joined her mother who lived in the same apartment house as Elsa. Mother and daughter were hidden by Elsa in several apartments that were under her supervision. During that time, Elsa also secretly penned anti-Nazi poems in which she denounced the persecution of Jews. Her mother often warned her that her involvement with Jews would eventually cost her life, to which Elsa responded: "Then I'll know for what." She took care to cover all traces of her rescue efforts, and succeeded in avoiding detection.[28]

Jetty Organek was born to a Jewish father and a Christian mother. In 1941, her father committed suicide in order to avoid further persecution. A family acquaintance, Hans Sieber, formerly a flight captain with Lufthansa airline, sheltered her and her brother in his Berlin apartment in 1943 for several weeks. Sieber was later arrested and imprisoned for his role in effecting the flight of Poles and political fugitives to Spain. To a friend he confided that the senseless destruction of parts of Belgrade in April 1941, during the invasion of Yugoslavia, in which he participated, and which he saw from the air, as well as the view of the destroyed Czech village of Lidice (in revenge for the slaying of SS second-in-command, Reinhard Heydrich), had turned him against the regime.[29]

As for Helmut Karnop, he was involved in several "subversive" activities that made him suspicious in the eyes of the authorities. Immediately after World War One, in which he served as a soldier, he joined the Freemasons – considered by many Germans as a subversive group, in collusion with the "International Jewry" that was conspiring against the country. He also studied law, but his Freemason association barred him from practicing law during the Nazi period. During World War Two, he served in Holland, Belgium, and France as a military officer. He and his mother, Maria, lived in Berlin, where they had as neighbors the Thiemke family, who were of mixed Jewish-Aryan background, and that led to Herta Thiemke's father being deported to Dachau camp where he died in 1941. Herta and husband Max Thiemke belonged to a church also attended by Helmut Karnop. When her father was first arrested and sent to Buchenwald during the Kristallnacht pogrom of November 9–10, 1938, Karnop accompanied Herta to the Gestapo to plead for her father's release, thus exposing himself. When the Gestapo demanded a huge ransom sum for the release, Karnop contributed the major part, but still the release was held up. On his second visit to the Gestapo, he was warned to stop interceding on behalf of Jews, or else be classified a "friend of the Jews." Her father was not released, and Herta dared not ask for a refund. Earlier, Karnop's home also served as a haven for other Jews (or half-Jews), who spent a night or two before leaving Germany during the late 1930s, such as Fritz Koch, born to a Jewish father and non-Jewish mother. While with the military in Holland, during the war, Karnop also helped persons of mixed origin, such as the half-Jewess Liesel de Vries (born Vogelsang), from Zeist, near Utrecht. In July 1944, while Helmut Karnop was on duty in Belgium, the Gestapo raided his home in Berlin in search of hidden half-Jews. Failing to find anyone, they severely beat Helmut's elderly mother Maria (who was seventy and blind in one eye), inflicting on her severe injuries, including several broken ribs and a sprained arm. For several weeks thereafter, the Thiemkes, who came out from hiding, nursed Mrs. Karnop's wounds. Then, in July 1944, Helmut was arrested in Belgium for mainly political reasons, and held until September, when he was taken prisoner by the liberating Allied armies.[30]

Ilse Moslé (Baumgart), who was born to a Jewish mother and a Christian father, was sheltered by the sisters Gitta Bauer and Maria Schwelien in their

Berlin home from the summer of 1944 until the war's end. In another story, one of the persons helped by Paula Hülle of Berlin was Charlotte Schaefer, who was of mixed Jewish–non-Jewish parentage, and her daughter Jutta. During a raid by the Gestapo, in December 1943, Charlotte's Jewish mother slashed her wrists and was taken to a hospital where she died. Paula then moved with the two women in hiding to a farmer's home in Lewenberg for a while, until they felt safe to return to Berlin. In the village of Niederroth, north of Munich, as already told, Leonhard and Maria Gailer sheltered little Hannelore Bach, daughter of a Jewish father and Christian mother. After her father left the country just before the start of the war, Mrs. Bach withstood Nazi pressures to divorce him. Fearing for her daughter's safety, she had Hannelore hidden with Gailer, a customer of her husband's previous household goods store in Munich.[31]

The previously mentioned Countess Maria von Maltzan sheltered in her Berlin home Wolfgang Hammerschmidt, born to a Jewish father (murdered in camp Schwetig, near Frankfurt/Oder, in December 1944) and a Christian mother. Up until 1944, Wolfgang was assigned various forced labor duties. In August 1944, he escaped from a camp in Rixheim, near Mulhouse, France, and made his way to Berlin, where his brother Helmut provided him with addresses of persons with whom he stayed intermittently – he moved from place to place, including a stay in the cellar of the Swedish church, and with the Pastor Wendland family. In between, he also hid in cellars of bombed-out buildings. Suffering from a lung inflammation, he finally headed for the home of Maria von Maltzan, where he had earlier stayed with his brother, and remained hidden there from March 15 until late April 1945. He then ran into Ruth Wendland, who (as earlier related) had in the meantime been released from prison and was looking for him. She hid him in her home in Turmhelm, until the place's capture by the Russians on April 30.[32]

We shall later have occasion to speak at greater length about Hans von Dohnányi, who, with the backing of his superior Admiral Canaris, arranged the flight to Switzerland, in September 1942, of a group of *Mischlinge* persons and baptized Jews. Also, of Hans Georg Calmeyer and Gerhard Wander, two German officials in occupied Netherlands who helped full and semi-Jews avoid deportation to Nazi death camps.[33]

In the following story, a traveling circus was thought to offer a better chance of keeping several steps ahead of the Gestapo. Irene Danner originally belonged to the Jewish Lorch family, which operated a circus in the

Darmstadt region. When the Nazis closed the circus (a *Gauleiter,* a Nazi regional leader, told Irene: "I forbid you to tempt our German men with your Jewish body"), Irene, whose mother, Alice, was Jewish and her father, Hans, a non-Jew and, at the time, a soldier in the German army, approached Adolf Althoff, who owned a traveling circus and had known Irene's family, and she was admitted as a rope jumper (previously she was also a horse rider). There she met Peter Storms, who performed as a clown. The half-Jewish Irene bore Peter two sons, born secretly, while at the same time eluding the Gestapo, who had been tipped off by an informer. The persons sheltered included Irene's Jewish mother and her soldier father, who had received leave from the army in order to divorce his Jewish-wife but, instead, decided to desert and go into hiding. All survived thanks to Althoff's ingenuity, courage, and determination.[34]

To close this section, we relate in quick succession a few more rescue stories involving *Mischlinge* in search of shelter and succor. Baroness Maimi von Mirbach sheltered in her home during 1941–1945 the piano student Prof. Gisela Distler-Brendel, a half-Jew. Walter Czok, the earlier-mentioned SA man in Vienna, is reported to have aided Maria Feldman, a *Mischling* born to a Jewish father who was previously a major in the army. Similarly, as already mentioned, Anastasia and Severin Gerschuetz, in the Mainz area, sheltered Eva Schmalenbach, daughter of a non-Jewish father and a Jewish mother. In Cologne, a clandestine group calling itself *Edelweiss Piraten* sheltered in their secret hideout several *Mischlinge* Jews, who had been interned in Müngersdorf camp, awaiting deportation, and had made their escape in September 1944. Some were eventually recaptured by the Gestapo.[35]

D) BAPTIZED JEWS

Jews who had freely chosen to convert to Christianity, or had been baptized at birth, before the advent of the Nazi regime, were in much greater danger of deportation than the *Mischlinge*. In fact, the Nazis fully disregarded the religious profession of these people and considered them as "fully" Jewish if they claimed three or four grandparents, including imposing on these self-declared non-Jews the obligatory wearing of the Yellow Star, and they shared the same fate as all Jews. According to a certain study, in 1933 the number of baptized Jews, officially known as "non-Aryan Christian" (*nichtarische*

Christen), was at the very least 228,000, but this may be an exaggerated figure. Six years into Nazi rule, in 1939, when hundreds of thousands of Jews had already left the country, the number of baptized Jews in the now-enlarged Reich was still significant – running into tens of thousands.

Baptized Jews experienced various forms of discrimination – even by their own churches, in glaring contravention of Christian teaching! For instance, a 1939 law stated that no Jew could become a member of the Thuringian Evangelical Church, and no pastor was to be obliged to minister to non-Aryans who were already Church members. Four other regional churches in Saxony, Mecklenburg, Anhalt, and Luebeck followed suit. The Synod of the Old Prussian Church resolved that anyone of non-Aryan descent may not be appointed as minister or official, whereas clergy or officials of Aryan descent who marry non-Aryans were to be dismissed. Most churches adopted the so-called Aryan Clause, which closed the doors of the church to baptized Jews – a violation of the church's most traditional and fundamental principles. Pastors Martin Niemöller and Dietrich Bonhoeffer vehemently attacked this violation of Christian teaching. To Bonhoeffer, the threatened exclusion of Christian non-Aryans was nothing less than the undoing of the work of Paul (born Jewish as Saul). Hermann Sasse, a Bavarian Lutheran theologian, stated that the Aryan clause had the effect of outlawing Jesus Christ Himself, born Jewish, from the preaching ministry. But most churches in Germany fell in line with the Nazi exclusion of non-Aryans from the community of Church fellowship.

In July 1933, a group of baptized Jews founded the Paulus Bund to struggle for their Jews, and the authorities tolerated this organization until August 1939, when it was ordered to disband. The Bund's point of view was that its members were "sincere Christians. . . . The Christian baptism has permanently cut all ties not only to Judaism but also to the Jewish people. We are absolutely loyal to the National Socialist government." The Paulus Bund claimed to distance itself from anything "un-German", such as liberal, pacifist, left-wing, and democratic ideas – which it attributed to Jewish and communist influences. To further curry favor with the authorities, in April 1937 the Bund expelled from its ranks members who were more than 50% of Jewish descent. This, however, did not stay the government's hand in closing the organization two years later.

Protestant Pastor Heinrich Grüber had the welfare of the baptized Jews very much at heart, and established an evangelical welfare office for their benefit. He was arrested in 1940, and his post was taken over by Werner Sylten, himself of Jewish descent. In fairness to Grüber, he and his team were also prepared to act on behalf of full Jews, not even necessarily Jews who had passed through the portals of the church. In these efforts, Grüber had a confrontational meeting with Adolf Eichmann, who cautioned him to cease and desist. Having disregarded this warning, in December 1940, he was arrested and interned in Sachsenhausen, then Dachau camp, and released in 1943. In 1960, he testified at the Adolf Eichmann trial in Israel.[36]

We have already noted, in a previous chapter, Gertrud Luckner's involvement in helping both Catholic-baptized Jews, as well as full Jews, through the Caritas organization with which she was affiliated. She sent packages to baptized Jews who were deported to Łódź ghetto, and helped smuggle others across the Swiss or French borders – herself occasionally accompanying persons in this dangerous undertaking. Arrested in March 1943, she was sent to Ravensbrück camp, which she luckily survived.[37]

An additional dramatic story in this regard is that of Beate Hecht, who at the age of sixteen freely converted to Christianity and married Fritz Steckan. After being decorated for bravery, he fell in combat during the First World War. Years later, with the start of Nazi rule, Beate suffered increased deprivations, including the loss of her pension and widow payments. Then came the wearing of the Yellow Star and forced residence in a Jewish-designated home in Berlin. Pastors of her church, affiliated with the Confessing Church, Grüber's *Büro,* and Prelate Hermann Maas's circle, helped supplement her reduced rations (such as milk, eggs, and meat – items forbidden to Jews). When she received the dreaded deportation summons in September 1941, she was told by Pastor Friedrich von Rabenau to report, who assured her she would be released as a decorated war widow, and she was indeed permitted to go home. She continued attending Bible classes, with von Rabenau accompanying her home, despite her wearing the Jewish star. It was then decided to move her out of Berlin, first to the Württemberg area, where she rotated from place to place. One of these stops was the home of Pastor Richard Goelz in Wankheim, near Tübingen. She was at first introduced as a refugee fleeing the city bombings, but after a while she disclosed to him her Jewishness ("after much inner struggle"), to which he responded: "Now you fully belong to us. Next Sunday, we have to intone a Te Deum in church, for the honor of hosting a daughter of the House of Israel in our home." From that moment, he made great efforts to find alternative hiding places for her. Pastor

Goelz belonged to a secret society in Württemberg, which included many pastors who answered the call of Swiss theologian Karl Barth to help Jews. The Gestapo eventually found out about the society and arrested many of its members. Goelz was denounced and arrested on Christmas day 1944 and jailed in Welzheim camp until the end of the war.

As told, Beate moved from one pastor's home to another – altogether some twenty-three stopovers. Arriving in Heidelberg, she met Prelate Hermann Maas, who was involved in helping Jews and was eventually imprisoned. A certain vicar, named Margarete Hoffer, at first contemplated Beate's flight to Switzerland, but this was dropped when a group of Jews was arrested during an attempted crossing there in August 1942. At each place she stayed for only four weeks, which was the permissible grace period for not reporting newcomers at the local police station. In Prenzlau, near Munich, she was invited by a certain Countess von Arnim (first name not given) to stay in her home, a place regularly visited by many Foreign Office, SS, and SA officials, one of whom inquired about the dark-haired guest in her house. Mrs. von Arnim replied she was a visitor from the French-annexed Alsace region. The von Arnims were reportedly also involved in the anti-Hitler conspiracy of July 1944 and miraculously were not suspected. In all those places, the hosts, at some point and time, discovered the true identity of their guest, the formerly Jewish Beate Steckan. Beate stated: "I should like to unequivocally and clearly reiterate: all that was done by German people to save me, happened because I was persecuted by the Nazis as a Jewess. My religious belief had mostly nothing to do with it." She listed twenty-five persons who helped her in one way or another to survive the Nazi period.[38]

Martha Levy was similarly baptized when she married Friedrich Steeg in 1926. During the Nazi rule, he withstood pressures to divorce her, and as a result lost his job in Oberdollendorf, Bonn region, and in 1944 their son was expelled from school. Then, in September of that year, Martha and her son were arrested and taken to Köln-Müngersdorf camp. After a two-week stay there, Martha was moved to the Henschel-Werke labor camp in Hess-Lichtenau. Her son Gunther (classified a *Mischling* Grade A), being under sixteen, was released and placed under the care of his grandmother. Martha was able to flee from her workplace, and as prearranged was hidden by her friend Wilma Groyen in her home cellar. There she remained until the area's liberation in mid-March 1945.[39]

Up north, in Bremen, Elisabeth Forck was active in the St. Stephani evangelical church. When Jewish converts active in this church were threatened by the Nazi regime, Forck with others tried to ease their plight with material aid and words of comfort. When these Christian-Jews received their deportation orders to Minsk, in October 1941, the St. Stephani church supplied them with warm blankets and gave them a moving farewell party in the church hall. The Gestapo reacted by arresting several of the church members, and its head Pastor Gustav Greiffenhagen was sent as a chaplain to the Eastern front, because "he gave Jews to eat from his bread, and allowed them to drink from the same cup." Four of the church teachers were dismissed from their post for showing sympathy to baptized Jews, such as donating clothes and visiting the Jewish converts in their homes. Four Jewish members of the church who were married to Aryan spouses were allowed to stay and survived. Three women sent to Theresienstadt survived. However, most of the other baptized Jews were deported and perished.[40]

Mention has already been made of Esther Seidel who helped Valerie Wolffenstein, who as a child was baptized into the church; of Reverend Alfred Dilger who, with his wife Luise, sheltered a Jewish Christian convert in their Stuttgart-Bad Cannsstatt home; of Maria Hueren who found a sheltering place for Gertrud Schnellen (born Beer, she converted upon her marriage to Franz Schnellen in 1912) with relatives in Hinsbeck-Orlig, on the German-Dutch frontier; and of Sibylle Dierke's help to Clara von Mettenheim (born Hirschhorn, and raised in the Christian faith) in 1944. Equally, the earlier-mentioned Father Heinrich Middendorf, in Stegen (near Freiburg), sheltered a group of baptized Jews in his Stegen church compound, beginning in 1944 – a group that included Irmgard Giessler (born Freitag), who converted to Catholicism upon her marriage to Ruppert Giessler, and her daughter. Also included were: Gerhard Zacharias, son to a Jewish-born mother and a Catholic father – soon after his mother Helene died in an air raid ("What a macabre thing to say, that she was lucky to be killed by bombs before being deported," Gerhard noted), as well as Dieter Bachenheimer, who became a Catholic upon his marriage to Hildegard. His father managed to flee Germany before the start of the war; Dieter lost his mother in an air raid on Dortmund in 1944. He too was hidden in Middendorf's monastery in Stegen.[41]

Baptized Jews who survived in Germany through the help of fellow Christians proved the exception to the rule. Most churches abandoned their converted Jews, who suffered martyrdom as full Jews. Their remains are mixed with those of Jews in the open fields and pits in Eastern European execution sites, and the ashes of the Auschwitz, Treblinka, Sobibór, and Bełżec death camps, and other camps in Nazi-controlled Europe.

Elisabeth Abegg

Oskar Schindler greeted by his
many survivors, Tel Aviv

Adolf & Maria Althoff (right)
holding Yad Vashem
Certificate of Honor; Irene
& Peter Storms (left);
Israel ambassador Avraham
Primor (second right).

Maria Nickel (right) and
Ruth Abraham (left)

Esther-Maria Seidel planting
a tree at Yad Vashem

Otto and Gertrud Mörike

Otto Busse & women he saved. Aryeh
Kubowy, Yad Vashem CEO (first left)

Berthold and Else Beitz, and daughter Barbara

Hermann Graebe   Hans Georg Calmeyer

Otto Weidt (2nd row, 3rd right)
and Jewish blind workers
Alice Licht (2nd row, 2nd right);
Inge Deutschkron (1st row, 2nd left)

Eberhard Helmrich (right)
holding Yad Vashem medal.
Michael Arnon (left), Israel
consul-general New York.

Wilhelm Hammann

Anton Schmid

Armin T. Wegner

Bernhard Lichtenberg

CHAPTER 7

Subverting the System – Persons in Positions of Authority and Influence

* * *

IN PREVIOUS CHAPTERS, WE HAVE noted cases in which certain German entrepreneurs and managerial trustees, in charge of assigned Jewish workers, went beyond the call of duty, or of profit considerations, to try to save their Jewish workers. We will briefly recap the names of these rescuers before moving on to other, no less fascinating accounts of Germans in high positions who also used various unorthodox methods to save Jews. As already told, Otto Weidt, who operated a broom and brushes manufacturing firm in Berlin, tried to keep his many blind Jewish workers safe from the grip of the Gestapo for as long as possible. In the Rovno region of Ukraine, Friedrich Graebe tried likewise to save his Jewish workers from SS killing units – he, too, for as long as possible. To the south, in Boryslaw, Berthold Beitz tried to hold on to his 1,500 Jewish workers with the excuse of needing them for the proper functioning of the city's oil refineries, although most of these workers were hardly fit for this type of work. When necessary, Beitz used bribery to buy off the goodwill of SS chief Georg Hildebrand, by lining his pockets with various highly prized gifts. In Kraków, Julius Madritsch and Raimund Titsch employed several thousand Jews in their uniform mending firm, thus securing their survival – in no small measure by play-acting a buddy-buddy attitude toward Płaszów's notorious camp commander, Amon Göth. The legendary Oskar Schindler was a master in the art of pulling the wool over the eyes of top Nazi commanders. To save his Jewish workers, who eventually counted 1,200 men and women, he used deception, bluff, lies, buffoonery – all of these laced with gifts to the right people. By the time the war ended, he had singlehandedly saved 1,200 Jewish lives, a feat unrivaled by any other German rescuer.[1] We continue with other stories of German officials, mostly in the occupied countries, who tried within the limits of their authority to save Jewish lives through the contrived use of all kinds of subterfuge and excuses.

a) Wielded Power and Subterfuge to Help Save

Josef Meyer, a trained agronomist, was a civilian administrator in charge of agricultural products in Złoczów, Poland (today, Zolochiv, Ukraine). One day he confided to the Jewish Solomon Altmann, a former attorney who now supervised a local bakery, his strong opposition to the Nazi regime. "I am a believing Catholic and a strict and uncompromising opponent of this criminal regime," Meyer told the startled Altmann. "Please inform your friends, with precaution, that within the purview of my duties I shall do everything in order to help." This was no mere blustering, as Meyer proved true to his word. He subsequently increased the food quota for the city's Jews by fictitiously doubling the number of persons listed as productively employed, telling Altmann: "I am aware that this is opposed to law and punishable; but the purpose of saving human lives justifies the means; hence, my conscience is perfectly clear." Meyer also made sure that sufficient food be made available to various Jewish institutions in the city, still allowed to function, and gave his consent to the setting up of a free kitchen for the ghetto's Jews. The additional food allocations were listed in the books under fictitious names of firms and army units. When he learned that the SS planned to liquidate the 1,000 Jewish laborers in a nearby labor camp because of a typhus epidemic, he arranged for a big consignment of soap and other hygienic equipment to be smuggled into the camp to help local doctors combat the spreading disease and thus spare the imprisoned camp workers from immediate execution. Suspected of help to Jews, Meyer was arrested by the Gestapo in January 1943 and taken to Lwów, but was released after three days of grueling cross-examination for lack of evidence. After his release, he told a worried Altmann: "Don't be afraid, I shall continue to help, but we will have to take more effective precautionary measures."

When the Nazis moved to destroy the remaining Jews in Złoczów (7,000 of an original 14,000-strong Jewish population), Meyer worked out a scheme together with the Jewish Strassler brothers, who earlier operated a candy factory, to secretly expand a series of underground caverns beneath the main market square, large enough to contain some 30 people. Meyer promised to supply the hidden people with the necessary food for an indefinite period. A trusted Pole served as liaison between Meyer and one of the hidden women. He also arranged for Solomon Altmann's wife to be cared in Warsaw, armed with false credentials. As for Solomon, his father and son were hidden in a hole behind a barn belonging to a Pole, who in return was given a permit to operate a pub. After the war, Altmann stated: "The fact that he saved us is in itself important. However, the fact that Herr Meyer preserved our belief in humanity is even of greater importance."[2]

In the following story, even greater subterfuge was needed to gain the freedom of a group of fourteen full and half-Jews, in a plan hatched by a senior officer at the highest levels of Germany's military intelligence service, the formidable Abwehr.

Hans von Dohnányi at first worked in the Ministry of Justice. Dismissed in 1938 because of his anti-Nazi views (a Nazi colleague in the Ministry testified against von Dohnányi that he had no understanding of the racial policy of his country, but was consciously opposed to them), he was admitted in the Abwehr by Hans Oster, head of the military intelligence's foreign department and a staunch opponent of Hitler. Von Dohnányi's duties included drawing analytic reports of political developments in surrounding countries. His brother-in-law, Dietrich Bonhoeffer, also officially listed within the Abwehr, besides being a noted theologian, was one of the principal spirits behind the creation of the Confessing Church and a diehard anti-Nazi. At Bonhoeffer's prodding, von Dohnányi decided in 1942 to save a group of full and half-Jews in Berlin, some of whom were married to non-Jewish spouses. Following a carefully devised plan, these persons were to be allowed to leave the country under the guise of Abwehr agents for supposedly undercover assignment in Switzerland. This came to be known as Operation 7 (*Unternehmen Sieben*), because it originally was to include only seven persons, but later was enlarged to fourteen persons. Admiral Wilhelm Canaris, head of the Abwehr and a man of considerable power and influence in the Third Reich hierarchy, gave his blessings to this operation, but only after he added to the list two Jewish friends of his. Canaris had already acted in like manner in a previous incident, when he effected the release and emigration, mainly to South American countries, of some 468 German and Dutch Jews and half-Jews, as "agents" of the Abwehr (known as *Aktion Aquilar*) – overriding the protests of SS officer Adolf Eichmann, who justly questioned the authenticity of these so-called agents.

The Abwehr people involved in this rescue conspiracy claimed that the people to be saved had made valuable contributions to Germany in the pre-Nazi period and therefore merited special consideration. Included on this list of privileged Jews and half-Jews were attorney Dr. Friedrich Wilhelm Arnold, a "full Jew" by Nazi definition, who had sustained severe wounds in the First World War (he lost a leg); his non-Jewish wife; and their two half-Jewish sons. Arnold's mother was deported to Theresienstadt camp, where she died. Similarly, attorney Dr. Julius Fliess, equally a "full Jew," was severely wounded in the First World War, where he fought on both the Western and Eastern fronts as a lieutenant, and suffered injury to his head that also left him blind in the left eye. After he had sufficiently recovered, he volunteered again and was sent to the Serbian front. Accompanying him now on the escape venture were his wife, Hildegard, and their daughter, Dorothee, all classified as "full Jews." Years earlier, during the start of Nazi rule, Fliess had protested to President Hindenburg his disbarment from practicing law, and he was referred to the Justice Ministry, where he met von Dohnányi. When, in November 1941, he learned that he and his wife were soon to be deported, he immediately appealed to von Dohnányi, and the latter, through the intervention of Canaris, effected the cancellation of the summons. As a result of the head wound sustained in the previous war, Fliess suffered from severe headaches. His doctor, Professor Karl Bonhoeffer, who happened to be von Dohnányi's father-in-law, interceded with his son-in-law on Fliess's behalf. In the meantime, Fliess's daughter, Dorothee, was expelled from school and assigned forced labor in a Berlin steel firm.

Also included on this list of privileged Jews was Dr. Ilse Rennefeld (née Bobrecker), a "full Jewess" and by profession a medical doctor, who left Germany for Holland in 1939, leaving behind her blind author, and non-Jewish, husband Otto. When the Germans occupied the Netherlands, she was ordered back to Germany and again felt threatened, this time with deportation. Ilse and Otto belonged to the Anthroposophist Society, where they meet Erika Canaris, wife of the Abwehr head, and she interceded with her husband to help the Rennefeld couple.

We continue with Annemarie Conzen (née Benzinger), a "full Jewess" but baptized into the church and widow of a non-Jewish husband, who lived with her two daughters in proximity to Canaris. Gabrielle, one of Annemarie's daughters, befriended at school Brigitte Canaris, daughter of Wilhelm Canaris, and this led the two mothers to meet and become friends. When in 1942 Gabrielle was expelled from school, Annemarie appealed to Mrs. Canaris, and through her husband, Annemarie's family was added to the list, including her "fully Jewish" mother. Also included was Charlotte Friedenthal, also a born Jewess but Evangelical by faith, who was active in the Confessing Church and in Pastor Grüber's help organization (earlier mentioned) and was an aide to Superintendent Martin Albertz. As a "full Jewess" by Nazi definition, she was made to wear the Yellow Star. Dietrich Bonhoeffer interceded with von Dohnányi on her behalf, and she was added to the Operation 7 group.

The above persons learned only after the war of the Abwehr connection and their supposed "enlistment" in the German military intelligence, as a ploy to facilitate their clandestine and at the same time official exit from Nazi Germany. Before leaving Germany, they were made to sign over their personal property and belongings to the Abwehr. In return, the Abwehr allocated for them funds in Switzerland. Previous to that, von Dohnányi journeyed to Switzerland to make the necessary arrangements, in collusion with Hans Bernd Gisevius, the German vice-consul in Zürich (who was later to become a contact person of the Allies with the anti-Hitler conspirators). Swiss Police chief Heinrich Rothmund gave his approval, after he was assured that these new arrivals would be well provided financially and not become a burden on the host country. On September 21, 1942, the Swiss embassy in Berlin affixed the visa on the passports of the group, and a week later, they left, accompanied by an Abwehr agent to protect them against red-tape entanglements and other last-minute hassles while en route to the Swiss border, which they crossed on September 30, 1942. Thus, at the highest level of Germany's intelligence service, an operation was carried out in which a group of fourteen persons, on the Nazi danger list as Jews, were spirited out of the country at a time when the official policy called for the murder of every and all living Jews on the European continent. One wonders how many more Jews could have been saved through similar ruses by persons in positions of authority such as von Dohnányi. Unfortunately for him, he was later arrested in April 1943 on charges stemming from foreign currency violations with relation to the U-7 operation. In truth, it was merely a pretext for the Gestapo to nibble away at the anti-Nazi ring operating inside the Abwehr. Von Dohnányi was kept imprisoned until December 1943, and was rearrested after the failed July 20, 1944, coup on Hitler's life. He remained in jail until his execution in Sachsenhausen camp in April 1945, weeks before the end of the war. He was declared a Righteous Among the Nations by Yad Vashem.[3]

Ferdinand Georg Duckwitz was another German in a position of power and influence, who wielded his authority – sometimes secretly and some-times openly – to defy and subvert the Nazi attempt to destroy' a country's Jews. He was a diplomat, serving as a maritime attaché in the Germany embassy in Copenhagen, Denmark, a country that, under the terms of the German occupation in April 1940, was allowed to remain nominally inde-pendent with its government and laws intact, with a German embassy func-tioning in Copenhagen, the country's capital. In summer 1943, the tranquil situation prevailing until then evaporated, as the Danish underground car-ried out sabotage raids against German installations. In response to this, the Germans clamped down with a curfew and placed the country under direct military control, with Dr. Werner Best of the SS acting as Hitler's personal representative for internal security matters.

Much earlier, before assuming his diplomatic post in Copenhagen, Duckwitz was active in various commercial undertakings, including as man-ager of a coffee firm. At the urging of Gregor Strasser, one of Hitler's ear-lier lieutenants (killed in 1934 on Hitler's orders), Duckwitz joined the Nazi party and for a time worked in Alfred Rosenberg's Foreign Department. However, he soon became disenchanted with Nazism and secretly became an opponent of the regime. Up until the war, he worked for the shipping firm Hamburg-America Line.

When in September 1943 Duckwitz learned that a large raid was planned in several weeks' time to net and deport all of Denmark's 8,000 Jews (until then not at all harmed), he decided to blow the whistle to friends in the Danish underground. At first, he tried to prevent this action by going to Berlin in the hope that Best's request for the raid had not yet reached Hitler's desk – but the order had already been given. According to another version, the events unfurled slightly differently. After he had asked permission for the raid, Best had a change of heart and asked Duckwitz to fly to Berlin to try to retrieve Best's cable to the Führer. Whatever the true version, when it proved too late to recall the order, Duckwitz flew to Sweden in order to facilitate a foreign intervention. Then, returning to Copenhagen on September 28, Duckwitz met with Hans Hedtoft, a leading Danish underground operative, and warned him of the imminent raid, slated to start on the evening of October 1, only 72 hours away. Ships were already anchored to take the Jews away. Duckwitz, according to Hedtoft, "was white with indignation and shame." Hedtoft, who knew Duckwitz well through their secret contacts during the occupation period, related that Duckwitz told him that "all leading Germans here, with the possible exception of the Gestapo people, were in their innermost hearts against the Jew pogrom and exerted all efforts to prevent a similar outrage from happening in Denmark." Hedtoft first alerted his underground friends, then sounded the alarm to the president of the Jewish community, Supreme Court barrister Carl Bernard Henriques. His reply to Hedtoft's warning was: "You are lying." It took some talking for Hedtoft to persuade Henriques, who claimed that he had just spoken with a high official in the Danish Foreign Ministry, who assured him that nothing of the kind was being planned.

Duckwitz's timely intervention succeeded beyond the wildest expectation, since his advanced warning made it possible for the Danish underground to organize the flight of almost all the Danish Jews to Sweden. The Danish underground, following Duckwitz's tip, organized a massive escape of thousands of Danish Jews, involving Danes of all walks of life including many fishermen (some of whom were handily rewarded for their services), who ferried the Jews across the Sund, the water channel separating Denmark from Sweden, which was patrolled by the German navy. Of Denmark's Jewish population of close to 8,000 persons, some 7,200 were able to flee the country in time, in a single operation, entirely planned and orchestrated by the local underground movement – and they were saved. This constitutes a feat unparalleled in any other European country. A German diplomat, and former Nazi, was instrumental in making this happen.[4]

Help was given in an altogether different way through Eduard Schulte. He was a German industrial magnate who operated a big mining firm near Breslau (today Wrocław, Poland), in Silesia province, which employed thousands of workers. Schulte's business was important to the war effort, and he had access to classified information on the conduct of the war. In 1942, he learned of the existence of a master plan for the total extermination of European Jewry within the shortest time possible, to be carried out under the cover of the war. He was told that this plan was under discussion in Hitler's headquarters. In conferences attended by SS heads, he heard more about this, and he became convinced that such a fiendish plan indeed existed. Driven by his conscience, Schulte decided to alert Allied leaders of this nefarious plan, so they would make it public and threaten Germany with dire consequences and thereby scuttle the plan in its embryonic stage. But how was he going to get this doomsday message to the Allies? He thought of the following plan.

As Schulte regularly travelled to neutral Switzerland for business purposes, he would try to pass on this frightful information to Jewish organizations there, in the hope that they would then refer it to world leaders. Indeed, in mid-1942, he went there twice to meet with his Jewish business acquaintances in that country. Schulte did not know that this master plan had already been given its seal of approval at the highest levels during the Berlin Wannsee Conference on January 20, 1942, and by the time of Schulte's second trip to Zurich, in July 1942, the mass exterminations were well under way. In Zürich, Schulte contacted his business friend Isidor Koppelman, who passed on the information to Dr. Benjamin Sagalowitz, the press secretary at the Jewish Federation. Sagalowitz alerted Gerhart Riegner, the representative of the World Jewish Congress in Geneva. Riegner was not too sure about the veracity of this frightful news, which came from an undisclosed source (Schulte asked that his name not be divulged), but a steady stream of information on Nazi anti-Jewish atrocities in Poland received recently through other channels pricked his ears and alerted him to the new alarming item just received. At any rate, he decided that it was best to pass it on immediately to the Allied governments, which is what Schulte had hoped would happen. Approaching the U.S. and British vice-consuls in Geneva, Riegner asked that their governments be informed about the Nazi extermination master plan without delay. As it turned out, the U.S. State Department received Riegner's missive, but did nothing to alert the U.S. government on the message's content, nor did it deliver it to Dr. Stephen Wise (President of the Jewish World Congress), as requested by Riegner. The British Foreign office after some hesitation informed Sydney Silverman, a member of Parliament and the chairman of the British section of the World Jewish Congress, to whom Riegner had also addressed the frightful message. Silverman, in turn, informed Rabbi Stephen Wise, in New York. By then, several crucial months had been wasted. Even after Wise learned of this information, doubts continued to prevail about the credibility of the message, especially after the

State Department asked Wise not to make it public until further efforts of verification. This was partly due to a general disbelief about the scope and terrible nature of the Final Solution, a disbelief that paralyzed effective action until very late in the war.

For years, people speculated on the identity of the emissary who revealed the "terrible secret," which is also the title of book by Walter Laqueur. He was known to be an important German industrialist. Even as late as 1981, historian Laqueur admitted that despite long research, he had not yet been able to establish the man's identity. Finally, in 1986, in his book *Breaking the Silence*, he identified the man as Eduard Schulte, and Gerhart Riegner confirmed it to me (Paldiel), at Yad Vashem, in a 1987 letter. Riegner wrote,

> We had, of course, many reports before, and we followed what was going on all over Europe and particularly in Eastern Europe and in the occupied Russian territories. But this was the first report from a responsible German source with access to the highest German authorities, and this was the first report that spoke of an overall German plan aiming at total extermination of all the Jews of Europe. Schulte came especially to Switzerland driven by his conscience, to communicate what he knew to the Jews and through them, to the Allies. . . . We knew at the time that Mr. Schulte was the head of a big mining company which occupied 30,000 workers in the war effort and that he had access to Hitler's headquarters. . . . In his first communication Schulte had told us that the plan of total extermination was under discussion in Hitler's headquarters and that he was not sure whether there existed an order by Hitler. About six weeks later, he came for a second time to Switzerland, this time confirming that he now was sure that such an order existed. . . . There is no doubt for me that in bringing us the information on the Final Solution, Schulte acted as a convinced anti-Nazi who tried to avert the catastrophe and to save Jewish lives. He was a very courageous man and risked obviously his life in pursuing his activities during a long period. His information played a decisive role in the activities which the World Jewish Congress pursued during the latter part of 1942 and which led finally to the publication of the Declaration by the Allied governments on December 17, 1942, on the extermination of the Jewish people.

At the time, Riegner was not privy to another secret: that Schulte was passing valuable information to Allan Dulles, the head of U.S. intelligence in Europe, stationed in Bern, and he was also involved in the anti-Hitler conspiracy taking shape at the time. When Gestapo suspicions against him mounted, he fled in time to Switzerland in January 1945, where he remained until the war's end. As far as is known, Schulte was the only and lone influential German who tried to do something to scuttle the Nazi plan to murder all of Europe's Jews. Yad Vashem awarded him posthumously the honor of Righteous Among the Nations.[5]

B) WIELDED AUTHORITY TO SUBVERT NAZI ANTI-JEWISH MEASURES

Germans in positions of authority could also help by craftily undermining the very Nazi rules with regard to Jews that they were obligated to faithfully implement, but which they actually subverted. Thus, while outwardly abiding by anti-Jewish legislation, these persons were in fact turning them upside down or otherwise disregarding them. We have on record only two such examples – which point to what could have been achieved if more highly placed officials had followed a similar lead.

With the rank of major in the army, Wilhelm von Hahn was advisor on Jewish affairs in the Brussels headquarters of General Alexander on Falkenhausen, military commander-in-chief of occupied Belgium. Per agreement between Hitler and Queen Mother Elizabeth, native-born Belgian Jews (who numbered some 8,000 out of a total Jewish population of 60,000 in 1942) were not to be deported. The Germans respected this agreement until September 1943, when all remaining Jews, irrespective of their nationality, were slated for deportation. In his position as chief ranking officer on Jewish affairs in the military government (not to be confused with the SS apparatus that was headed by Ernst Ehlers, who reported directly to Adolf Eichmann), von Hahn wielded considerable influence and was able to effect the release of Jews slated for deportation on various dubious pretexts.

His principal partner in this endeavor was Leon Platteau, a department head in the Belgian ministry of justice, who continuously interceded with von Hahn to secure the release of Jews, mostly on the false claim that they were Belgian nationals, and therefore not momentarily slated for deportation – with such lucky persons numbering into the hundreds. According to Platteau, von Hahn always sought bureaucratic excuses and doubtful legal loopholes to justify delaying or freeing certain Jews from deportation. Although he had no final authority on the matter (he was after all only an advisor to the German commander-in-chief), he managed to get around and obtain his objectives. Platteau also mentions that von Hahn knew Gestapo officials who were on the take, and he probably used this information as a weapon to effect the release of Jews.

Elisabeth Trainin-Kohn, a Red Cross representative of Jewish refugees' affairs, was one of the persons referred by Platteau to von Hahn to help release her husband, arrested by the Gestapo in January 1943 for supposedly not wearing the obligatory Yellow Star (the Gestapo had actually removed the patch from the man's coat to justify his arrest). Von Hahn suggested she file a claim against the Gestapo for vandalizing her home during the arrest. He then arranged for a witness to testify that he saw the defendant wearing the Yellow Star just before the arrest. But the military tribunal, in spite of Mrs. Trainin's complaint, accepted the Gestapo version, and her husband received a nine-month prison term. To prevent the man from being arrested again by the Gestapo on the day of his release, von Hahn arranged for a medical report to be submitted to the jail authority, asking for the man's early release due to a supposedly severe diabetic attack. This was carried out two days before his scheduled release – unbeknownst to the Gestapo. In the meantime, Mrs. Trainin was herself picked up by the Gestapo and conveyed to Mechelen/Malines detention camp, but von Hahn secured her release as well. Thereafter, Mrs. Trainin continued serving as a liaison between Platteau and von Hahn for the freeing of other arrested Jews.

Another witness testified that von Hahn secured her release from Mechelen/Malines detention camp on the strength of her false Haitian visa. Still another witness related that his deportation was postponed indefinitely and he remained in the detention camp until the end, due to von Hahn's intercession. Von Hahn also secured the release of Belgium's chief rabbi Solomon Ullman, upon the intercession of his wife, in December 1943. Mrs. Ullmann testified how she overheard von Hahn arguing with Gestapo officers over the phone, in her presence, in the attempt to free her husband. Other witnesses likewise linked their release from Mechelen/Malines to von Hahn's intervention. They also noted that within Jewish clandestine circles it was known that one could turn to von Hahn as a last resort. When seeing him, they were always received with great courtesy, something unusual by German officials at the time.

The following story illustrates further von Hahn's benevolent attitude. During one visit to von Hahn's office, Platteau accompanied a certain woman to plead for her husband's release. As required, she left her ID card with the guard at the entrance and received a slip with her name on it and the name of the man she was seeing, which she would later return to the guard, counter-signed by the man she had seen, and retrieve her ID card. On this occasion, after presenting her ID, the woman frantically realized she had given the false one, in which she appeared under a different name. Platteau: "I told her it was too late to retreat. There's no choice. If you want to save your husband, we must go see him, for he is the only one who can do something. We entered, with the lady trembling terribly. From the referral slip, von Hahn must have known that she was equipped with a false ID, which she had given to the guard, that she is Jewish, and she's circulating without the Yellow Star – a most serious offense in those days, for which he was required to arrest her on the spot. He disregarded this, dealt with her request, signed the document which helped liberate her husband, a document which could have testified severely against him, and all this without lifting an eyebrow." One must add that there was never a question of any payment for his help.

Felix Meyer, who served as spokesman for the Jewish population in Belgium before the German Military Administration, stated: "He [von Hahn] ignored on many occasions the cruel orders which came from the *Reichssicherungshauptamt* [The Reich Main Security Office, headed by SS head Heinrich Himmler] in Berlin. . . . In order to save Jews from arrest, he has under his own risk exempted them from wearing the David Star. He has been of the greatest help to me in my endeavors to create homes for aged Jews and a Jewish hospital, where Jews were protected against arrest. When after a grave operation I was unable to go and see Dr. von Hahn, he has risked to come to my house, in uniform, in order to establish a list of persons, who were to be de-ported and whom he tried to liberate from the camp at Malines. Dr. von Hahn will always be remembered as a great benefactor to the population in Belgium during the hard years of [the] German occupation."

The danger that von Hahn faced for his help to Jews cannot be lightly dismissed. Talking about this after the war, he minimized these dangers, stat-ing that the Gestapo agents in Belgium were not of the same brutal caliber as elsewhere, and he therefore found it easier to sway them to his point of view. "I pretended as though I had the authority; in cases where it succeeded, it succeeded. When it did not succeed – I could only regret it. And the number of cases in which I did not succeed was greater than those [in which] I succeeded." The greatest danger facing him, according to Platteau, was to be relieved of his post and sent to fight on the Eastern front. His working relationship with the Gestapo had its tense moments, and they no doubt would have grabbed at any opportunity to undercut and remove him from the scene. Von Hahn may not rank high in the roster of anti-Nazi heroes, but the little that he did to hobble the Nazi killing machine was not matched by other officials in high positions in the German hierarchy. There can be no denial that his timely interventions to save those he could stands in his favor.[6]

Immediately to the north, in occupied Netherlands, another German official was achieving even greater results with subverting Nazi rules and regulations in order to save Jews. Hans Georg Calmeyer was the top man of a special section in the German civil administration of Holland that dealt with an issue that was of the highest importance to Nazi policy makers: deciding who's a Jew and who's an Aryan, where doubts existed. An edict of January 1941, signed by Arthur Seyss-Inquart, the Nazi governor of the occupied country, required all Jews – full or partial – to register with the authorities. Doubtful racial cases were to be referred to the *Reichkomissar's* (German-appointed governor's) office, and Calmeyer was the man in that office who had the final word in these doubtful racial matters.

Calmeyer's duty was to decide whether persons listed as Jewish but claiming Aryan parentage should still be considered as full Jews or reclassified as only semi-Jews. Such reclassification, especially during 1942 and the following two years, when Dutch Jewry was being decimated, could make the difference between life and death for the petitioner. In Germany, Hitler arrogated to himself the role of final arbiter in cases of doubtful racial affiliations; in the Netherlands, it was the sole reserve of Calmeyer, a German-appointed attorney. What then took place is a rescue operation without parallel in Nazi-dominated Europe. For, instead of scrupulously applying Nazi racial principles, Calmeyer astutely subverted them – this by abetting the use of false statements and credentials, so as to make it possible to reclassify "full Jews" as only "half"- or "quarter"-Jews – thereby removing them from the deportation lists.

Born in Osnabrück to a father who was a judge, Hans Georg Calmeyer lost two brothers in World War One. After the war, as a law student in Munich, he witnessed Hitler's failed coup ("Beer Hall" putsch) of November 1923. Before that, although socialistically inclined, he had a short stint with a semi-military *Freikorps* regiment. After graduation, he practiced law in Osnabrück, but with the Nazi takeover in 1933, he was temporarily disbarred because of his defense of communists and his refusal to fire a Jewish employee. In May 1940, he participated in the invasion of the Netherlands as a *Luftwaffe* (German air force) ground soldier. Then, his Osnabrück colleague Dr. Stueler, who held an important post in the civil administration of occupied Holland, enlisted him as an aide and specialist (*referent*) to deal with doubtful racial cases. Thus, unbeknownst to him at the beginning, the fate, indeed the life and death of many Jews was placed in the hands of this nondescript attorney.

Calmeyer asked and was granted sole prerogative over an important issue that in Germany, as mentioned, was reserved for the Führer alone. He created a special team of German and Dutch aides in whom he placed his trust, and at the same time maintained pretenses that he was doing nothing but applying Nazi regulations in the interest of a racially pure Reich (to which the Dutch, as an originally pure Germanic tribe according to the Nazis, were to be absorbed). However, soon the word went out that Calmeyer was willing to stretch to the limit the accreditation of doubtful documents for proving one's semi-Aryan origins in order to reclassify someone as only partially Jewish, even as fully Aryan. The Nazi police in the Netherlands, suspecting Calmeyer's tactics, asked that the whole issue be turned over to their hands, but Nazi governor Seyss-Inquart, for tactical reasons of his own, refused. The SS then sought the aid of Ludo ten Cate, a Dutch Nazi genealogist, who before the war lived in one of the American Dutch colonies and had assembled much information (such as newspaper clippings of births, marriages, and deaths) on Jews living there, some of whom he suspected were now living in the Netherlands and claiming non-Jewish paternity. Ten Cate placed this information in the hands of the SS as a counterweight to those petitioning for exemptions to deportations on the strength of doubtful documentations originating in the overseas territories. Bowing to pressure from the SS, Seyss-Inquart allowed ten Cate to examine the persons on Calmeyer's list. Ten Cate followed up with a report on Calmeyer's mistakes, which he turned over to SS head in the Netherlands Hanns Rauter, who then asked from Seyss-Inquart for a thorough investigation of Calmeyer's list, a demand rejected by the Nazi governor. At the same time, Seyss-Inquart asked Calmeyer not to add names to his list after the December 1, 1942, deadline – a date disregarded by Calmeyer, who kept adding names on his special protected list. Even after ten Cate was removed from the scene (he had embroiled himself with the SS and was sent to the front in August 1944), the pressure on Calmeyer did not let up. By January 1944, 4,787 cases had been decided by Calmeyer, as follows:

Changed to Half-Jews	2,026	42.3%
Changed to 1/4 Jews or Aryans	873	18.2%
Cases rejected	1,868	39.5%
Total	4,787	100%

In other words, 2,899 Jews were saved from deportation. Calmeyer also demanded that the property and personal belongings of these persons, already impounded by the Nazis, be returned to them. SS chief in the Netherlands Rauter fumed, but Nazi governor Seyss-Inquart backed Calmeyer. To protect his rescue operation, Calmeyer presented figures showing the many cases that his office had rejected. He astutely gambled on the premise that Seyss-Inquart, a Nazi party stalwart, would not allow Himmler's SS, the party's main contender for power in Germany, additional ground in the Netherlands, a country considered part of an eventual greater German Reich. At the same time, to safeguard his credentials, Calmeyer could not save all – and in order to save a greater number, he had also to deny a somewhat smaller number. At the same time, to those denied reclassification, Calmeyer gave ample time for them to seek alternate escape plans, such as seeking shelter with non-Jews, before making his decision formal.

In this rescue conspiracy, Calmeyer was assisted by several trusty German and Dutch aides. Outside his office, his protected Jews soon became known as *Calmeyer Juden*. One of the Dutch confidants in this rescue conspiracy was the attorney Antonius Mom, then an official in the national population registration office. One method used by Mom was to remove the registration papers of Jewish persons and loan them to Cornelis Teutscher – one of Calmeyer's Dutch aides. Mom instructed Teutscher how and where to make special annotations showing that the person in question was a descendant of only one or two Jewish grandparents. A police confidant then reported to the registration office the loss of the Jewish person's identity card. Thereupon, a new card was issued but without the fatal large black J sign. The man would then report to Calmeyer, who then confirmed that a mistake had been made and he was only partially Jewish. The result? One more person saved from deportation.

Another method was to encourage Jewish women to somehow bring proof that their child was the result of an illicit relationship with an "Aryan" – not of their legal Jewish father. The son or daughter was then reclassified as "half-Jewish" and spared deportation. This proved to be an expertise of one of Calmeyer's aides, the German Dr. Gerhard Wander. It went so far that Wander one day ironically remarked to Benno Stokvis, who had come to plead his mother's case, "I never suspected that Jewish women are so unfaithful." Jews claiming to be the illegitimate offspring of non-Jewish fathers had become so much the fashion that it proved quite impossible for Wander to accept all their claims – doing so would have played into the hands of the SS, undermined the whole operation, and placed in jeopardy those already entered on the special exemption list. Men who were prepared to swear that they were the Aryan fathers of Jewish children were in great demand, but they could not always be found. Such as with Mrs. Polak who claimed her late departed Jewish husband was really not the father of her four children, but an earlier first husband, a certain Muller, whom she never married, and who she swore abandoned her after cohabiting with her for a long period – and he was now presumed dead.

The Dutch-Jewish historian Jacob Presser is convinced that Calmeyer was skating on exceedingly thin ice; he was working under duress, and had he gone any further than he did, he would, in fact, have scuttled what little he (as an official in the Nazi governor's office) was able to do to help the Jews. Luckily for him, the destruction of the Central Population Registry in The Hague in April 1944, in a British air raid, made it more difficult for Nazi agents who distrusted Calmeyer from verifying their allegations.[7]

It was sometimes facetiously said that the Jews suffered from not having an Eleventh Commandment: "Thou shalt convert thy grandfather and thy grandmother from Judaism." At any rate, this is what many Jews now did. Though Calmeyer knew that many applicants were trying to pull the wool over his eyes, he nevertheless let all of them go unpunished, although he did not necessarily accept their dubious claims. Moreover, he went to endless trouble to prove helpful to all petitioners. If an absolutely hopeless petition was presented to him, he would do his utmost to look for a possible loophole. He once described his position as that of a doctor in a lonely post, cut off from the outside world, and left with a mere 50 phials of medicine for the treatment of 5,000 critical cases. Since he could not save all, he did what he could for those few he could save.

Other than the Calmeyer Jews, there were other special-category Jews administered by him who, for a time, were spared by him from deportation, such as: Protestant-Jews, Catholic-Jews, ammunition factory Jews, mixed-marriage Jews, Portuguese-descendent Jews, World War I veterans, and exceptionally talented Jews ("Blue Knights"). The latter were a group of privileged Jews whose record cards at the *Zentralstelle* (the official Jewish registration bureau) bore a blue marking. They included thirteen ex-members of the Dutch Nazi party (which for a time, before the war, admitted some Jews to its ranks); five married to non-Jews and had sons fighting on the front; three art experts working for Nazi chief Hermann Göring; three married to members of the Conservatoire Orchestra; a German Olympic champion of 1896; the wife of a leading Dutch economist; and a son-in-law of a former librarian of the Royal Library in The Hague. Only 45 such cases were accepted out of twice that number. Those accepted were allowed to emigrate.[8]

The Portuguese Jewish community in Amsterdam, in trying to save its members from deportation in whatever way possible, commissioned a genealogist to prepare a scientific document proving that they were not of Semitic but of Iberian stock and should consequently not be identified with Jews – they were in truth racially Iberians, so they claimed, but of the Mosaic faith. One of Calmeyer's Dutch aides, Jan van Proosdij, handled the cases of this stricken community, and in that endeavor falsified documents for several persons without Calmeyer's knowledge – who then approved their reclassification as non-Jews. Calmeyer, in his attempt to help this community, wrote that a number of them might well have less than 25% Jewish blood and should therefore be sent to the "Celto-Iberian area" for possible exchange against Germans or Dutchmen. Calmeyer's department had investigated 1,015 of the 4,000 or so Portuguese Jews, of which 400 Calmeyer recommended should already be considered for special exemption. But SS chief in Holland, Hanns Rauter, suspecting another Calmeyer trick, insisted on screening even the favored 400. Calmeyer was asked to prepare a memorandum for SS head Himmler with whom the ultimate decision lay. This pleased Calmeyer, who anyway was playing for time. On February 20, 1944, the long-mooted inspection of these Jews finally took place. Two-hundred seventy-three families were paraded before three high SS commanders: Wilhelm Zöpf, Aust, and Albert Gemmeker (commander of Westerbork camp). The ruling was negative and harsh: "A sub-human race." The Portuguese Jews were doomed; Calmeyer could only ask that their deportation be postponed, and when this no longer proved possible, that they be sent to Theresienstadt rather than Auschwitz.[9]

As mentioned, Dr. Gerhard Wander was one of Calmeyer's principal aides. He was an attorney by profession and an officer in the German army. He was principally active in dealing with the out-of-wedlock birth cases. In this endeavor, he was not beyond accepting forged documents and statements. It was not always smooth walking with him. Dr. Benno Stokvis remembered that in 1942, at their first meeting, Wander irritatingly asked him: "Dear colleague, why are you making such major efforts to turn Jews into Aryans?" Stokvis responded: "You are wrong; I am not changing Jews into Aryans. I want to prevent you from carrying off to the East Aryans as Jews (*ich möchte verhüten dass sie Ariers als Juden nach dem Osten verschleppen lassen*)." Wander then laughed, and the ice between both men was broken. "We stared at each other, and from this moment on we knew that we understood each other well." Wander provided him with credentials establishing the Aryan parentage of Stokvis's Jewish clients, as well as of Stokvis's own mother.

Stokvis also related the following incident with Wander over a Russian woman. "One day I came to him to plead for a woman who was born in Russia in 1870, who claimed to be the offspring of full Aryan parents, but out of solidarity with her Jewish husband, had herself registered as Jewish." Earlier, after the death of her parents, a Jewish couple had adopted her. In Tsarist Russia, there existed no ethnic registration, but the woman's birthplace was now under German occupation. Stokvis: "Dr. Wander ordered a special investigation, which produced very good results. However, in this case, Dr. Wander was opposed. He strongly emphasized the fact that the petitioner married in 1899, and that seven rabbis had declared that she was indeed the daughter of the parents who she claims adopted her. . . . I was at my wit's end, and I slammed my right hand on the table and screamed at him: 'Since when, Dr. Wander, is a statement by seven rabbis accepted as credible in the Greater German Reich?' Wander suddenly turned speechless, and he gave in." Stokvis added, "This was not the only case where I had difficulties with him. In general, he was always prepared to make himself available to me. He helped wherever he could. In more than 20 cases that I referred to him, he took care to arrive at a favorable decision. He intentionally shut his eyes in the face of clearly false ancestry documents – also false documents which I placed before him. He was an honest person. He was a courageous man. He was a rescuer, out of compassion and love for fellow men. Hundreds of Jews owe him their lives."[10]

As suspicions mounted against him, Wander was called back for active military duty and sent to the Russian front. He managed to return several times and make contact with the Dutch underground. In September 1944, he returned to Holland on false papers and was sought as a deserter. He became active in the Dutch underground (under the codename Jonas); he helped smuggle out Jews and negotiated with other clandestine groups. Long on the wanted list, he was finally cornered on an Amsterdam street, and in a shootout with the Gestapo he was shot dead on January 22, 1945.

With the liberation of Holland, Calmeyer was briefly detained; then, in the fall of 1946, he was allowed to return to his hometown of Osnabrück, and after a certain interval he resumed his law practice. He then began to feel deep remorse and pain at not having saved more people and was also dejected at the mild sentences meted out to former Nazi criminals. In a letter to historian Jacob Presser in 1965, Calmeyer wrote: "Every action, every helping deed was one too little, too little! We did everything wrong, when there was suffering everywhere, of which the earth is full to the brim. . . . I still feel despair about it. Despair to be, despair to have remained. This is the only worthy and honorable attitude which we are obligated to adopt in the face of what happened and the attempt to try to evaluate it and make sense out of it." Calmeyer, speaking in the third person, added: "He was then in despair as today. He already knew then of the folly and insufficiency of all deeds and all undertakings. But he did, and omitted to do, what he did and failed to do, with a full heart." In an earlier letter to a certain Dr. G. Prey (1951), Calmeyer stated: "The Good Samaritan must not ask if the person whom he helped was worthy of such help. The one who was helped only represented the great number of those who had to be helped."[11]

The Calmeyer story is a striking example of a conspiracy of rescue, right out of the offices of the Nazi administration in an occupied country. In spite of the extensive danger to himself, instead of weeding out definitely Jewish elements from the Aryan stock, as his mandate called, he in fact acted not to purify the Aryan race but to save as many Jewish lives as possible, to the best of his ability. All this, against the setting of an SS hierarchy that sought to scuttle his operation and nab him, and the uncertain support of a boss who was a Nazi stalwart. The Calmeyer story suggests that officials in sensitive positions linked with the Jewish issue could, with fewer risks than those faced by Calmeyer, through a combination of inventiveness and astuteness try to save even a fraction of Jews if, like Calmeyer and the others mentioned in this chapter, they were willing to make an effort in that direction.

CHAPTER 8

Open Defiance of Nazi Antisemitism

∗ ∗ ∗

THERE WERE ONLY A HANDFUL of persons in Nazi Germany who went beyond merely contravening or deliberately misinterpreting the government's antisemitic policy but, rather, openly defied it. In contrast to the rescuers in this study who mostly, in order to succeed in their rescue mission, had to act surreptitiously and clandestinely, the following five persons did not assume the mantle of rescuer but wished to make known their moral disapproval of the antisemitic policy of their government. Unsurprisingly, the authors of these actions faced severe retaliatory measures by the authorities.

The first case in this series involves a non-Jewish professor who declined the offer of a university post that had been vacated by the dismissal of a Jewish scientist. In the spring of 1933, while engaged in research in the department of physiology at Göttingen University, Otto Krayer, acting head of the Department of Pharmacology and Toxicology at the Berlin University, was asked by the Prussian Department of Education to take over the Chair of Pharmacology in the Medical Academy of Düsseldorf. The vacancy had been created by the dismissal of the Jewish incumbent, Professor Philipp Ellinger, under the initial Nazi anti-Jewish measures of clearing the universities of Jewish academicians. Krayer declined this offer, and on May 15, 1933, he penned the following explanation, which he wrote to Wilhelm Stuckart, the Prussian Minister of Science, Art, and National Education in the new Nazi regime:

The primary reason for my reluctance is that I feel the exclusion of Jewish scientists to be an injustice, the necessity of which I cannot understand, since it has been justified by reasons that lie outside the domain of science. This feeling of injustice is an ethical phenomenon. It is innate to the structure of my personality, and not something imposed from the outside. Under these circumstances, assuming such a position as the one in Düsseldorf would impose a great mental burden on me – a burden that would make it difficult to take up my duties as a teacher with joy and a sense of dedication, without which I cannot teach properly. I place a high value on the role of university teacher, and I myself would want the privilege of engaging in this activity to be given only to men who, apart from their research capabilities, also have special human qualities. Had I not expressed to you the misgivings that made me hesitate to accept your offer immediately, I would have compromised one of these essential human qualities, that of honesty. . . . [I] therefore prefer to forego this appointment, though it is suited to my inclinations and capabilities, rather than having to betray my convictions; or that by remaining silent I would encourage an opinion about me that does not correspond with the facts.

Stuckart's reply was not long in waiting. He wrote back on May 20, 1933:

In your letter of 15 May, you state that you feel the barring of Jewish scientists is an injustice, and that your feelings about this injustice prevents you from accepting a position offered to you. You are of course personally free to feel any way you like about the way the government acts. It is not acceptable, however, for you to make the practice of your teaching profession dependent upon those feelings. You would in that case not be able in the future to hold any chair in a German university. Pending final decision on the basis of section 4 of the Law on the Restoration of the Professional Civil Service, I herewith forbid you, effective immediately, from entering any government academic institution, and from using any State libraries or scientific facilities.

Barred from the use of public libraries upon returning from Göttingen to Berlin, Krayer made use of private libraries to continue his research work. Later in 1933, Krayer's academic privileges at the University of Berlin were restored. However, sensing he could no longer freely continue his scientific work in the climate existing then in Germany, he left the country on the last day of 1933. He moved to London, then Beirut, and eventually settled in the United States in 1937, where he took up a post at the Harvard Medical School. During his lifetime, Krayer wrote some 120 research articles on cardiovascular pharmacology. Krayer's moral stance is in sharp contrast to others in the scientific community in Germany during the Nazi period, most of whom took advantage of the vacancies made available by the dismissal of Jewish academicians.[1]

An even more outspoken and provocative stance was that of Armin T. Wegner. He was an author of some repute in Germany, and had also written extensively on the slaughter of the Armenians by the Turks during World War One, which he witnessed while on a tour of duty with the German military in the Near East. Repelled by the vulgar antisemitism of the new Nazi regime, which assumed power on January 30, 1933, he penned an open letter to Adolf Hitler in April of that year, in which he asked him to stop the recently begun persecution of Jews – for the sake of the German people, if not for humanitarian reasons. Following are excerpts from this long letter:

> Herr Reichskanzler! On March 29 of this year, you announced that the government was imposing a boycott on all shops owned by Jewish citizens. Offending inscriptions such as "Deceivers!" "Don't buy here!" "Death to the Jews!" . . . appeared on shop windows. Men armed with clubs guarded the entrances to shops and the capital city was transformed into an entertainment arena for the masses. . . . Jewish judges, prosecutors and physicians are being forced out of their justly-earned positions, their sons and daughters expelled from schools and university teachers ejected from their chairs and sent on vacation (a reprieve not fooling anyone); stage managers, actors and singers are deprived of their careers, publishers of their newspapers. . . . Thus the Jew is attacked, not necessarily in his profession, but in the area that is his most noble contribution to society – his spirit.
>
> Herr Reichskanzler, it is not merely a question concerning our Jewish brothers; it is a question concerning the German people. In

the name of the people whom I have not only the right to represent but the obligation to raise my voice like everyone who has been formed through its blood – as a German whose heart is contracted with indignation – I turn to you. Order the stoppage of these doings! Judaism has survived the serfdom of Egypt, the Spanish inquisition, the sufferings of the Crusaders and sixteen hundred pogroms in Russia. The Jews will also survive this threat due to that toughness that has contributed to this people's maturity. But the shame and misfortune that have befallen Germany will be remembered for a long time. Who will one day be hit by the blow that is now aimed at the Jews? Only we, ourselves. Just as the Jews have adopted German ways and increased our wealth, their destruction must necessarily bring about the destruction of German property. History has taught us that countries that expelled Jews from their borders were made to suffer poverty; they became miserable and despised. . . . A hundred years after Goethe and Lessing we are returning to the most cruel suffering of all times, to blind superstition. . . .

For what must be the outcome of all this? In the place of the moral principle of justice we find [the highest value] in membership to a tribe. . . . As from today, even the unqualified and amoral person may say: "Only because I am not a Jew am I permitted to hold this office; it is enough that I am a German – I may even do an evil deed without being punished for it, because I am German." . . . As distinctions between good and evil are eliminated, we must ask ourselves, what will become of the unity of our people? . . . I feel that we are much more obligated to fight for the Jew than against him. It may be true that there are not many heroes of the sword among the Jews compared with our own warriors. But they have produced many wise men, martyrs and holy men. Even the saviors of this awakened [German] people must admit that they cannot do without righteous persons, just as they equally need this [Jewish] people whose voice has never been silenced as they perpetuated an age-old prophecy and the highest moral law. I ask: why are these curious strangers in the world persecuted and hated? It is because this people has placed law and justice above everything else, because it has always loved and honored the law like one's own bride, and because those who pursue evil detest nothing more than this people who demands justice.

Herr Reichskanzler, from the depth of a tormented heart I turn to you with words that are not only my words but which express the voice of fate which exhorts you, through me: protect Germany by protecting the Jews. Do not permit those who fight alongside you to mislead you. They give you bad advice. Consult your own conscience as you did when you started your lonely fight upon your return from the war in a world that was in turmoil. It has always been the privilege of great men to admit having erred. The masses are in need of a visible act. Lead back to their offices the men who have been cast out, the physicians to their hospitals, the judges to their courts. Do not keep the schools closed to their children, heal the troubled hearts of the mothers and all the people will thank you. For even if Germany may be able to do without the Jews, it cannot do without its honor and virtue! . . . I beseech thee: maintain the noble-mindedness, the pride, the conscience that we need in order to exist. Preserve the dignity of the German people.

This letter was written on Easter Monday 1933, shortly after the first government-orchestrated boycott against Jewish businesses. As no German newspaper was willing to print it, the author mailed the letter directly to the Brown House in Munich, the Nazi party headquarters, with the request to pass it on to Hitler. Wegner received an acknowledgement letter, signed by Martin Bormann (later to become Hitler's chief adjutant). Soon thereafter, Wegner was arrested and interrogated by the Gestapo, and subsequently brutally beaten. As he got up, staggering, the officer in charge told him: "Now you will never again write anything against us!" That night of horror was followed by a dolorosa trail that lead through several concentration camps. He was eventually released in the spring of 1934, emigrated from the country, then returned to it (he stated: "this is the country that I still love"), finally leaving in 1937 for the village of Positano, on the Gulf of Salerno, in Italy. In August 1940, under pressure from the Germans, Wegner was incarcerated in the Potenza detention camp, but he was able to obtain his release. He then worked on and off, and feeling threatened again, he fled to southern Italy with his wife, where he remained until the area's liberation by the Allies.[2]

Our next story is of a person who combined a moral condemnation of the Nazi regime with an unsuccessful rescue attempt, and which proved calamitous to its author. Ilse Sonja Totzke lived in Würzburg and was suspected of entertaining friendly relations with Jews. Neighbors reported to the police that she was a loner, was not very enthusiastic about the new regime, and failed to return the Hitler salute when greeted with it, as customary. In September 1941, she was summoned to the Gestapo. She admitted her friendly relations with the Jewish family Ottenberg and of contacts with other Jewish acquaintances, adding that she did not take an interest in politics and this explained her indifference toward the new regime. However, she added, she felt the anti-Jewish measures were unjust and she could not come to terms with them. "I consider every honest person to be in good standing, irrespective of whichever nationality he adheres to."[3]

While being questioned by the Gestapo, her home was raided, and the following "incriminating" books were listed: *Die Mutter*, by Schalom Ash; *Der Gezeichnete*, by Jakob Picard; *Eine Zeit stirbt*, by George Hermann; *Jüdische Geschichte*, by S. Mueller; *Theodor Herzl, Biographie*, by Alex Bein; *Palästinisches Tagebuch*, by Manfred Sturmann; *Der neuer Kreuzzug*, by Benjamin Disraeli; and several brochures of *Um die Frau*. In October 1941, she was called in for further questioning by the Gestapo and made to sign a statement that she was aware that in the event of further contacts with Jews, she would be immediately arrested and taken to a concentration camp.

In March 1943, she tried fleeing to Switzerland in the Mulhouse-St. Ludwig region of occupied France, in the company of a Jewish woman, and was shoved back across the border by Swiss border guards. She made a second attempt and was again apprehended. This time, the Swiss custom officials turned her over directly to the German police. Transferred to the Gestapo, Ilse Totzke did not use diplomatic language and mitigating excuses for her recent behavior. She made her position clear: she was staunchly anti-Nazi, in particular because of the regime's antisemitic policy. She gave a detailed account of her flight attempt in the company of a Jewish woman, giving the following reason. "I've already been considering for a long time to flee Germany, since I do not feel comfortable under the regime of Adolf Hitler. Above all, I find the Nuremberg Law incomprehensible. For this reason, I considered it right to maintain relations with my Jewish acquaintances. In the face of the renewed summons by the Gestapo, I made the final decision to flee to Switzerland."

As to the escape plan, she added: "I was not charged by anyone to fetch the Jewess Sara Basinsky to Switzerland. I only had compassion for the above-named Jewess and wanted to protect her from the evacuation [i.e., deportation]. I admit that it was I who persuaded the Jewess to flee. For my effort, I received no compensation, neither from Basinsky nor from any other person. I likewise deny that, before this event, I was engaged in aiding Jews to leave the country illegally. The escape plan was my own decision; I was aided by no one." She ended her statement with the following ringing words: "I wish to repeat that I wanted to flee Germany because of my rejection of National Socialism. Above all, I cannot approve the Nuremberg Laws. I had the intention of having myself arrested in Switzerland. Under no circumstances did I wish to remain any longer in Germany."

In his evaluation of this case, a Gestapo official wrote that with Totzke one deals with an obstinate person, oblivious to any form of persuasion. Another Gestapo agent added: "It is clear from the above statement that Totzke apparently from the start was a person opposed to National Socialism, and makes no secret of it. She is a Jew-woman, and based on her confirmed behavior is beyond any remedial action." Two months later, on May 12, 1943, the thirty-four-year-old Ilse Sonja Totzke was ordered deported to Ravensbrück camp. Her fate remains unknown. Her fearless stand is significant for a lone person who must have been fully aware of the consequences to herself for her anti-Nazi public utterances. There were not many persons to be found in Nazi Germany of the moral caliber of Ilse Sonja Totzke.[4]

A similar defiant stand taken by a lone person took place in the village of Oberlenningen, Würtemburg region. There, Protestant pastor Julius von Jan reacted to the Kristallnacht pogrom in very strong terms in his sermon on November 16, 1938. Paraphrasing the Hebrew prophet Jeremiah (22:29), he despairingly asked:

> Where in Germany is the prophet sent to the king's house to utter the word of the Lord? Where is the man who in the name of God and of justice, will cry like Jeremiah, "Maintain righteousness, rescue those deprived of their rights out of the hands of the transgressor? Do not oppress the stranger, the orphan and the widow. Do no one violence, shed not the innocent blood." God has sent us such men. They are today either in a concentration camp or reduced to silence. . . . Our bishops have not recognized it as their duty to stand shoulder to shoulder with those who have spoken the Lord's Word. . . . Wild passions have been released, God's Commandments disregarded, Houses of God which were sacred to others razed to the ground

without punishment, men who have served our German people loyally, and have conscientiously fulfilled their duty, have been thrown into concentration camps, merely because they happened to be of another race. A dreadful seed of hatred has been sown. A frightful harvest will grow out of it, unless God in Grace allows and our people to show sincere repentance. . . . Thou, O earth, earth, earth, hear the word of the Lord. Amen.

A few days later a mob of about twenty Nazi party members raided the vicarage. Von Jan was forcefully removed from his Bible class and hauled on top of the roof of a shed, where he was publicly whipped, and then hauled off to prison. The police did not intervene. But he survived, as a soldier on the front line, and returned in 1945 to his former parish. His was a lone voice in an otherwise cacophonous approval by many of that violent outrage, and a much larger thunderous silence by most secular and religious leaders.[5]

The final episode under the defiance category takes us to the story of another religious figure – Bernhard Lichtenberg. Born in 1875, he took his vows as a Catholic priest in 1899. In 1931, Nazi Propaganda Minister Josef Goebbels's newspaper, *Der Angriff*, viciously attacked Lichtenberg for sponsoring a private showing of the film *All Quiet on the Western Front*.[6] In 1926, Pope Pius XI honored Lichtenberg with the title of Monsignor, and in 1931 he was appointed to head Cathedral of St. Hedwig, in central Berlin. Two years later in 1933, with the Nazis in power, upon the announcement of an official government boycott of shops and businesses owned by Jews on April 1, Lichtenberg provided the Jewish Oscar Wasserman, Director of Deutsche Bank in Berlin, with a recommendation to see Cardinal Adolf Bertram to request church intervention in the boycott – which Bertram declined.[7] Lichtenberg made no secret of his disagreement with Nazi policies on a whole range of issues, such as the euthanasia program, as well as the persecution of Jews. Immediately following the November 1938 pogrom known as Kristallnacht, Lichtenberg publicly stated: "We know what happened yesterday. We do not know what tomorrow holds. However, we have experienced what happened today. Outside, the synagogue burns. That is also a house of God." During the evening prayer in St. Hedwig Cathedral, Lichtenberg then began to insert a daily prayer for both Jews and Jewish Christians as well as imprisoned priests and opponents of the regime, a practice that he faithfully adhered until his arrest in 1941. Lichtenberg also worked actively on their behalf as advisor to the Relief Agency of the Berlin Chancery (*Hilfswerk beim Bischöflichen Ordinariat Berlin*) and often wrote letters of recommendation to assist Jewish-Christians and Jews alike with issues of employment, often in church institutions.[8]

Previously, in November 1940, Lichtenberg took up Karl Adam on his espousal of the Nazi State. Adam, a professor of Theology at the University of Tübingen and a catholic priest of the diocese of Rottenburg, had lectured on a "positive" aspect of Nazism and the duty of Catholics to observe the regime's laws. In his rebuttal, Lichtenberg argued that one "must obey God more than humans" when people stray from moral commandments. Quoting directly from Hitler's *Mein Kampf*, Lichtenberg pointed out that Hitler had argued that the Christian ideology (*Weltanschauung*) could be broken and replaced by a new *Weltanschauung,* namely National Socialism. On November 23, 1940, Adam responded to Lichtenberg's critique in language that revealed more clearly than before his support of the Nazi sate. "The highest earthly worth remains for me – and for those who do not want to be unfaithful to their German blood – the unity of the German Volk in the new Reich. . . . Whoever sabotages this racially ethnic community (*Volksgemeinschaft*) directly or indirectly is to me neither a German nor a Christian." To this Lichtenberg responded, on November 30, 1940, that the idea of the *Volksgemeinschaft* is unchristian; that the Holy Spirit goes wherever it wishes, irrespective of whatever Volk." Lichtenberg was clearly on a collision course with one of the leading theologians of his own church.[9]

On August 29, 1941, two women decided to visit the St. Hedwig Cathedral to observe the architecture there. At that precise time, Lichtenberg, while officiating over the daily evening prayer, was heard also praying for the "poor persecuted Jews." Upset by this prayer, the two women immediately left the Cathedral and reported the information to the police, and this subsequently came to the attention of the Gestapo. On October 23, 1941, the Gestapo searched Lichtenberg's home and then arrested him "on account of hostile activity against the state." The Gestapo officers found a declaration that Lichtenberg had written and planned to read from the pulpit the upcoming Sunday, in which he denounced a recently published antisemitic pamphlet that Goebbels's Propaganda Ministry had distributed throughout the country in an effort to stir hatred against the Jews. In his penned comments, Lichtenberg had written: "An anonymous smear against the Jews is being distributed to Berlin houses. This pamphlet states that every German who supports Jews with an ostensibly false sentimentality, be it only through friendly obligingness, practices treason against his *Volk*. Let us not be misled by this unchristian way of thinking but follow the strict command of Jesus Christ: 'You shall love your neighbor as you love yourself.'"[10]

At his interrogation, Lichtenberg declared that since the world view (*Weltanschauung*) of the regime as portrayed in *Mein Kampf* stood in contrast to Christianity, he must refuse it "as a Catholic priest . . . and also refuse it de facto." As a Catholic priest, he could not say "yes and Amen to every decree and measure that comes from the government." As an example of his disagreement, he cited his letter to Dr. Leonardi Conti, the regime's health minister, against the euthanasia (mercy killing) of the country's mentally ill, but he also pointed out among others, the persecution of the Jews. With regard to Jews, he stated "I spiritually oppose the deportation with all its consequences, because it goes against the chief rule of Christianity: 'You shall love your neighbor as you love yourself,' and I consider the Jews also my neighbors who have immortally created souls after the image and likeness of God." Lichtenberg also admitted to praying regularly for "the severely harassed non-Christians, for the Jews, for prisoners in the concentration camps, particularly for the imprisoned priests and religious persons," as well as praying for the country's political leaders. In answer to the questions in relation to his notations in his copy of *Mein Kampf*, Lichtenberg stated: "Hitler is not an infallible prophet. . . . I do not consider Hitler as a prophet sent by God. . . . I state with steadfast conviction that the National Socialist ideology is incompatible with the teaching and commands of the Catholic Church."[11] On March 21, 1942, the State District Attorney's Office charged Lichtenberg with violation of the pulpit law and the law against treacherous attack on state and party. This charge stemmed specifically from Lichtenberg's intercessory prayers for the Jews and for his written and planned pulpit declaration against the Ministry of Propaganda's antisemitic pamphlet. Found guilty, he was sentenced to a two-year prison term.

While in prison, Bishop Konrad von Preysing interceded for him on several occasions and wrote to the Pope informing him of Lichtenberg's arrest for praying for the "arrested Jews." Pius XII wrote back to Preysing on April 20, 1943: "It gives us . . . solace to hear, that Catholics, specifically Berlin Catholics, have shown the so-called non-Aryans so great a love in their distress, and we say in this connection a special word of fatherly appreciation as well as intimate sympathy to the imprisoned Monsignor Lichtenberg."[12]

But other than expressing sympathy, the Pope took no action to try to effect the man's release. As for the Gestapo, it stipulated that if Lichtenberg would remain silent and abide by a prohibition against preaching during the war period, he would be a free man upon the end of his two-year prison term. Lichtenberg, however, refused and stated: "What better can happen to a person than to die for his holy Catholic faith? Today, I am ready, in fact, to die for it!" He requested to be allowed to accompany the deported Jewish Christians and Jews to Litzmannstadt (the Łódz ghetto) in order to serve as a pastoral minister to the people there.[13] Preysing, however, attempted to dissuade him from such an undertaking because of his heath. Lichtenberg adamantly stood firm in his decision.

When, on October 22, 1943, Lichtenberg was released from prison, the Gestapo was waiting at the gate and forced him into a waiting car. Taken to a nearby camp, he was pushed into a garbage room and severely beaten. He was left in that room for two days. On November 3, 1943, Lichtenberg was transported to a collecting point for prisoners on their way to Dachau camp. As he grew very ill, he was moved to a nearby state hospital, where he died on Friday, November 5, 1943. In the words of historian Guenter Lewy, "Lichtenberg's protest remained a solitary act of witness. His bishops remained silent in the face of the burning temples and the first roundup of the Jews."[14] In 1996, Bernhard Lichtenberg was beatified by the Catholic Church, under Pope John Paul II. In 2004, the Yad Vashem Holocaust Memorial, in Jerusalem, declared Bernhard Lichtenberg a Righteous Among the Nations.[15]

CHAPTER 9

Possible Motivations

* * *

IT WOULD NOT BE DIFFICULT, understandably, to describe the rescuers of Jews in our study as altruistic persons. This term was coined in the eighteenth century by the French philosopher Auguste Comte and came to denote the antithesis of egoism; that is, a behavior that was directed toward the benefit of others and that had the good of others less fortunate as their object rather than personal recognition or material rewards. Accordingly, altruistic persons were perceived as having internalized higher and more universal standards of justice, social responsibility, and modes of moral reasoning, and to be more empathetic to the feelings and sufferings of others.

This original description of the altruistic person implies a special behavior that is also guided by rational principles, at which the altruistic person has arrived after a certain amount of thought and reflection, presumably in the quiet repose of one's home. Such a person then chooses a course of action and behavior that coheres and harmonizes with his philosophy of life – in our case, by committing himself/herself to the welfare and good of others in need. Granted that such persons are to be found in all societies, do the Righteous in our study embody the aforementioned attributes? Are they the deeply emotive persons, who through a process of reasoning and moral self-education have attained a level where they place the good of others as their primary goal, and not necessarily their own good and prosperity? Laymen and scholars have pondered the mystery of the ulterior motivations that prompted these plain and unassuming people of the Holocaust period to place their lives at risk in order to save people toward whom they had no personal obligation. What is it, we wonder, that made them suddenly decide to brave the risks to themselves for the sake of others – neither family members nor, in many cases, even persons of their immediate circle of friends? Although none of the theories advanced have satisfactorily cleared up this enigma, three recent studies deserve special attention.

a) Some Studies on the Altruism of Rescuers of Jews

Sociologist Nechama Tec, in her study of the Polish Righteous, distinguishes between two fundamental types of behavior: "normative" and "autonomous."[1] Whereas the "normative" type is a behavior that is sanctioned and rewarded by society, the "autonomous" type is characterized by a behavior that runs the risk even of social ostracism. The Polish rescuers in her study were mostly of the "autonomous" type; that is, nonconformists and highly individualistic. This caused them to stay somewhat aloof from their immediate society; in fact, their individualistic temperament made it difficult for them to blend with the surrounding larger group. Moreover, in researching their past before the onset of the Holocaust, Tec found a high level of independence and self-confidence, and a reliance on their own moral imperatives, not those set by their society.[2]

An autonomous person, Tec points out, is someone who finds it difficult to blend into his or her environment. For example, a foreign-born spouse residing in an ethnically homogeneous location, or an unmarried woman living in a small town while having an open love affair with a married person, might be considered autonomous.[3] Being a bit of an outsider within one's immediate community contributes to developing an independent frame of thinking on various subjects, even when such thinking does not cohere with acceptable ideas in the surrounding community. "Those who are on the periphery of their community are not strongly controlled by it," Tec underlines. Rescuers of Jews had had such an independent frame of mind, and followed their own moral imperatives, even when these were in opposition to the values and norms pervasive in their environment.[4] Briefly put, such persons have the following personality traits: a strong sense of individuality, a high level of independence and self-reliance, an enduring commitment to help the needy, even before the war, a matter-of-fact attitude toward rescue, which they see as a mere duty, and a universalistic perception of the needy. In fact, Tec found that "in case after case, there is a long history of giving aid to those in need" by the rescuers of Jews, even before extending aid to Jews.[5] In summary, "the less integrated into a community people are, the less constrained and controlled they are by the community's norms and values," and the more likely they are capable of resisting the pressures of the community and acting independently.[6] This is especially so in a country like Poland (Tec's restricted study), where, as Tec admits, a very pronounced antisemitism was shared by large swaths of the population – even by some rescuers of Jews. Hence the significance of the individualistic and contra-society nature of most rescuers of Jews in that country. One wonders whether such conclusions can also be drawn with regard to German rescuers of Jews, many of whom were comfortably ensconced in their society. But no such study has so far been undertaken.

Samuel and Pearl Oliner, in their study of rescuers of Jews from various European countries (not only Poland), arrived at different conclusions, also from a sociological perspective. They found that a significant number of rescuers, while harboring some individualistic traits, had (contrary to Tec) mostly fully integrated the norms of their society, such as kindness, helpfulness, and tolerance, to which others only paid lip service but hardly applied in their daily activities. He termed this type of behavior "normocentric," that is, a behavior that is motivated by the social group rather than by the individual, in which the individual either knowingly or unwittingly acts on the group's stated norms of conduct. With the rescuers, the Oliners point out, these social norms were so strongly internalized that their behavior appeared to be individualistic and self-driven, but in fact it was not.[7]

In a "normocentric" setting, the larger group imposes norms for behavior and proscribes action that is considered a violation of the group's code of proper conduct. The Oliners underline that "helping Jews was less a decision made at a critical juncture than a choice prefigured by an established character and way of life," largely influenced by the behavioral norms and ethical codes of the surrounding society"; as Iris Murdoch writes in the *Sovereignty of Good*, "at crucial moments of choice most of the business of choosing is already over."[8] For it is the larger group's code of ethical behavior that is at play here, not the individual's self-coherent thinking. Many of the persons in this category were also committed to the improvement of society and supported various causes. They were "outreach" persons, with extensive attachments, involvements, and commitments. Their "altruistic act of rescue was not a radical departure from previous ways of responding but an extension of characteristic forms of relating to others," in accordance with what was inculcated to them by the society at large.[9] Nechama Tec would probably also agree with the Oliners' characterization of the rescuer's code of moral behavior, but she would attribute it to a self-imposed, individualistic state of mind that does not necessarily cohere with the surrounding society and may even be opposed to it.

When "normocentric" persons (52% of the Oliners' sample) witnessed the arrest or persecution of Jews, it automatically triggered a response based on the norms of the social group with which they strongly identified, and to whom they looked for moral guidance. Responses arose not from their connection with the victim but from feelings of obligation to the group or community. Less "normocentric" persons are those moved by empathic feelings (38% of the sample), such as concern with the fate of another in distress, and feelings of compassion, sympathy, and pity. Such a spontaneous reaction could be caused by a face-to-face encounter with a distressed person. Those whom the Oliners described as "autonomous/ principled" were aroused to help Jews because their persecution was a violation of the rescuer's own moral precepts, and did not need validation of their actions from the outside – but these constituted only 11% of the Oliners' sample.

The Oliners also found that most rescuers were not only outreach persons with extensive attachments who sought out opportunities to help, but they were also adventurous and risk-taking, more self-confident in meeting challenges, and more likely to evaluate themselves positively. Most of the values, though socially rooted, were acquired directly from parents. They had closer family relationships in general than non-rescuers. Also of significance, parents of rescuers were less likely to emphasize obedience. Instead they provided an education based more on reasoning than on physical punishment.

As for bystanders (the control group in the Oliners' study), who refrained from helping, the Oliners found that they were unaffected by the suffering of others and led a constricted and detached life, bordering on self-imposed exclusivity. The outside world was experienced as peripheral. As self-centered persons, they paid scant attention to others or to the norms of their immediate society. They also were suspicious of others, blaming others for their own insufficiencies, and shared a sense of impotence and victimization. Such persons were not predisposed to get involved in helping others, especially when this entailed discomforts and personal risks to themselves.

Another study undertaken by Eva Fogelman offers a psychiatric perspective, as well as sociological insights, on the behavior of rescuers of Jews.[10] Some of her conclusions align with those of Tec and the Oliners, but with some reservations. In the introduction to her book, she makes it clear that while altruism is a stable personality characteristic, altruistic behaviors are jointly determined by the combination of personality and situational factors, and one should not look at rescuers of Jews as "saints"; nor were they particularly heroic or often all that different from others. Though laudable, they were in fact ordinary people.[11] As for those who withheld themselves from helping, it is not necessarily that they were opposed to it, but that they lacked a "needed opportunity"; they did not always have the occasion to offer help because of the circumstances of their lives and professions. The bystanders' situations may have been too dangerous or uncertain to be of any help, not that they were opposed to it.[12] Supported by Elizabeth Midlarsky's study of altruistic behavior, Fogelman asserts that responsibility involves competence – and the confidence that you can control events to bring about the desired outcome, an attribute that not all would-be rescuers shared. In Fogelman's words, "Rescuers were not about to offer help unless they felt there was a very good chance that they could pull it off. They needed to have faith in their capacity to assess the situation and find solutions." But there was seldom time for measured thought. No one knew how long the commitment would last, or how long the war would last.[13] Therefore, some bystanders wanted to help, but the fear of endangering their own children or themselves immobilized them. Fogelman agrees that that action may come from the core of one's self, but it is inhibited or reinforced by situational factors, and this explains why persons with rescuer attributes (according to either Tec or the Oliners) found themselves incapable of carrying out their inborn wish to be of help.[14]

Fogelman underlines that the first step for any would-be rescuer was awareness; that is, they must note that something was amiss and be aware of the imminent danger to and probable death of Jews.[15] At the same time, there is no single set of attributes that will predict helping behavior. Often, subtle elements of the situation play predominant roles in determining whether the individual will intervene in a specific situation. What also prompted rescuers to get involved is their realization that others would not take care of the problem. Rescuers felt that unless they, personally, did something, those seeking help would probably die.[16]

Also worth nothing is that most rescuers did not initiate the rescue. A friend, an acquaintance, a friend of a friend came and asked for help.[17] Also, we should take account of the importance of the gradual nature of help. In the words of Dutch rescuer Johtje Vos: "You don't get up one morning and say, 'Now I'm going to hide Jewish people.' It's something that grows. You start with a suitcase and a child and a piano."[18] Fogelman qualifies this as "the foot-in-the-door effect." When people are asked for a small favor and comply, they are more likely to agree later to a larger favor than they would be if they had been asked first for the larger favor. For example, asking to stay just for one night could lead to a longer stay.[19] This is also borne out by many other rescue stories in many countries, including those mentioned in this study of German rescuers.

But once the decision to help had been reached and the rescue had begun, a different self – a *rescuer self*, in Fogelman's words – emerged to do what had to be done. "A 'transformation' had taken place." Rescuers "became, in effect, different people." That new "self" allowed them to do what was necessary, including plotting, stealing, lying, taking risks, enduring hardships, putting loved ones in jeopardy, and living in fear – all that was needed for the success of the rescue operation.[20] Fogelman supports this thesis with the story of Tina Strobos, in the Netherlands. She once attended a funeral and waited until all the mourners were in the chapel. She then sneaked into the coatroom, went through their coats, and stole all their identification cards.

It was heartbreaking when such anti-social actions had to involve one's children. "We had to teach our children to lie," said Johtje Vos. "On the one hand, we had to punish them or reprimand them when they lied for other purposes. We had to make them understand the difference between the lies."[21] One may also use the example of Oskar Schindler, of a total transformation taking place gradually, with his ever-mounting interventions in the rescue of his Jewish workers. An original, self-centered bon vivant, over the years he became obsessed with one sole goal – the rescue of his Jewish wards, even to the detriment of his accumulated monetary gains. Schindler acted out the part of a German *bon ami* so convincingly that Amon Göth, the brutally sadistic labor camp commandant with whom Schindler socialized, considered calling him as a character witness at his postwar trial.[22]

Fogelman also points out that "most rescuers were not loners or people who felt alienated from society" (as advanced by Tec). It was the act and secrecy of rescue that effectively isolated them from everyone else, not necessarily a characteristic predisposition.[23] True enough, there were also those termed by Fogelman as "moral" rescuers who – as Tec would argue – shared an autonomous-acquired morality. They had a strong sense of who they were and what they were about. Their values were self-sustaining, not dependent on the approval of others. What mattered to them was behaving in a way to maintain their integrity. Scenes of Nazi brutality touched their inner core and activated their moral values, which had been developed early in life and may have remained dormant or simply untested. When asked to help, moral rescuers could not say no.[24]

In agreement with the Oliners, most rescuers in Fogelman's study came from loving families that instilled in them a sense of self-worth and love. As children their interests were encouraged and their talents praised. A nurturing, loving home, an altruistic parent or beloved caretaker who served as role model for altruistic behavior, and a tolerance for people who were different were also contributing factors.[25] Also, as the Oliners argue, rescuers had parents who reasoned rather than threatened, explained rules, and used inductive reasoning instead of harsh punishment (although, in many cases, rational conversation did not always carry the day, and some punishment came in handy). This type of background led to the formation of the ability to think and act independently, and not necessarily based on what others thought or what the laws mandated. However, Fogelman warns, not all rescuers were raised in lenient, democratic homes, and she gives a few examples of contrary backgrounds.[26]

To summarize, both Tec and Oliner place rescuers on a high pedestal: they are special, out-of-the-ordinary, highly self-reliant, and strongly self-motivated persons, not the run-of-the-mill one generally meets. Likewise with Fogelman's theory; once the person has acted altruistically, he/she is transformed into a "rescuer self." The Oliners expand on this description by portraying the Righteous rescuers in laudatory terms. They are outreach persons with broad social commitments; they evaluate themselves positively and seek out challenges.

Mention should also be made of two others studies, which also originate from a sociological perspective. Perry London based his research of social deviance on interviews with 27 rescuers and 42 rescued persons – all of whom moved after the war to the United States.[27] He found it enormously complex to define altruism and study it meaningfully. He could come up with no easy criteria for deciding on the motives of the rescuers' actions. In his words,

"Motives were still less easily classified than were activities – because motives change, because they were conflicting, or because they were obscure." Some rescuers got involved with what London termed "benevolence aforethought." Others acted in response to social pressure and to social reinforcement for doing so; still others, for selfish reasons. Some rescuers were fanatically religious; others devout atheists. Some had close ties with Jews; others were antisemitic. And so on and so on, with multiple motivating factors.[28] London proposed three possible structural motivational hypotheses: (a) a spirit and fondness for adventurous acts; (b) an intense identification with a parental model of moral conduct; and (c) a sense of being socially marginal (although, he cautions, this may have a bit to do with the fact that his sample were no longer residents of their countries of origin where the rescue took place).[29] All of the rescuers interviewed also tended to have very strong identifications with parents, usually with one parent more than the other, usually a parent who was a very strong moralist – not necessarily religious, but holding to very firm opinions on moral issues and serving as a model of moral conduct.[30]

Finally, a few observations on the study undertaken by Kristen Renwick Monroe. She found that rescuers come from a wide range of educational backgrounds, socioeconomic classes, religions, and types of relations with parents and role models (including, strangely, antisemitic and alcoholic parents). "You could hardly find a more disparate group of individuals."[31] She states that rescue behavior does not corroborate the belief that moral actions arise from the dominance of reason over the baser passions. Decisions to help were spontaneous and simple, not the outcome of prior reasoned thinking. In fact, most rescuers found it hard to give a logical explanation for their life-threatening involvement in the rescue act. They innocently and seemingly naïvely state: "But what else could I do? They were human beings like you and me." However, non-rescuers give a more reasoned and negative explanation: "But what could I do? I was one person, alone against the Nazis."[32] Here, the sense of helplessness.

Monroe adds that most persons would probably behave likewise if they were in the same straits as the non-rescuers. "We are the norm. We, the non-rescuers." She did, however, find one factor that differentiated the two groups: "cognitive orientation," which is the perceptions each group had of themselves in relation to others. Non-rescuers saw themselves, as earlier noted by the Oliners, as powerless and lonely, usually as isolated individuals or as members of a group of helpless people. Rescuers, by contrast, saw themselves as individuals strongly linked to others through a shared humanity. Rescuers perceived themselves as part of a common humankind; non-rescuers, simply as members of their immediate family, or of a religious, national, or ethnic group. "Rescuers simply had, if you will, a different way of seeing things."[33] She closes her observations with a warning, by quoting Dutch rescuer Tony van Renterghem: "Every time you see the monster, you basically are looking in the mirror. . . . You have many times to look in the mirror to make very sure that he [the perceived enemy] hasn't crept into your head. . . . Good and bad are in all of us. You have to look in the mirror."[34]

With respect to German rescuers, important for our study, it is worth noting the conclusions drawn by Daniel Fraenkel, who made a thorough compilation of the acts of German rescuers – but only of rescue acts, not their personal backgrounds and motives.[35] He found nothing to suggest that as a group they stood out from their environment either before or after the rescue. They were ordinary human beings who dared to act humanely in a society in which racial persecution culminating in state-organized mass murder had become the perverted norm. It is in a sense easier, Fraenkel suggested, to account for the apathy, acquiescence, and complicity of the overwhelming majority than to explain the goodness of the few. The presumption of constructing an all-encompassing theory of the rescuer personality, which would also serve as a sort of educational blueprint for preprogramming altruistic personalities in the future, seemed dubious at best, in Fraenkel's estimation. We can perhaps educate individuals to become more useful members of a better society; we can hardly train them to become rescuers of human beings in critical times. Though some of the most notable rescuers did indeed possess unique and distinctive personalities, many others would have been indistinguishable from their environment and fellow countrymen in more normal times.[36]

b) The Altruism of the Righteous Among the Nations and Levinas

Returning to our opening question, do the rescuers in our study fully meet the criteria of a simple, literal definition of altruism? Perhaps not. To begin with, the overwhelming majority of the rescuers in our study did not have the luxury of reflecting over an extended time before deciding on a course of action, as would apply to ordinary altruists such as, for example, Mother

Teresa, when she made a rational decision to dedicate her life to helping others in need, in a faraway and distant country. Many were, so to speak, minding their own business, when suddenly the question of intervening to help others in distress was thrust upon them; that is, they were challenged to get involved or not, to help someone survive or decline that person's request for immediate help (in many cases, the needy person was literally standing before the prospective helper, begging for help).

We are therefore concerned here with a different form of altruism, and with altruistic deeds by persons who otherwise did not perceive themselves as altruists and were not in any particular way predisposed to seek out those in need of help, if not under pressure to do so. Many, especially in Eastern Europe, simply responded to situations of frightening confrontations with persons pleading for help – to be allowed to live. In other instances, especially in Western Europe, including Germany and Germans in responsible positions in the occupied countries, the decision to help was spurred by the sight of the brutality of the Nazis' behavior and the inhumane treatment of the Jews in their proximity. This led to the resolve to oppose this terrible humanitarian infraction in whatever way possible – including help to Jews. In some cases, the decision by religious-minded persons was perhaps prompted by theological considerations – to help God's elect people, who although they may have "sinned" by not accepting the Christian faith, were nevertheless an integral and indispensable part of the divine dispensation for the salvation of mankind. In the face of the Nazi plan to root out all Jews, which was taking place before their very eyes, devout Christians, according to this thinking, had a religious obligation to preserve the Jews at all costs.

The type of behavior peculiar to the actions of our Righteous is therefore not to be linked to a simple altruism, in the narrow sense of the term. It is rather to be viewed as a confrontational type of altruism – you're challenged, you respond affirmatively, and, unbeknownst (even surprising) to yourself, you discover you're as capable of charitable deeds as any self-proclaimed altruistic person. At the same time, let us not forget that in most cases the first move in this direction was usually not made by the rescuer, but by the rescued person – totally helpless, fleeing for his life, and desperately in need of a helping hand. The rescuer responded to the appeal of the hapless rescued, and exhibited an altruism of the most elevated kind – risking one's life for the sake of others – a danger not always faced by other altruistic persons not contending with a challenge as threatening as the Nazis.

In the very short moment of confrontation with a person pleading for help, there are some questions that may suddenly and intuitively have crossed the mind of the potential rescuer and that caused him to respond one way or another. Some of these questions were: Is the situation really that serious (for the first prerequisite for helping is to define the situation as an emergency); will my personal intervention make a difference (the answer to this must be positive); if I don't help, will someone else do it (quite possibly not, so it's up to me)? Defining the situation as an emergency is the first step; assuming personal responsibility for intervening is the next. Then comes the sudden awareness that "I, at this time and place, can really make a difference between that person's life or demise." At this totally unprepared and unplanned point, a new self-worth and self-confidence is born or given added strength. This description of the rescuer's response is particularly true for rescue situations in Eastern Europe. In West European countries, decisions to intervene were also prompted by the unprecedented wave of Nazi terror – such as the sudden enforcement of the Yellow Star in September 1941 in Germany, followed by the start of the mass deportations. This was especially so in Germany, as rescuers were also prompted to get involved by the shameful sight of their own country presiding over the liquidation of another people. The Holocaust rescuers, consequently, have shown us that persons not necessarily of an altruistic temperament, nor uniquely individualistic, highly self-reliant, or prone to outreach were nevertheless capable of acting in a highly altruistic manner – perhaps because this type of action is a potentiality endemic in human behavior and shared by most people, but only comes strongly to the fore and assumes concrete form in unique, irregular, and highly inordinate human situations, such as during the Holocaust. However, it only comes to the fore with persons not otherwise constrained by deep prejudices (such as a profound antisemitism) nor overcome with fear for their own personal safety. Most persons would also not become rescuers unless initially confronted with direct appeals for help by Jews on the run for their lives.

The face-to-face encounter between victim and rescuer that was in most instances the opening stage that led to a positive response by the rescuers, has led me to consider one of the central ideas advanced by the French Jewish existential philosopher, Emmanuel Levinas. Diverging from other self-centered philosophies in the search of an authentic personal Self, Levinas states that the ethical responsibility for others should be the starting point and primary focus for philosophy: "ethics precedes ontology" (the study of Being). For Levinas, the search for one's true Self is possible only with its recognition of the Other, a recognition that carries responsibility for the other person. That other person, in Levinas's thought, is irreducibly different from one's own selfhood and yet is part of one's self, in the sense that a true evaluation of one's individuality is only possible by integrating within oneself the presence of the other person without necessarily trying to control and dominate him. In this context, "ethics begins with the face of the other," which includes a recognition and respect of the other's selfhood or, in Levinas's words, the other's Alterity. This recognition of one's relation and obligation to the other is what allows a person to attain a full individuality – the state of being at one with one's Being. According to Levinas, the face-to-face encounter is the beginning of such a personal and authentic ethics, which exists beyond every form of a socially conditioned ethics. So viewed, the face of the Other has a special metaphysical and moral significance. The tangible presence and proximity of the Other's face evokes, on a pre-cognitive level, the realization of the Other's and one's own mortality, coupled with a recognition of one's own individuality, and precludes turning the other person into a tool for the fulfillment of one's egotistical needs. It also evokes the realization of the primordial importance of life itself.[37]

In addition, on a very deep level, the other person's face is a reflection of an Otherness (or "alterity" in Levinas's language) that is within the person himself when facing the other person, coupled with a realization of one's own mortality. As phrased in philosophical language by one interpreter of Levinas's thought, the Other "is my standing-outside-myself-calling-myself-into-question."[38] The face of the other, coupled with an authentic relationship with the other, the stranger, integrates his presence inside myself and makes him an "insider," a part of my own worth and self-estimation – or my Being. This, without my being able to fully apprehend that other person. At the same time, insofar as the Other is within me, that is, an element of my consciousness, this inability to fully comprehend the other person is also part of me. It expresses itself as a limitation of my ability to completely synthesize, grasp, and objectify the other person.[39]

A true ethics, according to Levinas, begins with a turning toward and responding to the Other, since I am only true to myself as long as I carry the other's presence in myself. This encounter with the Other makes possible a true self-dialogue with one's conscience – the soul's dialogue with itself. That takes place when I question myself in light of the Other, who is somehow also present in me, in my consciousness, yet is not of it. This apprehension of the Other necessitates a commitment to caring for the other person's needs when such a necessity arises. This obligation is non-symmetrical, in the sense that my help to him is not conditioned by a similar reciprocal obligation by the assisted person.[40]

The record shows that the face-to-face encounter in most of our stories, during the height of the Nazi persecution of Jews, was the primary cause that prompted the would-be rescuer to suddenly and intuitively agree to respond favorably to the request of aid. Oskar Schindler, Berthold Beitz, and Otto Weidt were not prompted to aid Jews from a safe and invisible distance to the persons needing such help; rather, their response was triggered by close proximity, by the daily face-to-face encounter with the Jewish workers under their supervision and the realization that only their intervention could make the difference between their Jewish workers' life and death. This form of situational altruism, under extreme emergency conditions, only took place during the Holocaust.

c) Group Versus Individual Behavior

The record presented here demonstrates that it is possible (though not as a widespread phenomenon) for the individual person, even under a totalitarian system, to deviate from the larger group's suffocating ideological embrace in at least one important domain, when it is perceived to violate something basic to the very core of human existence and human justice. Beyond all social constraints, there exists an archetypal (to use a Jungian term) human wisdom to which people can lay claim, and which helps them to differentiate between what is ultimately right and wrong, just and unjust, permissible and forbidden, good and evil. Such realization does not always lead to concomitant action, due to a whole array of inhibiting factors: fear, loss of social status, and one's inherited bag of stereotyping prejudices.

We have also found that even in a totalitarian state such as Nazi Germany, individual open protest was possible, but as noted in our opening chapter, only when the individual joins others, as happened during the Rosenstrasse demonstration by hundreds of women who asked for the release of their Jewish husbands. This confirms the observation noted earlier by social scientists about the possibilities of variant forms of disagreement or protest against the larger group in all societies – even in totalitarian ones.[41]

The examples brought to light in this study, of help by persons of various callings and walks of life, suggest that it is possible for the individual person to adopt a viewpoint different to the one upheld by the larger society, without necessarily having to disagree with all of the larger group's laws and norms. Such disagreement need not take the form of outward disobedience, or rather cannot for obvious reasons, but may be acted upon secretly and in contrived ways. While social conformism remains a powerful inducement to coerce people to toe the official line, it does not necessarily rule out manifestations of opposition to some elements of the ruling group's policies. With dictatorial regimes, this will not take the form of outward defiance but of subterfuge – of outward compliance but secret disobedience. Help to Jews, considered a serious offense in Nazi Germany, was possible to many if not most persons; more so to those in civilian dress and less so to those in uniforms. Help to Jews came in two principal forms: hiding Jews in one's home and providing them with false identities, or sheltering them from violence by utilizing various ploys that could be translated into acceptable excuses to Nazi authorities to justify a temporary halt to the killing of Jews in a particular place. Both of these forms were surreptitious by nature, and not a few Germans employed them. However, they were not enough to make a dent in the overall Nazi plan to destroy the Jewish people.

Rescuers were not challenged to obey or disobey in the sense described by Christopher Browning in his study of Police Reserve Battalion 101.[42] Outwardly, rescuers of Jews were obedient citizens of the Reich; secretly, they disobeyed with regard to the Jewish issue. Their actions were of a surreptitious nature; no open defiance in the isolated cases discussed in chapter 8. Even Battel and Liedtke did not justify their standoff with SS troops as defiance. Schindler continued to play up his good camaraderie act while he saved, and Calmeyer is proof that autonomous moral behavior is possible, even while outwardly playing out one's act as a cog in the ruling bureaucracy.

An additional distinction is in the area of personal responsibility for one's deeds. Whereas the perpetrators were part of organized and regimented units, with group discipline a top priority, rescuers had only themselves and their conscience to obey, not any civilian or military bureaucratic machinery. Perpetrators, consequently, "passed the buck" of responsibility to others, while rescuers took it wholly upon themselves. It turns out that the highest form of personal responsibility, which entailed risking one's life for the sake of saving someone else's life, was during the Holocaust the reserve of people who acted strictly as individual persons, responsible only to themselves, to their conscience, and to their estimation of themselves as purposeful human beings. By contrast, "free-floating" responsibility, which during the Holocaust went hand-in-hand with inflicting senseless pain and death on totally defenseless people – this was the reserve of persons who were "under the influence," who acted upon orders and at the behest of others, and were therefore able to discharge themselves of any responsibility for their reprehensible acts. The rescuers, by contrast, took all responsibility upon themselves, and when asked claimed that by saving a fellow human life, they were "only" doing what was "natural" to themselves as purposeful human beings. Here we have human behavior at perhaps its most elevated and sublime form.

This leads us to the thought that when the individual person is locked in what Stanley Milgram defined as an Agentic State, which in practical terms means being at the total behest of another agency's will and divested of any personal responsibility for one's behavior, we then have a situation that to a large extent explains the behavior of the perpetrators of the Final Solution.[43] On the other hand, when the individual person is in a situation where he can act independently, and without having to worry how his action will measure up to the expectations of others but only to himself and his conscience – there we have the type of rescuer described in this study.

An additional observation is that while some rescuers were card-carrying members of the Nazi party, one would not expect to find among the rescuers dyed-in-the-wool Nazis, for that would have meant that the person must violate a most fundamental tenet of their party's ideology, the special virulent brand of Nazi antisemitism. But even here, exceptions to the rule were possible, and a Nazi of the type of Ludwig Clauss, who in his writings advocated the elimination of Jews from German society, could justify to himself violating Nazi laws and saving at least one Jewish person, to whom he felt personally obligated. This brings to mind the words of SS chief Himmler in his Posen speech of October 1943, in which he bewailed the fact that every German had his "good" Jew, who ought not to be harmed. At the same time, it is best to remember that in spite of Himmler's concern, most Germans were not prepared to act for their "good" Jew, inhibited as they were by a combination of fear of retribution, a too-strong identification with the larger group, and their own socially inbred anti-Jewish prejudices – or, perhaps, they were not approached by a Jewish person whom they knew who asked for help, as in many cases in our study, and therefore they remained aloof from any form of self-initiated assistance.

To summarize, from whichever way one looks at it, the Holocaust is also the story of behavior in a group setting, under group control, where the herd instinct predominated. The inhumanities were committed in the presence of others. It seems that the beast in us manifests itself more strongly in group-controlled situations. Evil is best propagated when egged on by others, and in the presence of the many. Evil is most potent, danger-ous, and destructive when carried out under group control, where a person is most divorced from his or her true self, which may lead to a different type of behavior.[44] Goodness, on the other hand, is mostly the product of an individual endeavor; under tyrannous regimes, it is a concealed, usually clandestine act. But it is where man is truest to himself. Goodness during the Holocaust (in Germany and elsewhere) was the domain of the individ-ual person, who in the majority of cases acted out his humanity secretly, in contrast to the isolated cases, such as that of Armin Wegner, characterized by open defiance to the ruling system. In all such cases, it proves that the human person possesses an individual intelligence and morality, indepen-dent of the larger group, with the capacity to distinguish between what is ultimately right and wrong, just and totally unjust – if and when a person is given the chance to look himself in the mirror, so to speak.

d) Some Final Observations

Our own findings with regard to the study of German rescuers may be put as follows:

(1) Those who actually rescued may be divided into the following groups:
   (a) People who saved Jews with whom they entertained some kind of previous relationship, business or personal. This, by far, rep-resents the most common factor of all rescue stories. Rescuers who knew the rescued party before the start of the rescue opera-tion – either through friendship, family relationship (mixed

marriages and *Mischlinge*), business relationships, and (in the occupied countries) supervisor/administrator-laborer relationships – developed a special affinity with them and saw themselves as responsible for their continued existence. This previous acquaintanceship represented an important incentive to future acts of assistance. Otto Weidt, in Berlin, and Dorothea Neff represent two of many similar examples.

(b) People ideologically opposed to Nazism, either from religious (such as members of the Confessing Church) or political convictions (socialists and communists). Helping Jews was one sure method of opposing the regime in an area of great importance to the Nazi leadership. Examples include Pastor Otto Mörike and Wilhelm Hammann.

(c) Persons who may have been more or less content with the general policies of the Nazi German state in the economic and political spheres, perhaps even agreeing with a mild form of antisemitism, but sharply disagreeing with the virulent antisemitism of their regime and morally repelled by the mass murder of Jews, which they judged as a criminal act of historic proportion – such as the cases of Hans Georg Calmeyer and Wilhelm von Hahn. This especially applies to Germans who employed Jews as forced laborers; through time, they grew attentive to their needs, commiserated with their suffering, and lightened their burdens, and in some cases went to great lengths to save their lives. Persons under this category could save great numbers of Jews. Oskar Schindler and Berthold Beitz represent two prominent cases.

(2) In addition, rescue operations were, in almost all cases (with the notable exception of the Confessing Church), initiated by individual persons, not by groups or organizations.

(3) Furthermore, it goes without saying that in order to ensure the success of the rescue operation, rescuers had to act in total secrecy, or surreptitiously, by camouflaging their true intentions or by subverting existing laws and regulations vis-a-vis Jews. The success of the rescue operation depended on that secrecy, or that "deviant" behavior.

(4) The situational factor and proximity to the victimized person were important stimulants to the rescue operation. Most rescue undertakings were triggered as the result of a close encounter between the

potential rescuer with the totally helpless Jewish victim, whom he may have known before.

(5) To make a decision to get involved, at great risk to the acting person, one had to conclude that this was an emergency situation insofar as the victimized person was concerned (a conclusion not difficult to draw in Nazi Germany), that one had to act immediately, and that one's decision could make the difference between life and death for both the rescuer and the rescued. For perhaps the only time in their lives, rescuers wore the mantle of God – of deciding between life (by helping) and death (by declining to help). The decision to help was born as a result of a confrontation with something terribly upsetting – of a great evil before one's eyes, whatever one's inbred prejudicial ideas, and the belief that the potential rescuer had the capacity to do something about it. The knowledge that one's action was directly linked to the saving of another person's life is undoubtedly one of the most rewarding feelings one can hope to obtain.

(6) Rescuers had to have some flexibility and freedom of movement in order to ensure the success of their rescue operation. Persons in tight-knit military or civilian units and organizations, constantly under watch and observation, with little room to explore, experiment, and maneuver, and with no freedom for personal evaluation, judgment, and decision-making – such persons could become rescuers only with great difficulty. To hide a Jew, one needed a self-assurance (realistic or not) that it stood a good chance of success, with contingency plans in cases of emergency – whether in the privacy of one's home or other forms of sheltering and rescue. For persons in positions of authority or influence, such as those in charge of Jewish labor, help meant stalling, inventing excuses, and utilizing discretionary prerogatives, so as to be able to subvert and distort orders and regulations in order to produce a contrary and beneficial result.

All these aforementioned factors help to explain the phenomenon of German rescuers of Jews, inside Germany and Austria (which was part of Nazi Germany during the most important years of the Holocaust), or in countries occupied by Germany. The proximity factor – the eye to eye contact with the victimized Jew – and the instinctive realization that the potential rescuer could make a difference between the life and death of that person and that a decision could

not be postponed, coupled with the belief that everyone had a right to life –
these appear to have been the most dominant factors that overshadowed all
other considerations militating against getting involved (such as one's baggage
of prejudicial stereotypes and/or the more serious fear of risk and retribution by
the rescuer's own regime). They propelled the potential rescuer to take up the
challenge: to intervene and help out.

AFTERWORD

*   *   *

WE ARE NOW AT THE close of our study, and some final lessons and observations are in order. Before we analyze the results of our findings, let us briefly recap some issues mentioned in our opening chapter, especially Nazi antisemitism.

It is true that other than Nazi Germany, there were quasi-fascist movements in many European countries. In Poland, for instance, the mood among conservative and rightwing elements was in favor of the expulsion of Jews. The difference was that in Germany a radical antisemitic party was in power and held on to it. Moreover, Nazi antisemitism went beyond anything advocated by antisemitic movements elsewhere. It was what Saul Friedländer qualified as "redemptionist" antisemitism; in other words, the belief that the physical removal of the Jews from the world would usher in an apocalyptic millennium, never seen before, as it would free Germany and other nations from a destructive stranglehold, embodied in the presence of Jews. This was an antisemitic novelty not copied by antisemitic movements in other countries.[1] In addition, this type of antisemitism was then translated into political action – expansion of German borders, the establishment of a New Order on the continent – simultaneous with the implementation of the Final Solution. All these were inextricably bound one to another.

Let us also not forget that the idea of the "Jew" in Nazi Germany had assumed demonic and cosmic proportions. It was a hallucinatory form of Jew-hatred not witnessed in recent times. He was the universal enemy of mankind, the great Satan. He came in many forms and under different mantles but always remained elusive: communism, plutocratic capitalism, democracy, and the parliamentary system – and among die-hard Nazis, even

Christianity – were seen as nothing other than a Jewish front to achieve world domination. World Jewry was believed to be currently at the helm of a worldwide conspiracy against Germany. The Nazis propagated the belief that it was not the Jews but the Germans who were the real victims. It is instructive to see in this regard Hitler's Reichstag speech of January 30, 1939, and his Political Testament of April 29, 1945, in which the Jews are blamed for egging the nations of the world to a crusade against Germany. It is no wonder that earlier-held prejudices now became translated into a self-defensive crusade to save the Aryan race from a demonic force, a struggle where no holds were to be barred. This apocalyptic thought pattern undoubtedly affected the thinking and behavior of wide strata of the German population, but not necessarily the majority. Yehuda Bauer has noted that one tremendous success of the Nazis was to draw the elite toward them, not because they identified with the Nazis, but because of the common, and general, search for Utopia.[2]

John Weiss, writing independently from Daniel Goldhagen on the origins of Nazi antisemitism, arrived at a surprisingly similar conclusion: what we term "eliminationist," or a radical form of antisemitism, indeed became part and parcel of the German elite at the end of the Wilhelmine Reich – including academia. Goldhagen also underlined the voluntary nature of behavior of the perpetrators, which included Germans from many walks of life, including killing and torturing beyond the call of duty. Weiss's explanation is that antisemitism was an expression of a collective national will; Germans killed Jews because they believed that they were guilty and deserved to be destroyed They had internalized a demonic image of the Jew, which factored in the general wish to do away with them, in one way or another, either by forced expulsion or physical liquidation – first, from Germany proper, the homeland of the so-called Aryan races, then from the rest of Europe. In other words, the Holocaust was an explosion waiting to happen.[3]

Some of the rejoinders to this apocalyptic imagery (not by Hitler but by the German people) was to point out the high intermarriage rate between Jews and non-Jews just previous to the Nazi takeover, as a sign that antisemitism was not really endemic in the population. Moreover, in all free elections, and even in the Nazi-controlled last election of April 1933, the Nazis failed to poll a majority of votes, and a year previously, in the second elections of 1932, the Nazis lost many seats in the Parliament. This, however, cannot be construed as an indication of the strength of antisemitism in the country, as antisemitic sentiments of one form or another were shared by various political parties other than the Nazis. Even the less radical, the antisemites of the old school, wished to see the Jews removed from German soil – witness the antisemitic opinions among the anti-Hitler conspirators of 1944. So statistics about the votes in the Reichstag do not tell us everything we ought to know about the spread and impact of antisemitic ideas.

As also pointed out by David Bankier, Nazi propaganda did not fully captivate the minds and thinking of large segments of the population. As the prospects of victory dimmed, especially from 1942 onward, which corresponds to the Holocaust crescendo, growing numbers of people silently became disaffected with the regime. So, while most people supported the policy of ridding the country of Jews, only a minority favored what Bankier terms the regime's "aggressive antisemitic policy," that is, the actual killing of Jews. Antisemitism was indeed rampant in German society even before the Nazi radical anti-Jewish input, and most people favored the exclusion of Jews in one way or another; but this fell short of supporting the mass murder of Jews as a solution to the presence of Jews, and the public withheld its support from it, although preferring not to display such opposition in public. This, at least, according to Bankier, was the position of most Germans with regard to the Jewish question.[4]

It has also been noted that there was no tradition in German thinking for the protection of minority groups. Even the Confessing Church, which was opposed to the Nazis, claimed that the State had the right to enact laws vis-a-vis minority groups as it saw fit. Moreover, the idea of the individual person questioning the legitimacy of actions by the State did not figure much in German philosophical thinking. Quite otherwise – most saw the State as the repository of law and order; it was to be obeyed, no matter what. So it may not only be a question of antisemitism, but of a collective mentality that made it difficult to criticize the Nazi state. Things were accepted as long as they were done within the framework of the law. This is borne out by the events of Kristallnacht. There was a condemnation of the disorder and senseless destruction. But when the Jews were taken to the camps, this was perceived as not disturbing since it was done in an orderly fashion and was a right reserved by the State.

The antisemitism, however, absorbed by millions of Germans during the Nazi rule was of a most vicious and vitriolic nature, which helped reinforce the traditional viewpoint of the Jews as a malignant and undesirable presence that could no longer be tolerated in the country. How, then, under these unpromising circumstances, was it be possible for people to even consider extending aid to Jews, let alone risking their own lives in that endeavor?[5] In the light of all this, how are we to explain the phenomenon of some Germans risking their lives and safety in the attempt to rescue Jews from their own government? Were they the small and insignificant exceptions to the rule? To try to answer this question, let us first examine the results of our findings.

Clearly, help to Jews was possible, even in Nazi Germany, as the record in this study illustrates. At the same time, the Nazi killing machine was too efficient and all-encompassing for individual persons to have made too much of a difference. But a greater involvement by many more people may have put a dent in the casualty rate. On the other hand, one must also bear in mind that most Germans did not experience that face-to-face encounter with a destitute Jew on the run, which would have presented them with the challenge to try to help, as with those examined in this study. At the same time, only a fraction of Germans who did experience such an encounter made the decision to help.

One will never know whether a public condemnation of the anti-Jewish measures from the pulpit by a venerable churchman, such as that made by the Münster bishop Clemens von Galen on the euthanasia issue, would have carried weight with top Nazi brass. In the euthanasia case, Hitler ordered a temporary suspension of the program until the war's end. Perhaps the anti-Jewish campaign, while not fully stopped, would have been reduced and assumed a less deadly form. We shall never know, for no high church dignitary publicly condemned the anti-Jewish measures. The Vatican too remained silent throughout the war years.

Even if one does not accept Goldhagen's reductionist explanation of a deadly antisemitic "eliminationist" drive within the German people as the root cause of the Final Solution, it is clear from all serious researches in this field that antisemitism of one sort or another had infested practically all strata of German society, from right to left, blue to white collar. In a country where Jews were depicted as the greatest enemy of the German people, as the ones responsible for the war and all its travails, it is a wonder that in this mass hysterical atmosphere there were to be found even people numbering close to 700 (587 for Germany and 107 for Austria) identified by January 1, 2016, as bearers of the Righteous title, and others who also aided but were not awarded that honor, as well as still unknown others whose rescue stories did not come to light. It is a wonder there were persons able to withstand the continuous poisonous propaganda, and capable of even considering extending aid to a Jewish person, let alone actually translating it into action.

Let us not forget that the rescuers had not decided on that course because of an ideological commitment to altruism. They were minding their business, so to speak, and then there either was a knock on the door, as in the stories of Erna Härtel, or a close encounter as with Dorothea Neff, as they stood face to face with a person whose only wish was not to be bodily hurt by the country's regime, for no other offense than simply of having been born. Arno Bach was on his way to cut trees when he met several Jews on the run asking to be allowed to live on. Hans Georg Calmeyer, Hermann Graebe, and Alfred Rossner, who wound up saving hundreds of Jews, at first simply thought of carrying out their specific assignments to the best of their ability before realizing that in their stations they had to play God in the best sense of the term. In going to conquered Poland, Oskar Schindler thought principally of enriching himself at the expense of the cheap labor available there. These not originally altruistically inclined persons were then suddenly confronted with the overwhelming catastrophe of the Jewish people, as a direct result of their own government's anti-Jewish policies, and a transformation took place in their thoughts and actions. They had decided to become rescuers.

Do they represent isolated cases, the exceptions to the rule, which only prove and reinforce the rule – that the majority of Germans supported a radical form of antisemitic persecutions? If so, what led the Germans in this study to act so differently from the larger group? Is it, perhaps, because the men and women in this study were not locked in tight-knit fool-proof Agentic State situations (as suggested by Milgram's study), as were the men of Christopher Browning's Police Reserve Battalion 101 (who curiously came from a city known for its support of socialist causes during the pre-Nazi era)? The rescuers in our study had some room to experiment and maneuver. They could explore and rediscover a humanity that is perhaps, after all, inherently humane, though not always actively so.

Some of the rescuers may even at some time have sympathized with the broad outlines of the political and social policies of the new regime; they may have favored a dominant and aggressive position for Germany on the continent and an autocratic regime at home. Some may have been in favor of some form of discrimination against Jews, but they were against murder.

Those who responded in the affirmative were able to see the human person and his needs before them – not the incessant, Nazi-drummed portrayal of the "demonic subhuman Jew."

To be able to identify with the suffering Jew was no mean achievement in the highly charged anti-Jewish atmosphere of Nazi Germany, where the Jew was ousted from the human species. The effects of this propaganda were telling even on good-minded people. The Quaker-affiliated Elisabeth Abegg, of Berlin, mentioned in an earlier chapter, confided to a friend: "Do you know, Gisela, one cannot perceive how much evil Nazism brought with it. I am, after all, a convinced opponent of this regime and am not easily swayed. Nevertheless, when I previously walked the streets, I saw persons about me without making any distinctions about them. When I now walk the streets, I see different types of persons. I say to myself, this man looks Jewish, poor fellow."[6] To be able to see the Jew as a fellow human being, having equal inalienable rights to life and happiness, and relate to him accordingly (the authentic I-Thou relationship, in Martin Buber's philosophy), was a perception that most Germans during the Nazi period were not able to have and retain. Hence, the greater significance of those few who did retain the idea of the brotherhood of all mankind.

For this attribute, however, to be triggered into action, it has to be aroused by outside irritants and special circumstances, usually of an emergency nature. Actress Dorothea Neff, in Vienna, could save but one person, but it lasted for a full three-and-a-half years, from the start of the deportations in Vienna in October 1941 to the fall of the city to the Russians in April 1945. Duckwitz, by a timely "blowing of the whistle," was instrumental in saving over 7,000 Danish Jews. Supervisors of Jewish forced workers continuously stretched labor time limits so as to keep their Jewish laborers working in war-related industries. Only an Oskar Schindler was able to go even beyond this and keep his Jewish laborers safe until the end of the war. But not everyone was cut out to be a Schindler and to possess the special personal traits (laudable during the Holocaust years; not so, under normal circumstances) to make it possible to succeed in such a superhuman endeavor. At the same time, if a card-carrying Nazi such as Oskar Schindler, initially thinking only of his own pleasure and self-gratification, could be transformed into a humanitarian par excellence, then this points to what could have been achieved by others, perhaps on a less audacious scale.

The story of the rescuers in this study (including also the many more stories appearing in the footnotes; see Sources section) is a vindication of the Judeo-Christian ethos of man as potentially a moral being who can do wonders, even under the most trying circumstances. What needs to be constantly emphasized is that goodness is as mysterious and inherently human as the other less salutary traits in human behavior, and man's potentiality for goodness is as promising as his more celebrated (and to a great extent socially conditioned) propensity for aggressive behavior. The Holocaust was a government-orchestrated orgy of mass murder on an unprecedented scale. But here and there, sparks of light kept the vision of man's humanity alive in this awesome darkness. The German persons portrayed in this study each, in their own measure, partook of these shining lights. These spark of lights, even in their diminished numbers, strengthen our belief and hope that man can indeed act differently and more humanely than the record of the Holocaust testifies, and this hope is what makes life worth living.

APPENDIX A
THE RIGHTEOUS TITLE
AND ITS CRITERIA

∗   ∗   ∗

As ALLUDED TO IN THE introduction, not all who participated in the rescue of Jews are necessarily awarded the title of "Righteous Among the Nations" by Yad Vashem. This program, initiated in 1963, was designed to honor rescuers who met certain criteria, which are prescribed by a special commission. These include the following: (a) that the rescuer was fully aware that he/she was placing his or her life and freedom in jeopardy in the attempt (successful or not) to save at least one Jewish person, without in any way being able to "pass the buck" to others; (b) that such help was not preconditioned by the promise of a substantial reward of money or in kind, or motivated by other considerations, save the rescue of the Jewish person; (c) that the initiator of the rescue operation was not part of an organization or agency that was directly implicated in harm to Jews (such as the German SS), and that the rescuer was not at any time implicated in causing harm to Jews or other innocent persons; (d) that as far as we can ascertain, we are dealing with a rescuer who was definitely non-Jewish, and of a rescued person who was definitely Jewish at the time in question; and (e) that evidence exists in the form of testimonies by the beneficiary party and/or of other incontestable documentary and archival evidence to substantiate the rescue story. These criteria were set by a special public commission, the Commission for the Designation of the Righteous, which is chaired by either a functioning or retired Israeli Supreme Court Justice.

There are, of course, many rescue stories that do not fit this prescribed model. Not a few rescuers took money above and beyond the amount needed

for the success of the rescue operation. There were also Nazis and other officials in well-positioned places who saved some Jews but caused harm to others,
and rescuers who saved persons who, although considered Jews by Nazi racial
definition, had left the Jewish fold before the rise of the Nazis to power, or
were born as non-Jews but had Jewish grandparents. The Commission's position was that persons who saved Jews who had freely and without constraint
converted to another religion before the start of Nazi persecutions certainly
deserve praise and recognition, since they risked their lives to aid persons persecuted by the Nazis because of their Jewish origins, but that this did not necessarily obligate the Jewish people to honor such a person. That being so, the
Commission felt that the Yad Vashem Righteous program, which is rooted in
the Israeli civil (not religious) law, was created to cite non-Jews who specifically
rescued persons (religious or not) who still considered themselves part and parcel of the Jewish fold at the time of the rescue operation, irrespective of whether
these persons were observant Jews or not – as long as they had not freely elected
to leave the Jewish fold. An additional reason for withholding recognition to
someone who rescued a baptized Jew was whether such a rescuer would have
equally extended his/her charitable aid to someone still Jewish – not merely to
a person who had severed all connections with his Jewish past and gone over
to another non-Jewish religious association to which the rescuer also belonged.
Not all Commission members are of the same opinion on this issue, and some
hold that anyone saving a person whom the Nazis considered Jewish, whether
or not that person agreed to this definition, merited the Righteous title. In this
chapter, we will cover some of these issues and attempt to explain to the reader
the considerations that led a majority of Commission members to decide this
or that way. Throughout its over-50-year existence, the Commission tried to
be consistent with previously established precedents and act in accordance with
what most Commission members perceived was the intent of the originators of
the Righteous program. But opinions differed on this point, leading to spirited
debates, with decisions made in special sessions by a majority vote of the 20–25
commission members usually present at these hearings.

a) Were Part of the System

As the reader will recall, Hans von Dohnányi, who worked for the Abwehr
(military intelligence) devised a plan for the rescue of a small group of Jews

(some of whom had left the Jewish fold) by moving them to Switzerland under the guise of counter-intelligence agents – in an operation code-named U-7. As the story unfolded, it became apparent that not only did this operation have the backing of Admiral Wilhelm Canaris, the powerful head (at the time) of the Abwehr, but that he himself was implicated in this rescue operation when he added several of his wife's Jewish friends to Dohnányi's list and simultaneously sought the silent support of SS chief Himmler. This then was not a rescue operation devised and carried out solely by von Dohnányi (an anti-Nazi, and at the same time a highly placed official in the Abwehr), but one involving top-echelon Abwehr officials. If von Dohnányi were to be awarded the Righteous title, could not a similar argument be made for Canaris, who was associated in this operation to the same extent as von Dohnányi – thereby raising the specter of the Jewish State of Israel honoring Nazi Germany's chief military intelligence officer whose agents were also implicated in various anti-Jewish brutal measures in the occupied East European countries? This would certainly be an absurdity. As for von Dohnányi's arrest in 1944 – this stemmed mainly from his entanglement in the anti-Hitler conspiracy, not the 1942 rescue operation. Had von Dohnányi acted alone, the case for his inclusion among the Righteous would have been much stronger, but this was rather an "inside" job, planned and carried out to its minutest details by the organization, which was no other than the Abwehr. Originally declining the Righteous title for von Dohnányi, due largely to the "organizational" nature of this daring rescue operation, several years later, the Commission reversed itself and, impressed by von Dohnányi as the prime mover and principal activist in the rescue of over a dozen persons – some fully Jewish, others only partly so – decided to award him, and him alone among other Abwehr conspirators of this rescue operation, the Righteous title.[1]

The Commission also was painfully troubled in the matter of Hans Walz, but from a different perspective. During the 1930s, when Walz headed the Bosch company in Stuttgart, he helped a group of seventeen Jews from Württemburg with money, making it thus also possible for them to leave for France in time. He also funneled secret funds to the Jewish community in Stuttgart, recipients of which included Dr. Leo Baeck, an important religious figure of German Jewry. With the consent of his boss, Robert Bosch, a secret bank account was opened in Amsterdam to help former Jewish employees of the firm to start a new life there. For all this, he was awarded the Righteous title in 1969. However, after his death in 1974, new information surfaced in which it turned out that not only was Walz a member of the Nazi party, he was even an officer (*Hauptsturmführer*) in the SS and very close to a group of people who raised funds to promote SS programs (such as SS housing retreats in the Stuttgart region). At the same time, a close investigation of the documentation revealed that Walz's SS rank was merely honorific, and he never donned the SS uniform to which he was entitled and hardly attended SS meetings. SS documents from April 1943 also revealed a growing frustration with Walz's anti-Nazi behavior, and discussions were underway whether to expel Walz from the SS because of his lack of enthusiasm for the SS ideology, his former pro-Jewish stance, and his close involvement in church affairs. Interestingly, Walz was close to Carl Friedrich Goerdeler, a main ringleader in the anti-Hitler conspiracy, whom he met in his Walz's home, on the eve of the July 20th aborted coup. In the event of success, Walz was to assume an important economic post in the new government. In 1976, the Commission felt there was no justification for revoking Walz's nomination to the Righteous title. Walz could not be considered an accomplice in the destruction machine, and his SS honorary title did not justify the cancellation of the Righteous title that he merited for his help to Jews in previous years, before the start of the war. However, doubts continued to linger. Whether Walz would have earned the Righteous title had his involvement with top SS brass been known to the Commission earlier, in 1969, before this revelation, remained an open question.[2]

In the case of Walter Czok, mentioned in chapter one, who sheltered a Jewish couple in his Vienna home and helped several other Jews and "half" Jews – he was not only a member in the Nazi party since 1930, but was also a Stormtrooper (SA - *Sturmabteilung*) from 1933 until the end of the war. Czok stated in his defense that he did mostly administrative work in that Nazi organization. After the war, he moved to Berlin, and sought recognition within the framework of the *Unbesungenen Helden* (Unsung Heroes) program by the Berlin Senate for persons having helped mostly Jewish persons persecuted by the Nazi regime (as further explained in Appendix B), but this was denied him. He then petitioned Yad Vashem for recognition. Such an honor would have helped him benefit from pension restitutions, which he sought at the time. The Commission declined this request. It was felt that being a member in good standing in a Nazi voluntary paramilitary unit cancelled his other meritorious deeds on behalf of some Jews, and that it would not be becoming of a Jewish national Holocaust memorial to honor a Stormtrooper who remained at his post until the war's end. Here, it could be argued, the man was, by his own free choice and not through constraint, an integral part of a hardcore Nazi unit.[3]

B) SAVED BUT ALSO HARMED

What was the Commission's ruling with regard to persons who saved some Jews but simultaneously also caused harm to other Jews during the Holocaust? Can such ostensibly contradictory behavior be acceptable, and could such persons be recognized as Righteous? Even in the matter of Oskar Schindler, when his name first came up for consideration, the Commission declined to honor him with the Righteous title although he had already planted a tree at Yad Vashem a year before the Commission came into existence. His membership in the Nazi party, coupled with his takeover of Jewish property in Nazi-occupied Kraków, is what troubled the Commission. It took thirty years for the Commission to reverse its stand, coincidentally with Steven Spielberg's film of the Schindler story, and award Schindler (posthumously) the full Righteous title. The large number of Jews saved by him over an extended period of time undoubtedly played a role in the final verdict – but it was not smooth sailing from the start.

It needs to be pointed out that mere membership in the Nazi party does not automatically disqualify someone from bearing the Righteous title, if such membership did not accrue to any harm to Jews. What we have in mind is quite paradoxically cases of persons who saved someone they knew from years before, or to whom they had become particularly attached, yet at the same went about their assigned task of rounding up Jews, or even worse. The general rule of thumb by the Commission is that anyone directly involved in causing harm to Jews or other innocent persons could not merit the Righteous title, even if he saved others at the risk of his own life. Having one's hands tainted with innocent blood annulled a person's claim to the title of "Righteous Among the Nations," even if his role was that of an accomplice, a cog in a larger murder machine. But how far was one to stretch this point? Would this also apply to a government official who otherwise shuffled papers and at the same time risked his life to save Jews? The answer to this depended on several factors: the importance of the man's job in the overall bureaucracy, whether he was directly involved in the execution of the Final Solution, and the number of persons saved.

The case of Alfons Zündler seemed at first sight intractable, but as more evidence poured in, it was clear where the decision would fall. As a Waffen-SS guard, he was part of an SS team guarding thousands of Jews who were taken to the former Dutch Theater in Amsterdam before their transfer to the giant Westerbork camp. From there, they were to be sent to either Auschwitz or Sobibór concentration camps, where most perished. About a dozen witnesses testified that Zündler released them, asking nothing in return. Other witnesses stated that he exacted sexual and other favors from those he helped (not necessarily those who testified on his behalf). More damaging to his case was evidence that he participated in raids on Jews, directing them to either the train station or the Dutch Theater. In May 1943, he and several other SS guards were arraigned before an SS court on charges of participating in a birthday party, which turned into a sort of orgy, and during which a semi-clad Jewish woman prisoner was made to dance before them. His death sentence by an SS court for the sin of "race pollution" (*rassenschande*) was commuted to a long term of prison, in view of a previous wound sustained on the Russian front. The Commission declined to award him the Righteous title for his help to those (some claim it amounted to several dozen) he freed. The major reason was not his cavorting with Jewish prisoner women, but the suspicion that their release was preconditioned by their forced submission to him. Also, the fact of his participation in the forcible roundup of Jews (even if his heart was not in it since he was ordered to do it) and guarding them until their deportation to the Westerbork camp, did not add merit in his favor. This made him, not a mere accomplice, but a prime participant of the Nazi destruction machine, and such a person could not, in the Commission's eyes, be the recipient of Israel's highest honor awarded to non-Jews. Those aided by him could, of course, in the Commission's eyes personally hold him in high esteem – but not an institution representing the Jewish State.[4]

In the case of Willi Friedrichs, a tragic postwar twist also caused the Commission to withhold the Righteous title to the man, although during the war he sheltered six Jews in his home in Brest-Litovsk, today in Belarus, where he worked as an auto mechanic for the Todt organization. He was by no means a Nazi, and his hands were not sullied with Jewish blood, but after the war, while out of a job and in desperate need of money, he decided to rob at gunpoint a bank clerk. A scuffle ensued during which Friedrich's revolver accidentally went off, killing the clerk. His original life sentence was reduced to eighteen years, and he was released in 1968. In order to help him with a new start in life, one of his beneficiaries asked Yad Vashem to award him the Righteous title for his rescue action during the war. The Commission declined the request, arguing that the Righteous title would not be fitting for a person who wrongfully caused the loss of an innocent life – even if it occurred not during the Holocaust but at a later period. At the same time, the Commission agreed to issue a letter of appreciation, spelling out Friedrichs's humanitarian aid to Jews during the war and thanking him for this – but not the Righteous title. One of the persons saved by him disagreed strongly with the non-recognition decision, and she invited him to visit Israel and plant a tree in her kibbutz, with the approval of her kibbutz elders.[5]

Would the same principle also apply to persons not directly involved in the Nazi Final Solution of the Jewish people, nor tainted with any innocent blood on their hands but holding senior positions in a German-occupied country, with a mandate to adjudicate questions dealing with the deportation of Jews? Here, after long debates, the decision was postponed until further clarifications could be made. In practice, the case was shelved and no longer dealt with. As the reader recalls, Major Wilhelm von Hahn served as special advisor on Jewish affairs to the German commanding general in Belgium, and in that capacity he tried as best as possible to help free Jews from deportation. His efforts were mainly limited to cases where Jews could produce foreign passports or show proof (authentic or not) of Belgian nationality. Belgium-naturalized Jews were not harmed until September 1943, per agreement between Queen Mother Elizabeth and Nazi Germany. Some of his methods were clearly unorthodox, such as advising a person how to spar with the Gestapo to avoid arrest and gain time, or seeking bureaucratic excuses for delaying the deportation of a particular person. Although he had no final authority on these matters (he was only an advisor), he managed to get around the system and get his way.

The Commission's debate on the man's merits was spirited. Some claimed that as a special counsel on Jewish affairs, von Hahn was part of the destruction machine. But others countered that he did not decide on deportations and did not draw up lists of deportees to the camps, since this was left to others who were responsible to Eichmann's operation, not the German military governor. Opponents responded that he held a high position in a department that had some say in specific deportation cases, and in this case he linked up with Eichmann's separate administrative apparatus. Those in favor of the man rejoined that von Hahn tried to save as many as he could, within the limits of his authority, at times jeopardizing himself in these endeavors. Opponents pointed out that Eichmann's 4b4 section of the RSHA (the central Nazi state security agency) was itself a subsidiary of the Belgian military government, as were similar departments in other oc-cupied countries that were headed by military administrations. As for the risks, these were minimal; at the worst, he would have been removed and sent to join others to fight on the Russian front. Two questions troubled the Commission's mind, which were not satisfactorily resolved: whether any person affiliated with a bureau that dealt with the deportation of Jews, even in an indirect manner, could possibly qualify for the Righteous title? And what sort of risks did the man face when he contrived the most liberal interpretations in certain doubtful cases concerning a person's eligibility to be deported or not. Moreover, were not those removed from the deporta-tion list due to his intervention replaced by others, since the fixed contin-gent assigned to each transport had to be filled so, statistically speaking, no Jews were saved? The Commission could not resolve these two matters, and decided not to decide, shelving the case for a future additional debate. In fact, no further action was taken, leaving von Hahn with no final decision on his merit to the Righteous title.[6]

These questions surfaced again, with renewed vigor, in the debate of Hans Georg Calmeyer. As previously described at considerable length, Calmeyer was assigned to deal with doubtful racial cases in the Administration and Justice Department of the occupied Netherlands. As the Dutch were held to be a pure Germanic tribe, the Nazis were anxious to cleanse it of non-Aryan blood as fast as possible before the planned induction of the country into the Greater Germanic Reich. This raised the question of what to do with persons of mixed blood, but with a "healthy" dose of Aryan blood. Calmeyer decided to exploit the uncertainty surrounding such racial questions and subvert its original intent by finding legal loopholes to allow him to declare "full" Jews as only "semi" Jews, or fully Aryan, and thereby exempted from deportation. Whereas in Germany only Hitler could make such reclassification decisions, in the Netherlands, Calmeyer asked for and was granted sole authority on similar cases – much to the chagrin of high SS officials. The word went out that Calmeyer was willing to stretch to the limit his acceptance of doubtful documents in order to prove that one was not a full Jew – perhaps even more

Aryan than Jewish. He employed clearly unorthodox and illegal methods, in collusion with Dutch attorneys who provided him documents with false information concerning a person's true origin. Calmeyer was able to save close to 2,900 Jews, and those on "Calmeyer's List" survived the Holocaust. Nothing was asked in return. As stated by Calmeyer after the war, he tried to save as many as he could, and in the interest of his operation, he was also forced to reject many applicants. In the opinion of one historian, Calmeyer was skating on exceedingly thin ice, and his personal freedom and security were not without risks.

Calmeyer's acceptance into the ranks of the Righteous did not go through smoothly. Opponents in the Commission argued that Calmeyer's very placement inside Nazi governor Arthur Seyss-Inquart's administration (a die-hard Nazi who was hanged in Nuremberg after the war), and his role in filtering racially doubtful cases disqualified him from bearing the Righteous title. Moreover, it was claimed that those rejected by him may have wound up being deported and perishing in the camps. Those favoring his inclusion countered that he exploited his high position in order to subvert the very intentions of the Nazis – to save rather than destroy inasmuch as he could. In this very risky operation, he had to reject many applicants in order to cover his tracks and use this as a weapon against those wishing to scuttle the whole operation and reveal the spurious nature of his work. In addition, the very number of persons saved should also be taken into consideration. The personal risks for Calmeyer were clearly much greater than for von Hahn, as top SS officers sought various approaches to unmask and indict the man. Calmeyer's further attempts to save special-category Jews, such as the Portuguese Jews, was a clear indication of the man's commitment to a consistent rescue policy, not to incidental rescue efforts as was the case with von Hahn. These considerations finally led a majority of commission members to vote for Calmeyer's inclusion within the ranks of the Righteous.[7]

Finally, Wilm Hosenfeld was a German military officer in occupied Warsaw, who in late 1944 and early 1945 accidentally ran into Władysław Szpylman, a famous Polish-Jewish pianist, in his hiding place in the ruins of a building in a city systematically leveled by the Germans when they reduced Warsaw to rubble in suppressing a Polish uprising. At first, unsure what to do with this man, Hosenfeld took a strong liking to Szpylman's rendition of a Chopin piece on an abandoned piano. This led Hosenfeld to help Szpylman with food, a coat, and words of encouragement. Hosenfeld was later taken captive by Russians, tried for war crimes (related to the interrogation of Polish prisoners during the 1944 uprising, when as a major he served as an aide-de-camp in the German command), and died in captivity. Testimonies were also received of his help to several other Poles. In his letters home from Warsaw he condemned the brutal German treatment of the Polish population, although he justified the occupation itself and had a good opinion of Hitler. Leading Holocaust historian Yehuda Bauer felt that the man deserved to be recognized, for if Schindler, an unrepentant trickster, Nazi Party member, and spy for the German intelligence, was recognized, certainly the more well-behaved and courteous Hosenfeld merited the Righteous distinction, although he too was a Nazi party member and previously also in the Nazi SA (Stormtroopers). One may counter this argument by pointing out the huge difference between these two persons: one who saved 1,200 lives (Schindler) as contrasted to the other who saved a single life (Hosenfeld). Those opposed to Hosenfeld's recognition pointed out that during his four-year military tenure in Warsaw, he steadily rose in ranks and is not known to have been involved in any rescue attempts of Jews during the terrible period for Warsaw Jews, except for this single rescue episode, in a city already bereft of Jews and its own inhabitants. The initial decision was to decline recognition. Here too, the Commission reversed itself and, based upon appeal by the relatives of Szpylman and non-Jewish Poles who also benefited from his aid, it decided to award him posthumously the Righteous title.[8]

c) WORK ADMINISTRATORS AND TRUSTEES (*TREUHÄNDER*)

Another issue dealt by the Commission for the Designation of the Righteous was how to relate to German civilians who operated or administered industrial facilities in the occupied countries in which many Jews were employed – especially in cases when they acted above and beyond their mandate in order to save their Jewish workers. The argument could be made that what really motivated them was the smooth operation of their business, and easy profits, through the use of cheap Jewish forced labor. Hence, they were principally guided by the incentive to hold on to these workers for as long as possible, and by derivation save them from death. But, argued others, things were really not as simple as that, and some entrepreneurs exerted themselves greatly to save their Jews from Nazi execution squads, without regard to their firm's profits.

As earlier told, Berthold Beitz headed the oil producing company *Karpatenöl A.G.* in Boryslaw, Poland, in which he employed over a thousand Jews from the nearby ghetto. He cared for their needs and was able to free them from deportation until his plant was closed in spring 1944 due to the approaching Russian army. Most of his workers were transferred to Płaszów camp, near Kraków; others, he aided in making good their escape. The debate in the Commission dealt mainly with the risks involved for Beitz in protecting his Jewish workers, contrasted with the self-serving interest in maintaining reliable workers for his plant's operation. Opinions were divided, with some emphasizing the crucial importance of oil production for the German war industry, hence the need for these workers, with others pointing to the many unqualified Jewish workers for this type of work who were kept by Beitz – most with a background as merchants and traders, or, in the case of many women workers, little more experience than doing household chores. A few of his former workers who declined to support his nomination to the Righteous title claimed that his help was linked to favors in the form of gifts he received from those he saved – a charge that could not be sustained. A bit more damaging to Beitz's record was his postwar testimony in favor of SS commander Fritz Hildebrand at his trial, where Beitz claimed that Hildebrand, otherwise implicated in the deportation of Jews to the Bełżec death camp, "closed his eyes" and overlooked the hiring by Beitz of unqualified workers for the oil-refining industry. In the end, the fact that he exerted himself to remove from the deportation trains to the death camps some of his workers, as well as hiding others during SS raids or encouraging them to flee before arrest, prompted commission members to overcome their original hesitancy and consider his case in a favorable light, and by a majority vote, Beitz was added to the list of the Righteous. The saving of not merely a few but of over one thousand persons for a long period – in fact until late in the war – tipped the scales in the man's favor.[9]

The same consideration applied in the case of Julius Madritsch. He was the trustee, then the owner, of a textile firm (which had formerly belonged to Jews) in Kraków, Poland, which manufactured uniforms for the German army. Like Beitz, he employed a large number of Jews, running in the several thousands, of which only about a third could be considered professionally qualified. While profit was surely an important incentive, other considerations came to the fore, all related to saving as many Jews in his shops as possible. As with Beitz, his plant (which after the liquidation of the Kraków ghetto in March 1943 was relocated inside Płaszów camp) was closed in 1944 and most of his workers were sent to others camps. He had tried to save his many Jewish workers as long as he could and was personally involved in several rescue operations. The scales tipped in his favor as well, and he was duly recognized.[10]

Such was also the case for Alfred Rossner, in Będzin, Poland. Profit may have been his original motivation, but he then literally exhausted himself in order to save his several thousand Jewish workers – unfortunately without much success. This was probably a factor in his undoing, as he was executed after a short trial in January 1944. As earlier related, Rossner was appointed trustee over two formerly Jewish-owned firms, which produced and repaired uniforms and army boots, and in that he capacity he employed thousands of Jews from the city's ghetto. Eyewitnesses testified not only to Rossner's especial care for his workers, but to his personal involvement in various rescue efforts, most of which failed, as the Nazis systematically clipped his work force from thousands to a bare several hundred. He constantly sought ways to fend for his Jews: he allowed them to build shelters on factory grounds, and financed the escape of others across guarded frontiers to Hungary and Romania. As told by Henrietta Altman, Rossner "had to maintain very good relations with them [the SS], in order to get a lot of work from them [for his Jewish laborers]. There is no doubt he lavishly entertained them and gener- ously bribed them. . . . It was a typical Catch-22 situation. The workshop, which belonged to the SS and was managed by a non-SS, was saving Jews from deportation, making them 'essentials' to the war economy. The same SS demanded from the Judenrat 'delivery' of Jews, which the Judenrat was unable to meet, because they were protected by working for Rossner!" If he also derived a personal profit as a result of his commanding position in the two firms under his responsibility (90 watches were found in his home during his arrest in late 1943), all witnesses lauded his selfless efforts to try to save them in whatever ways possible. His tragic death at the hands of the Nazis also gave impetus to those claiming he was Righteous, and the Commission acted accordingly.[11]

Slightly to the east of Bedzin, in Kraków, when the legendary Oskar Schindler first appeared on the scene, he at first also thought mainly in terms of personal gain at the expense of the cheap Jewish labor on hand. To the surprise of many recent observers, especially since the successful Hollywood film about the man, his inclusion among the Righteous did not come off easily. It seems that in the early phase of his wheeling and dealing in Kraków, during 1939–1942, he was not beyond using rough tactics against Jewish industrialists who stood in his way. During the hearings by the Commission in 1963 on Schindler's candidacy to the Righteous title, two former Jewish businessmen testified how they were brutalized by Schindler when they refused to sell their firms to him. Opinions in the Commission were divided, and some heated debates ensued. On the one hand, Schindler personally initiated a rescue operation, unique in its scope, length of time, and number of people saved. If, at the start of his business venture in occupied-Poland, he derived great profits from his enamelware factory in Kraków, allowing him the extravagant lifestyle that he so much craved, he later wasted his money in the sole endeavor to rescue his Jewish workers and their families. Here too, most of his workers were far from qualified for the specialized enamelware production, let alone for the so-called ammunition factory that he later set up in Brünnlitz, Moravia, and to where he moved 1,100 of his Jewish wards. One may add the 100 destitute, stranded persons from emptied Golleschau camp that he placed under his protection, and who were anything but fit for any kind of labor. On the other hand, doubts lingered among Commission members because of Schindler's boorish behavior in the early phase of his presence in Kraków. In 1963, the Commission followed a more hardline approach when dealing with German rescuers, and this led it to decline formally awarding Schindler the Righteous title, but only to acknowledge his rescue deeds in a written letter to him. This was corrected many years later in 1993, when full recognition was awarded him – quite late for him, as he was no longer among the living. That same year, his still-living wife, Emilie, who was active in the Brünnlitz phase of the rescue operation, was also given the Righteous title.[11]

The commission found it equally difficult to adjudicate the case of Karl Plagge. He was a major in the German army, assigned to a military motor vehicle repair workshop (HKP) in occupied Vilnius, with Jewish laborers from the nearby ghetto. In September 1943, when the ghetto was liquidated, the last 3,000 residents were spared. Half were assigned work in a fur-producing firm (*Kailis*) for the German army, and about 1,500 in Plagge's HKP workshop. These included 449 men, 554 women, and 190 children – for Plagge had asked that whole families be allowed to stay together, so that the working

men would be better motivated on their job. His workforce included men
with no professional experience in vehicle repair, such as former barbers,
shoemakers, and cooks. On one or two occasions, he also arranged medical treatment for two persons, one of whom was the mother of a youthful
worker. Yet, he could not prevent an SS raid on the children and other acts of
retribution on his site, for his workplace was guarded by over 200 troops (SS
and other), who had ultimate responsibility over these people. In June 1944,
with the approach of the Soviet Army, he gathered the workers and told them
he could no longer care for them, since the SS would take over, and added
derisively, "and as is known the SS takes care of its charges." Five hundred
persons understood the hint and went into hiding, and some 250 were able
to survive the SS hunt after them. In 1947, a denazification court ruled that
Plagge was a lower-grade *Mitlaufer* (a mere Nazi "fellow traveler") and fined
him 100 marks plus court costs of 9,000 marks. Several of his former Jewish
workers had testified in his defense.

With regard to Plagge, an otherwise good person who treated his workers well in job assignments sanctioned by the German army, the Commission
wondered where the risk had been for him. In the initial examination of this
case, the Commission ruled for only a letter of thanks. On appeal by some
of his Jewish beneficiaries, the case underwent a renewed examination. In
the end, the Commission reversed course and, bending to the appeals of
several of his former beneficiaries, decided to award the Righteous title to
this German military man – although the risk factor was clearly in doubt.
The unusually large number of Jewish workers and their families who were
under Plagge's protective umbrella for an extended period figured largely in
the Commission's positive decision.[13]

d) Help by Camp Inmate Officials

One of the unwritten rules of the Commission is that no concentration
camp staff personnel, administrative or otherwise, is eligible to receive the
Righteous title in spite of occasional help to one or several Jews. Exceptions
to this rule may be made for non-Jewish prisoners, incarcerated for political
offenses, who were then assigned administrative and supervisory functions
and were thus in a position to alleviate the sufferings of Jewish prisoners and
help them to survive. Thus, Ludwig Wörl and Hermann Langbein, interned

in Auschwitz for previous affiliation with socialist and communist movements, were awarded the Righteous title for their help to Jews in that camp, at considerable risks to themselves. As earlier recalled, for his intercession on behalf of imprisoned Jews, Wörl even found himself placed in the *Stehbunker* (a narrow cell with standing room only), which left him fully exhausted and almost blind.[14]

Similarly in Buchenwald camp, Willi Bleicher and Wilhelm Hammann held minor administrative posts and were part of a communist underground cell, and in this capacity exerted themselves to save Jewish children who arrived there from other places in Eastern Europe. Through the efforts of Bleicher and his comrades, a three-year-old Jewish boy survived the extremities of the camp. In addition, Wilhelm Hammann took special care of a group of Jewish youth by teaching them handy trades and enough German to be able to follow orders, thus bettering their chances of survival. As recounted earlier, their ages were falsified to make them appear older. In April 1945, when the SS planned the liquidation of the camp population, Hammann risked his neck to save the children in his care through the ruse of having them reregistered as non-Jewish. It could have cost him his life, but at the last moment, the SS guards gave up and fled the camp at the approach of the US Army. Hammann saved 159 lives and was awarded the Righteous title – as was equally the case for Bleicher. Some other non-Jewish camp inmates in some position of authority were also designated as Righteous for their assistance to Jewish prisoners.[15]

E) DEFIED THE SYSTEM

The Commission also took special note of Germans who may not actually have saved Jews, as required by the program's guidelines, but defied the system and protested the anti-Jewish laws of their regime. Professor Otto Krayer, who in the spring of 1933 declined a university chair made vacant by the dismissal of a Jewish professor, was not awarded the Righteous title, since no rescue action was entailed in the man's otherwise meritorious stance – although the Commission praised the man's moral courage.[16] However, when in the same year as Krayer's protest another German decided to take on Hitler directly on his antisemitic policy, the Commission acted more forthrightly. In the spring of 1933, Armin Wegner, an author of some repute, wrote a personal letter to Adolf Hitler, in which he asked him not to besmirch the honor of the German people by tainting their name with the persecution of Jews. Against the charge that the Jews, as a foreign entity, are incapable of true German patriotism, Wegner retorted: "Are not many tribes intermixed with the German people – Franks, Friesen and Wenden? . . . Have you yourself not come from a neighboring country?" He warned Hitler that the destruction of the Jews "must necessarily bring about the destruction of German property. History has taught us that countries who expelled Jews from their borders were made to suffer poverty; they became miserable and despised. . . . A hundred years after Goethe and Lessing we are returning to the most cruel suffering of all times, to blind superstition." Furthermore, "a homeland without justice cannot exist. . . . Does not a mighty nation degrade itself by abandoning helpless people to the hatred of the frustrated masses?" Finally: "I am turning to you not as a friend of the Jews but as a friend of the German people, as a descendant of a Prussian family which can trace its roots back to the days of the Crusaders; it is because I love my own people that I turn to you. Even if everyone remains silent at this hour, I do not want to keep silent in the face of the dangers threatening Germany because of that silence."

As a result of this letter, Wegner was arrested, tortured, and imprisoned in several camps. Thanks to his personal stamina and good luck, he survived the Nazi era. The Commission felt that Wegner's open defiance of the Nazi persecution of Jews from the very start, the blunt choice of words in his letter to Hitler, and the consequent sufferings imposed on him earned him the Righteous title. Here was a man who personally addressed Hitler, the highest authority in the country and the chief culprit in the anti-Jewish drive, in no uncertain terms and in pointed language took issue with him on his official antisemitic policy. Unlike Krayer, who merely declined the offer to assume a post vacated by a Jewish scientist, Wegner's protest was not prompted by any personal incident, only the tremendous moral issue that he felt was at stake and that forbade him to remain silent. Although no rescue operation was involved, Wegner's courageous attempt to stop in its tracks the Nazi onslaught on the Jews by a direct appeal to Hitler, unique in the annals of Nazi Germany, moved the Commission to award him the Righteous title.[17] The case of Ilse Sonja Totzke, from Würzburg, belongs to the same category. Her repeated declarations before Gestapo investigators that she did not countenance the Nuremberg Laws of 1935, the persecution of Jews, or the regime headed by Hitler – coupled with the failed attempt to flee the country in the company of a Jewess – eventually led her to be penalized by the Gestapo, and she was deported to Ravensbrück camp. She, too, was awarded the Righteous title.[18]

Of equal significance, in the Commission's eyes, was the behavior of the military officers Major Max Liedtke and his adjutant, Lieutenant Albert Battel. As the reader will recall, Liedtke was the garrison commander in Przemyśl, Poland, in July 1942. Learning that the SS planned a raid on the Jewish ghetto, he and Battel placed troops with orders to shoot in order to prevent the SS from carrying out the raid, on the pretext that some of the Jews were needed for Wehrmacht-assigned work details. Going so far as ordering German troops to shoot at the SS in the attempt to protect a group of Jews of a Polish-occupied city is by all accounts highly unusual, to say the least, by the standards of those days for German officers. The fact that both officers were reprimanded, and that Himmler ordered Battel to be court-martialed after the end of the war, added a touch of poignancy to the story. No known similar act of open defiance by German army officers to the persecution of Jews was recorded during World War Two, and the Commission decided that by awarding the two men the Righteous title, not only would it acquit itself of a moral obligation to both (one of whom died in Soviet captivity), but it would also call attention to the need of army officers to draw a line between permissible and clearly criminal behavior, even when ordered by superior commanders.[19]

Equally recognized was the Catholic prelate Bernhard Lichtenberg, who served as provost of the St. Hedwig Cathedral in Berlin. He stood out from the rest of the German clergy in taking a strong and unequivocal stand against Nazi antisemitism – in sharp contrast to even staunch critics of Nazi policies, such as Bishop Clemens von Galen and Pastor Martin Niemöller (whose only interest was for the baptized Jews). Lichtenberg took an outspoken stance during Kristallnacht, in November 1938, when he preached publicly from the pulpit: "Outside, the temple is in flames. That too is a worship place to God." The other church prelates kept their silence. With the start of the war, he wrote a letter asking for the cancellation of the regulation prohibiting Jews from visiting air raid shelters. The letter, mailed on September 6, 1940, remained without response. On October 23, 1941, he was arrested following a denunciation by two women who heard him praying during mass in church for the Jews – a custom he followed since Kristallnacht. During his interrogation by the Gestapo, he went on the attack. "I totally reject the 'evacuation' [i.e., deportation] with all the accompanying measures, since it stands in opposition to the Christian command of 'Love your neighbor as thyself.' And I consider the Jews also as my neighbor since they too were created in the divine image." He added, "I do not accept Hitler as a prophet sent by God," and "I declare out of inner conviction that the Nazi ideology does not accord with the teaching and command of the Catholic Church." After a two-year prison sentence, he was rearrested, beaten, and conveyed to Dachau camp. Already in declining health, he died before reaching that camp. He was sixty-seven years old. The Commission contrasted the man's outspokenness on the Jewish issue with the public silence of Pope Pius XII and decided to award him posthumously the Righteous honor. This was in line with the Commission's policy to include among the Righteous exceptional cases of persons who made a stand on the Jewish issue, with all the concomitant risks to themselves, such as in the case of the earlier-mentioned Armin Wegner – although they were not personally involved in the rescue of Jews.[20]

Similarly laudable in the eyes of the Commission was Eduard Schulte's attempt to stave off the Final Solution by making this plan public knowledge in the Allied countries through a Jewish business contact in Switzerland. Although his mission failed due to the lack of belief and proper action by Allied leaders, the Commission felt that Schulte was worthy of special merit. As a leading industrialist, he was privy to information on the planned gassing of all of Europe's Jews. He therefore made several special trips to Switzerland, ostensibly for business purposes, in order to pass on the frightful information to a Jewish business colleague, with a request to pass it on to world leaders – hoping for a robust response on their part to thwart this murderous design. Although not personally involved in the rescue of Jews, this desperate act by a German industrialist to trigger world attention to the planned destruction of the Jews, and thereby scuttle it, merited his inclusion among the Righteous.[21]

Finally, Gustav Schroeder, the German captain of the ill-fated *St. Louis*, was also recognized as Righteous. In May 1939, he sailed from Hamburg to Cuba, with over 900 Jews on board. While the ship was traversing the Atlantic Ocean, the Cuban authorities had added a further stipulation that led to the refusal to allow the passengers to disembark when the *St. Louis* docked in Havana, although the Jewish passengers were in possession of all accredited documents when the boat left Germany. Schroeder then took the boat off the coast of Miami, Florida, but here too the American authorities forbade the ship landing or visiting rights. Schroeder was forced to head back to Germany (which is what Nazi propagandists had hoped for, to give added impetus to their claim that the democracies that were flaying the Nazis for their antisemitism were themselves reluctant to admit Jews in their countries), but during the protracted voyage across the Atlantic, he began to devise plans to prevent his Jewish passengers from returning to Germany, where the concentration camps awaited them. One idea was to prolong the ship's voyage across the Atlantic, long enough to allow public opinion in the West to force the hands of their respective governments. Another plan was to scuttle the ship off the Scottish coast. This, hopefully, would force the British government's hand. As the *St. Louis* approached Europe, the US-based Joint Distribution Committee solicited the consent of England, France, Belgium, and the Netherlands to each admit an almost equal part of the stranded *St. Louis* Jews, with JDC financial support. In addition, during the voyage back to Europe, Schroeder had prevented some desperate passengers from taking their lives. Survivors testified to Schroeder's humanity and his care for the passengers. On June 14, 1939, the *St. Louis* landed at Antwerp, and all passengers disembarked and headed to the four aforementioned countries. The impact of the *St. Louis's* voyage on world public opinion, which highlighted the plight of Jewish refugees from Germany, coupled with Schroeder's initiative and well-nigh defiance in bringing about a resolution of this crisis to the benefit of the over 900 Jews on board during the long painful voyage of the St. Louis, led the Commission, after an especially spirited debate, and in view of the exceptional humanitarian nature of the boat's captain, to award him posthumously the Righteous title.[22]

f) Help to Baptized Jews

In the final topic in this chapter, we touch on a subject that has caused much misunderstanding and no little pain to the persons affected. It concerns Yad Vashem's policy vis-a-vis persons who had freely and under no constraint left the Jewish fold by the simple yet significant act of conversion to another faith and were later persecuted by the Nazis because of their Jewish origin. As a national Holocaust memorial charged with awarding honors to non-Jews for the rescue of Jews on behalf of the Jewish state, Yad Vashem found itself in the unenviable position of having to decide on a person's Jewishness insofar as the Righteous program was concerned. In this conundrum, Yad Vashem as a secular institution does not necessarily follow the Jewish religious law (the *Halacha*), which does not recognize one's departure from the Jewish fold by conversion to another religion. It is rather guided by the more secular viewpoint, which considers anyone born Jewish and a member of the Jewish people, however one interprets that membership and irrespective of whether one practices the religion or not, to still be considered as Jewish – for as long as that persons has not freely and under no constraint taken a step that has throughout Jewish history been interpreted as a severing of links with the Jewish fold, usually through conversion to another faith. Such a person, the Commission felt (although opinions were divided), although later persecuted by the Nazis, would not qualify as a Jewish rescued person for the purpose of the Righteous program. The following few examples will illustrate this complex and delicate point further.

Beate Steckhan (originally Hecht) was born into a Jewish family, but then at the age of sixteen she freely converted to Christianity – in her words, out of personal conviction. She then married the non-Jewish Fritz Steckhan, who fell in action during World War One. With the start of the Nazi persecution of Jews, she too suffered severe deprivations. A group of pastors, mostly affiliated with the Confessing Church, came to her aid. Threatened with deportation, Beate went underground, leaving Berlin and moving from place to place, mostly in the Württemberg area; she passed through 23 different homes, and mostly in the care of friendly pastors. Though appreciative of the pastors' help to this forlorn woman, the Commission declined to award the Righteous title to Mrs. Steckhan's many clerical rescuers for the reason stated above; namely, the petitioner's exit from the Jewish fold of her own free will, which was not due to any outside pressure. Some Commission members also speculated whether some of Beate's rescuers were perhaps motivated solely by the obligation to come to the aid of a fellow believer in distress, and not necessarily because of the rescued person's original Jewishness. At the same time, some of Mrs. Steckhan's clerical helpers were awarded the Righteous on the basis of help to other persons, that is, to Jews who still adhered to the Jewish community at the time in question.[23]

When a group of baptized Jews in Bremen received their deportation summons in October 1941, Elisabeth Forck, together with members of her evangelical church, St. Stephani, supplied them with warm blankets and gave them a moving farewell party in the church hall. The Gestapo reacted by arresting several of the church members, and the congregation's spiritual head, Pastor Gustav Greiffenhagen, was sent as a chaplain to the Eastern front because "he gave Jews to eat from his bread, and allowed them to drink from the same cup." Here too, the help was to baptized Jews who had left the Jewish fold not under constraint, but well before the advent of the Nazis. Instead of the Righteous title, the Commission sent Mrs. Forck a warm and thankful letter of commendation on behalf of Yad Vashem.[24]

Another similar case involved a girl, born to a Jewish father and a Christian mother, and raised in the latter's faith. In 1941, ten-year-old Hannelore Bach was sheltered by Leonhard Gailer, the mayor of Niederroth, a village in the Munich region, for the duration of the war. Here too, while appreciating the meritorious behavior of the rescuer, the Commission declined the Righteous title to the author of the rescue operation.[25] However, in the case of Father Heinrich Middendorf, the Commission acted otherwise. Beginning in the fall of 1944, he sheltered in his monastery in Stegen, near Leipzig, a Jewish woman who was married to a non-Jew, and her son. In this case, the woman had not left the Jewish fold; hence her rescuer met the criteria established for the Righteous title.[26]

The Commission similarly declined to award the Righteous title to the more illustrious and world-renowned Nazi martyr, Dietrich Bonhoeffer, a Protestant cleric praised for his uncompromising anti-Nazi stand, for which he paid the ultimate price – his life. However, when it came to the Jewish issue, Bonhoeffer's position was at best ambivalent. In a June 1933 article, he maintained the church's traditional theological anti-Jewish stance, viewing the Jews as a people "cursed" by God for having rejected Jesus and thus divinely punished with ongoing suffering, that would only end when the Jews "recant" and admit Jesus as their savior. Moreover, he even approved the initial Nazi anti-Jewish measures. His only concern was for the baptized Jews whom the Nazis wished to segregate from their fellow Christian believers. His arrest in 1943 and eventual execution in April 1945 stemmed from his opposition to the Nazi regime and were not linked to any direct involvement in favor of Jews. True enough, in 1942, when he learned that his brother-in-law, Hans von Dohnányi, an officer in the army intelligence (Abwehr), was organizing an escape group to be taken to Switzerland in the guise of spies, he asked to include Charlotte Friedenthal, a baptized Jewish person who previously held an important post in the governing body of the Confessing

Church. Otherwise, he was not involved in the rescue of Jews, nor did he retract his previous deicide charge and the supposed curse hanging over the heads of the Jews, although he was certainly opposed to the radicalization of the anti-Jewish measures by the Nazi regime, and hearing of the burning of synagogues during Kristallnacht, he was heard uttering, "Whoever does not weep for the Jews, should not sing Gregorian songs." However, to repeat, there is no record of Bonhoeffer's involvement in trying to help non-baptized Jews. Bonhoeffer's case was supported by a distinguished list of scholars, who urged his nomination to the Righteous title due to his uncompromising anti-Nazi stance, and also as a tool to help cement a better dialogue between Judaism and Christianity. For the Commission, however, while admitting that the churches had every right to honor this martyr of their faith, Bonhoeffer's words and actions with regard to non-baptized Jews during the Nazi period proved not to be consistent with the requirement of the Righteous title.[27]

When dealing with rescuers of Jews who were themselves born Jewish but had freely passed to another faith, the Commission had difficulties in deciding whether to view the rescuer as Jewish, and consequently not meriting the Righteous title, since that is reserved for only non-Jews, or otherwise. The following story, though not of a German but a Frenchman is emblematic of the conflicting opinions in the Commission on this issue. Born to Jewish parents in Zhitomir, Ukraine, Alexandre Glasberg was baptized as a child into the Russian Orthodox Church. Fleeing to France after World War I, he took vows as a Catholic priest, and during the German occupation of France, he initiated various rescue efforts in collaboration with fellow Catholic clerics and institutions, that led to the saving of many Jews. When, still alive, questioned on his own identity, he adamantly claimed that he was still part and parcel of the Jewish people, although donning the clerical garb of a Catholic priest. The request by some of his World War II Jewish rescued persons to award him posthumously the Righteous title led to a spirited debate inside the Commission. Finally, the Commission disregarded the man's claim, while he was still alive, to still be fully Jewish, from a non-religious perspective and awarded him posthumously the Righteous title, as asked and beseeched by those aided by him. The Commission may have been swayed by a 1962 Israel Supreme Court ruling in the case of Daniel Rufeisen (another Jewish convert and priest in the Catholic faith), that a Jewish person who freely converts to another faith and takes it a step further by taking priestly vows in that faith could no longer be considered a member of the Jewish people, in spite of that person's claim to the contrary.[28]

In closing, it is worth emphasizing that the Yad Vashem–sponsored Righteous program was not designed to pass judgment, or assign grades, on the merits of all those who aided persons persecuted by the Nazis, but solely to honor non-Jews who specifically aided Jews – so defined by themselves at the time. In a few exceptional cases, the Righteous honor was also accorded to persons who openly defied the Nazi persecution of Jews. Also worth remembering is that the decision to honor or not is the sole prerogative of the Commission for the Designation of the Righteous, most of whose members are not Yad Vashem employees. That Commission acts similarly to a jury in a court trial, but bases its decision on a show of hands – by majority vote. Also worth pointing out is that in many cases where the Righteous honor was declined, the Commission voted for a letter of thanks and appreciation to be forwarded to the author of a rescue operation as an acknowledgement of the person's meritorious deed. The Commission having ruled, Yad Vashem then acts as the executive arm by carrying out the decision taken by the Commission.

A final important observation – that whereas the greater part of the rescuers mentioned in this study were awarded the Righteous title, I felt it necessary also to mention other significant rescue stories, of those who did not merit the Righteous honor, for their stories also need to be told.

*　　*　　*

WHILE YAD VASHEM WAS HOLDING its breath on initiating its own law-pre-scribed Righteous program, during the 1950s, in the former capital of Nazi Germany a similar program had already been launched—in fact, the first of its kind. The Berlin municipality, in the western and free zone of the divided city, through its governing Senate, had in 1958 initiated a program of honor-ing its citizens who aided Jews during the Nazi period. The Berlin rescuer project was launched by a German of semi-Jewish origin, under the heading of *Unbesungene Helden*, which may be translated as Unsung, Unpraised, or Anonymous Heroes. It was limited to only Berlin residents who during the Nazi period aided persons persecuted for racial reasons; in other words, Jews. Begun in 1957, it lasted until end 1966—several years after the Yad Vashem Righteous program got under way. During that period, Berlin was divided in two, with East Berlin forming the capital of Communist East Germany (DDR) and West Berlin enjoying a special independent status, under the protection of three NATO power—the USA, England, and France—this, until the fall of the Berlin Wall in 1989 and the reunification of the city as the country's capital.

Thanks to a recent study of this program by Dennis Riffel, we know more about this program—its criteria and how many were honored.[1] Incredibly, the Berlin program was born of a combined initiative of two un-likely persons—Kurt Grossmann and Joachim Lipschitz: one Jewish, the other semi-Jewish.

A) Origin

Kurt Grossmann, born in Berlin in 1897, was a journalist involved in various human rights causes. In 1933, he fled the country upon the Nazi takeover and eventually settled in New York in July 1939, where he worked on various assignments for the World Jewish Congress.[2] On one of his postwar trips to Germany, Jewish survivors told him of their rescue by a certain Oskar Schindler, and this gave him the impetus to write a book on rescuers. Grossmann was one of the first to publicize the Schindler story in an article that appeared in the New York-based German language weekly Aufbau, on July 12, 1957.[3] In the process of collecting material and evidence for his book, he placed an article in the German *Süddeutschen Zeitung*, with an appeal for testimonies by rescued persons. The response was huge; more than one hundred wrote back. Choosing the most impressive stories, Grossman published a book in German, under the title of *Unbesungene Helden* (henceforth, UH), in 1957 (a new edition appeared in 1960). It was the first of its kind that addressed itself to stories of rescue of Jews by non-Jews during the Holocaust. From then to the end of his life, in 1972, Grossmann was consumed with the UH theme, since in his words they symbolized "the eternal humanitarian values…that in the period of the barbaric darkness, they maintained kindled the dimmed light of humanitarianism."[4] Most of the rescuers mentioned in his book are Germans, since understandably most of his inquiries were targeted to persons living in Germany.[5]

As for Joachim Lipschitz, he was born in 1918, to a Jewish father (a medical doctor; in 1934, the second year of Nazi rule, he committed suicide) and a non-Jewish mother, and was baptized into the Protestant church. In 1933 he was a member in the Social Democratic youth movement and, simultaneously, the Jewish Maccabi sports organization. Prevented from continuing his studies due to being classified as a half-Jew (*Mischling* in Nazi terminology), he worked for an electrical firm. Accused of *rassenschande* (race soiling) due to his friendship with a non-Jewish woman, he lost his job. He then became a locksmith apprentice in an auto firm. During the Kristallnacht pogrom of November 9, 1938, Lipschitz was brutally beaten and remained imprisoned until February 1939. Yet in spite of his Jewish origin, in August of that same year, he was drafted in the army (Wehrmacht) and took part in the campaigns of Poland, and Western Europe. Then in August 1941, during the Russian campaign, he sustained wounds on his left arm, which had to be amputated, and was then discharged in March 1942 as a noncommissioned officer.[6]

Due to his *Mischling* status, the law forbade him from marrying his non-Jewish girlfriend, Eleonore Krüger, which eventually only took place on May 29, 1945, three weeks after Germany's defeat. Earlier, as the situation for the *Mischlinge* deteriorated, in late October 1944 he decided not to respond to a forced labor summons and went into hiding in several locations, with the assistance of Eleonore and her parents (especially her father, Otto), including staying at times in their own home in Karlshorst.[7]

In June 1945, Lipschitz returned to activity in the Social Democratic party (SPD), and he soon filled an administrative post in the Russian sector of Berlin, with responsibility for over 4,000 employees. He then came into conflict with the Soviet commander, leading to a demand for his dismissal and a harsh prison sentence, in absentia, for he lived in West Berlin, out of Russian hands. Undeterred, Lipschitz moved up the scale of political activity in the SPD, and in 1955 he was appointed senator for the Interior, under Mayor Willy Brandt, and his successor Otto Suhr. In that capacity, Lipschitz was also responsible for the Berlin police.[8] West Berlin, at the time, enjoyed a special independent status, not part of democratic West Germany (Budesrepublik), nor of Communist East Germany, due to the ongoing stand-off between the Soviet Union and the USA, England, and France, which each controlled a separate sector of the divided city.

When he learned of Grossmann's book, Lipschitz wrote to him, on June 28, 1958, asking for corroborating material of the names appearing in the book. Lipschitz then decided not to rely only on Grossmann's conclusion but to undertake a separate investigation of each and every case of Berliners who had helped Jews.[9] When, on April 20, 1958, the Berlin Jewish community held its annual Warsaw ghetto uprising ceremony by announcing the setting apart of a special prize of 2,000 DM to assist non-Jewish Berlin rescuers of Jews, Joachim Lipschitz spoke up and called on the audience to salute the *Unbesungene Helden*, who in his words followed their conscience while braving the authorities, as contrasted with the contemporary custom of hailing the so-called war heroes, whom he termed "professional helpers of death."[10]

Back at the Berlin Senate, Lipschitz now in charge of the UH project decided that only Berlin resident rescuers of Jews, still alive, would be considered, since their honoring was inseparably tied with monetary compensation to them. A special section in the Berlin Senate was therefore delegated to deal with compensations to rescuers.[11] In each case under consideration, the UH team sought to solicit evidence from both sides of the story: the rescuer as well as the rescued, and-or their next of kin if the rescued was not alive or was otherwise incapacitated. Both the rescuer and the rescued were invited for a personal interview, which was recorded, and cosigned by the interrogated persons. Each request was checked with the proper archive centers for the person's possible membership in the Nazi party, or of having been penalized for having committed a criminal offense. For instance, in the case of Baumbach, who was married with a Jewess, and had sheltered a Jewish woman in his two-room apartment, he withdrew his request when he learned that the UH was investigating his Nazi past. In his defense, he claimed that many notable former Nazis, more distinguished than himself, were occupying ministerial posts in Berlin. Lipschitz tried to convince him, that notwithstanding his former Nazi affiliation, to allow his case to be processed, but without success.[12]

Lipschitz allowed himself the liberty to differ from the decisions of his underlings, although, formally, after 1960, he had to bring his recommendation before the Senate for its approval. Such as in the case of Maria Margenroth, who had sent material on her sheltering of a Jewish man. She had since died, and the UH team was about to decide in the negative, when Lipschitz intervened in favor of the case, represented by Margenroth's niece, whose only request was for the UH to pay for a tombstone of her recently deceased aunt. Lipschitz told his aides to approve the payment.[13] At first, no time-limit was established for UH program, but eventually December 31, 1963, was chosen as the deadline for the receipt of requests. All petitions after that date were to be returned, and this was announced in the press. After Lipschitz's sudden premature death on December 11, 1961, at the age of forty-three, he was succeeded in the Berlin Senate by Heinrich Albertz, and later by Otto Theuner.[14]

The Berlin Senate tried as much as possible to give preference to cases of old or sick persons. Naturally this caused a protracted time lag in the processing of other cases, which aroused the ire of petitioners, such as one person who angrily wrote, "if the petitioners had dragged their responses [to Jewish requests for help during the Nazi period] for so long a time, there would have been hardly any Jewish survivors."[15] In some cases, the seemingly inordinate length of time led to a request to discontinue the processing of their cases. Such as with Dr. Otto Ostrowski, the 1946 mayor of Berlin, who during the war hid Ella and her daughter, Inge Deutschkron, and who decided to with-draw his petition.[16] In another similar case, in January 1965, Attorney Walter S. complained on the long time it took the UH to deal with the case of his client, Donata Helmrich, submitted in July 1962. She was finally honored on April 20, 1965.[17] A total of 132 of the petitioners (or 12 percent of the total) died while their case was being processed, and they were therefore not honored, as it was decided at the outset that there would be no post-mortem honoring.[18]

As mentioned earlier, the attribution of the UH honor entitled the recipient not only to a special certificate but also to financial assistance, if the person's situation warranted it. The justification advanced was that whereas a Jewish person formerly in hiding could benefit from compensation by that very fact, his or her rescuer was denied such assistance—only, if he or she was otherwise part of an anti-Nazi resistance organization or involved in the failed July 20, 1944 plot to assassinate Hitler. This was felt to be an injustice toward the rescuers that needed to be corrected. Financial assistance, however, would only go to those in need, such as persons whose income was less than 400 German Marks (DM) monthly for singles and 460 DM for married couples. In some cases it was decided to limit assistance to a single payment, which varied between 300 to 1,000 DM.[19]

b) CRITERIA

Officially, the UH title was described as the honoring of Berlin citizens who during the Nazi period rendered selfless help to the persecuted.[20] The second criterion stated that aid given to the persecuted was done at personal risk to the helper, although they were not otherwise in immediate danger of arrest.[21] This remained the basic criterion. It was further decided that honoring under the UH program was to be limited to persons who were residents of West Berlin—not living in Communist-controlled East Berlin, anywhere else in Germany proper, or abroad. Also to be excluded were persons who helped and promoted the Nazi cause, were involved in anti-democratic campaigns in the postwar period (having probably in mind Communist activists), or were otherwise found to submit false statements.[22]

The most prevalent type of aid was shelter and hiding (84 percent of all submitted cases), taking place at the height of Nazi anti-Jewish persecutions—usually during the war years. Only three out of seven cases that took place before Kristallnacht (November 9–10, 1938) were recognized, one of which involved aid in flight across the border. During Kristallnacht itself, many Jews sought shelter with non-Jewish neighbors. Of the twenty such cases, fourteen were accepted as UH honorees, since it involved actual flight from homes under attack, of which twelve also assisted Jews later, during the war years.[23] As for the length of time of the rescue action—affording shelter for even several hours to avoid arrest during the period of mass deportations was considered more praiseworthy than shelter before that period. Still, a very short time sheltering period was generally considered less significant.[24]

As for help with provisions or nourishment, it was originally felt that this was not consistent with the UH honor, although such helpers could benefit from a one-time payment. For most, at first only persons who sheltered and cared for the persecuted in their own homes for some length of time were considered for the UH honor. In 1960, the UH decided to moderate its position on this point and honor persons who acted to supply Jews with provisions, but only if this was an ongoing, not one-time, activity—even if it didn't involve sheltering.[25] Persons who aided Jews with false credentials were also to be honored. Theodor Görner, who personally fabricated false identities, was thus recognized. So also was William Monnheimer, who handed over to Jewish persons new *Kennkartes* (identification cards) under different non-Jewish names, and also handed signed statements to Jews falsely stating that they were bombed out during air raids and thus lost their documents (known as *Bombenscheine*). According to him, he thus helped eighty to one hundred persons. Altogether thirty-five persons were honored for providing fleeing Jews with false identities.[26]

Persons who helped by gainfully employing Jews, at the time while this was still permitted, were generally not cited, other than in exceptional cases. In one such case, a woman employed a Jewish woman in her home for difficult household chores in exchange for food and provisions. She also charged the woman's children with various errands. It was a clear case of exploitation and compensation to the rescuer. The UH rejected the case, but in the rejection letter, a standard thankful note was added for her assistance to the Jewish woman.[27] With few exceptions, persons implicated in the attempts on Hitler's life but not having aided Jews were also denied recognition.[28]

What about romantic involvement between the rescuer and the rescued? When such a relationship evolved before the rescue period, the UH felt that it was the "moral obligation" on the part of the rescuing spouse to assist his or her partner, and such a person may not have been recognized.[29] In only four out of twenty-one cases of romantic involvement considered by the UH, was it decided to honor the rescuer. In the matter of a certain Gertrud, a non-Jewish woman, while employed as a housekeeper she met a Jewish man in 1909 who was then married to a mentally disturbed woman. The two fell in love, and Gertrud cared for him until his death in 1943 in a Jewish hospital. She had arranged for him to be kept there to avoid his deportation and visited him, in spite of the risks entailed for her. She was recognized because of the help and the risk of her being indicted for "race soiling" (*rassenschande*).[30]

As for mixed Jewish-non Jewish married couples, decisions varied. In one case, a woman was recognized since she continued to care for the relatives of her divorced Jewish husband. In another case, a non-Jewish woman and her Jewish husband adopted a Jewish child, before the Nazi period. The two then divorced during the early period of Nazi rule, and he wanted to give up the child, but she insisted on holding on to him. She was not recognized since it was felt that this was equal to the moral obligation of saving one's own child.[31]

The principal of moral obligation also applied to certain other cases. Such as for Erich Klamroth, a Protestant pastor in the Confessing Church, who cared for a baptized Jew. The UH title was denied to him, since it was felt that in aiding another person he was fulfilling his religious obligation. On the other hand, a woman, presently living in Berlin, who earlier worked for a Catholic institution in Hamburg that cared for baptized Jews, also sheltered Jews in her home—she was recognized since it was felt that having Jews in her home went beyond the moral obligation of her religious work.[32]

Those awarded the UH title received a standard confirmation letter, including thanks for having "opposed the Nazi authorities" and countered the Nazis' "merciless disregard of conventional human dignity and their cold-blooded destruction of innocent victims," and saved them from "a mad racial persecution." The letter ended by pointing out the significance of the honoree's humanitarian deed, and "as proof that in the Germany of a most radical dictatorship there were to be found dignified and self-sacrificial forces."[33] The letter did not make clear the type of help in mind; nor was the identity of the aided persons specified—although Jews were clearly in mind as the victims of the "mad racial persecution."

Some of those rejected the UH honor responded angrily and a few even sued the UH via an attorney. As a result, the UH moderated its non-acceptance letter, to read: "We do not belittle the fact that your behavior contributed to lighten the fate of fellow citizens. At the same time, I have to point out that since the number of Berliners who assisted the persecuted is quite large, this has forced me within the framework of this honoring to adopt very strict and sharp rules." The letter then mentioned the criteria adopted, such as the presence of personal risks and the scope of the help given, and ended with: "I must, therefore, regretfully inform you, that based on these criteria, you were not able to be considered for this honoring." In all such negative responses, the specific reasons that led to such a decision were not specified.[34] Some of those still unhappy with this outcome of their demands sued the Berlin Senate. But, in one such instance, on February 25, 1964, the court rejected the plea, since in the court's opinion the matter did not reside within its jurisdiction but was intimately linked with the criteria solely established by the Berlin Senate for the UH honoring. [35]

c) ISSUES

Rejection of petitions could be due to a host of reasons, including that the rescuer had died during the time of the case's processing; the rescuer currently lived outside West Berlin (since recognition was intimately tied to financial assistance by the city of Berlin); the story suffered from lack of specific information or of witnesses; help was extended to persons not considered victims of Nazi persecutions; the type of help was considered as insignificant; a help which also benefited the rescuer; assistance considered as obligated by the helper (such as husband helping his wife); rescuer was an active Nazi; immoral behavior of the rescuer at the time of the help or in the immediate post-war period; submission of false statements; and request by petitioners to withdraw their recognition application.[36]

Berlin Residency: The Berlin residency requirement gave cause to serious recriminations. Such as the person who, upon being notified of his recognition, asked for a family member to represent him at the ceremony since he had recently moved permanently to Munich. When informed of this, the UH decided to annul the recognition. Ruth Andreas-Friedrich, famous for her realistic wartime memoirs ("Berlin Diary"), was also denied recognition, although she helped many Jews during the Nazi period, since in the eyes of the UH staff her second residence in Munich (her husband was living there) appeared to be the permanent one, in spite of her statement that she also kept a rented apartment in Berlin. Persons receiving monthly stipends under the UH program risked a cut-off of their stipends if and when they moved out of Berlin, and the Berlin Senate kept tabs on the continued residence of the recipients of its aid.[37]

Already Honored: Another UH criterion was to decline the honoring of persons already previously honored by another agency. Such as with the already mentioned Pastor Heinrich Grüber, who at first dealt with facilitating the emigration of baptized Jews only, but later extended his aid to Jews of all categories. When, in December 1940, he protested the expulsion of Jews from the Baden and Rhineland regions, he was arrested and sent to Sachsenhausen and Dachau camps, where he remained until June 23, 1943, and was then freed. Similarly, Dr. Harald Poelchau (the wartime chaplain at the Tegel prison) who had sheltered Jews in his home. Both had already been cited by other agencies, and were therefore denied recognition by the UH.[38]

Nazis as Rescuers: Membership in the Nazi party did not automatically nullify the UH title, unless documentation showed that such persons advanced the party's cause by active participation in its programs. In each such case, the postwar Denazification file of such a person was carefully scrutinized. A harsher stand was applied against those who joined the Nazi party before it came to power in January 1933, for this indicated a certain ideological commitment. In total, thirty-five cases of persons who belonged to the Nazi party were rejected for the UH title. Decisions under this rubric showed a lack of consistency, at least at outward appearance. For instance, Walter Koch's recognition was rejected, although he sheltered many Jews in his pension house. He had joined the Nazi party in early 1933, simply for personal, not ideological reasons. In another case, a man had joined the Nazi party in 1932 and held there a minor position. The record showed that in June 1934, he was excluded from the party due to his "passive" demeanor toward Nazism, whatever that meant. He then sheltered Jews. He was recognized, plus a one-time payment of 1,000 DM. Likewise in the case of a dentist who hid a Jewish person for two years in his home. He had joined the Nazi party in March 1930 and remained there until 1939. He was recognized on the presumption that his joining the party before 1933 was not ideologically motivated.[39]

Communists as Rescuers: Persons active in the communist movement were also denied recognition in light of Berlin's rival front-line position vis-a-vis the East German communist regime. Lipschitz, who earlier experienced harassment by the communists in East Berlin, was quite adamant on this point. At the same time membership in East German communist organizations considered only as nominal, as opposed to membership in communist organizations in West Germany, were not automatically disqualified. Likewise, membership in a communist organization before 1949, or during the Nazi period, was disregarded when considered for recognition to the UH title. In light of this restriction, obviously many former communists did not indicate this fact on the questionnaire that they were asked to fill out. In general, a stricter investigation was undertaken of membership in Nazi movements than in communist ones. In nine out of eleven such communist affiliation cases, it was decided to proceed with the processing, since the applicants were found to have already left the communist party.[41]

Knowledge of Jewish Identity: It goes without saying that in all cases, it had to be established that the rescuer knew perfectly well that the person being helped was Jewish. What if he or she didn't know it, when extending assistance to a person in need? In one such doubtful case, the decision was not to recognize, but instead to award the helping woman with a one-time payment of 1,000 DM.[41]

"Insignificant" Aid: The UH program also differentiated between "significant" and "insignificant" assistance. Not recognized were persons who aided Jews to leave the country when emigration was still a possibility. Since, until the fall of 1941, the official Nazi policy was to force as many Jews out of Germany, helping Jews to leave through legal channels was not regarded as "significant" and dangerous to the rescuer.[42] When, however, it involved trespassing emigration laws, such as flight across borders, the decision could be otherwise. Such as Gustav Pietsch, who formerly lived in Danzig (a mostly German populated city, but enjoying a special status until the start of the war) and helped local Jews flee the area in 1938. As a ship captain, he taught some of them the art of navigation. Altogether, he is reported to have smuggled out several hundred Jews, some of whom continued on their way to Palestine, and he was recognized.[43]

Compensation: In most instances, when payment was involved in return for aid received, the cases were rejected out of hand. For this, the rescued person's testimony was critical. Most compensation cases dealt with rent in exchange for residence, and some with other forms of rewards. A certain woman handed over part of her ration cards to Jews, through middlepersons, in exchange for some other goods. The middlepersons did business by selling the ration cards to Jews. She added that she sometimes stopped Jews on the street and offered to sell them her food ration cards. She was eventually arrested and sentenced to two years in jail. She was not recognized. Another case involved sexual compensation, which even led to the helper's arrest on the charge of "race soiling" (*rassenschande*); the rescued woman was deported and died. The man had earlier also demanded monetary compensation. When she submitted to him, he no longer charged her for staying with him. This was a clear case of nonrecognition.[44]

Questionable Behavior: Hedwig Porschütz was denied recognition for active prostitution. Back in 1934, she also sat in jail for ten months for blackmail, and in 1944 she was condemned for hoarding food and other provisions, some of which she passed on to Jews in hiding; this time she was committed to a labor camp until the war's end. She also had sheltered from time to time Jews at the request of Otto Weidt, a brush and broom manufacturing entrepreneur who employed many blind Jews in his firm and saved them from deportation for a long time. In a slightly similar case, with an embarrassing different twist, Charlotte Erxleben claimed to have sheltered Jews in her private pension and was consequently betrayed and denounced. She received the UH honor and a monthly stipend. It turned out many years later that the "pension" was in truth a privately owned room where she brought in customers for sexual favors—in other words, prostitution. This new revelation came out in 1986, five years after the woman's death. Understandably, it was too late to overturn the original decision.[45] In general, persons who sat in jail for more than three years for various criminal offenses were also denied the UH honor—such was the result in sixty-six cases. However, persons fined for tax evasions but who aided Jews were not automatically denied the UH title.[46]

False and Contradictory Statements: When new revelations were at variance with statements submitted with regard to help the Jews, denial of recognition was immediate. Such as in the case of a woman who claimed to have sheltered a Jew (a *Mischling*), in late 1944, when it turned out that the person was at that time already away in a labor camp. Similarly, another woman produced a 1949 statement in which a Jewish person declared (evidently falsely) having been sheltered by this woman. It turned out that at that time he was in hiding in Warsaw and had only showed up in Berlin after the war, when he had rented a room at this woman's place. The request was denied. The UH policy was not to follow up with judiciary proceedings against persons who knowingly made false statements, although this was an offense punishable by law. The files were simply closed.[47] Another disturbing phenomenon was where accounts in the statements of the rescuer and the rescued conflicted or did not fully agree with each other. Such as in the case of a woman who stated she had sheltered a Jewish couple in her apartment for ten months. The rescued man denied ever having spent an evening in her home. The case was shelved.[48]

In the immediate postwar period, many persons appearing before a Denazification court took the easy way out by claiming that their adherence to the Nazi party was only nominal and not ideological (a *Mitlaufer*— "fellow traveler," not a hard-core Nazi). To shore up such claims, it served to invent or highlight acts of goodness toward a Jew. Suddenly everyone seemed to have had a Jewish friend. One could hardly find self-confessed hard-core Nazis; it seemed they had never existed. Such "nominal" *Mitlaufers* were usually forgiven and not denied important positions in the new civil service, and very soon many known Nazis filled important posts in the government and economy. Not surprising, testimonies given by persons at the end of the war before Denazification boards were not accepted for the purpose of the UH program, unless corroborated by other verifiable sources.[49]

d) Summary and Conclusion

A total of 1,864 requests were received, of which 1,524 cases were considered during the lifetime of the UH project, which lasted from 1958 to 1966. December 31, 1963, was the deadline for submission of requests, and the project was officially terminated on November 9, 1966. Ludwig Wörl was the last person to be publicly honored with UH title in November 1965. Paradoxically, and quite by coincidence, three years earlier, in 1963, he became the first person to be awarded the Righteous honor by Yad Vashem. The financial assistant aspect of those honored, naturally, was allowed to continue for the lifetime of the honorees. Of the 1,524 cases under consideration, a total of 760 were approved for the UH title; 846 were rejected and in 201 cases the processing was discontinued for various reasons, such as rescuers who had moved out of Berlin. Of the 760 honored, only 4 involved help to non-Jews. All others were principally help to Jews, and perhaps also to non-Jews. Statistically, more women than men were honored as UH. Rescuers came from all professions and walks of life. Some helped for long periods, while others, for shorter ones; some helped persons they knew from before; others, strangers to themselves. Most gave shelter; others provided food or false credentials, or helped to flee the country.[50]

Interestingly, no other German city followed the example of Berlin in honoring their citizens who aided Jews during the Nazi period. The Berlin Senate wrote to other German provinces to encourage them to initiate separate UH programs. The response was disappointing, citing various excuses. In March 1963, Frankfurt am Main asked Berlin for more specifics on its UH program, but it took them until 1990 to copy the Berlin example. Hamburg too initially showed an interest but then dropped the idea.[51] Only after the UH ceased operating—starting in 1967, the West German government began to include rescuers of Jews under its own *Bundesverdienstkreuz* (Order of Merit of Federal Republic of Germany) program. Up to as many as two hundred rescuers were honored under that program.[52]

Lipschitz was careful to emphasize what he called the "other Germany" which the UH recipients represented, who by their rescuing acts were the true opponents of the Hitler regime. This was to counter the general excuse given that, with the example of the failed July 20, 1944 plotters in mind, the individual person was helpless in the face of the brutal Nazi regime. The Berlin Senate UH program was meant to show, by contrast, that the individual person could strike back with relatively much success by helping Jews, even in capital city of Nazi Germany.[53] One still unanswered question is to what extent, if any, the Berlin Senate's initiative in honoring non-Jewish rescuers of Jews prompted the World Jewish Congress to initiate its own rescuers program in 1961, which in turn triggered, a year later, Yad Vashem's own rescuers' version, under the Righteous Among the Nations program?[54]

* * *

INTRODUCTION

1. Aharon Weiss, ed., *Yad Vashem Studies* 19 (1988). See the following articles: Martin Broszat and Saul Friedländer, "A Controversy about the Historicization of National Socialism," 1-47; Ernst Nolte, "Between Historical Myth and Revisionism?", 49-63; Jürgen Habermas, "A Kind of Indemnification," 75-92; Otto Kov Kulka, "*Singularity and its Relativization,*" 151-186.

2. Daniel Goldhagen, *Hitler's Willing Executioners: Ordinary Germans and the Holocaust* (New York: Knopf, 1996). Goldhagen rejects the thesis advanced by Christopher Browning and others who minimized the role of antisemitism as the determining factor in the Holocaust, and rather emphasized general behavioral tendencies, such as obedience to superiors, group and peer pressure, routinization, and fragmentization of the killing process. See for instance Christopher Browning's study of a Police battalion 101 that was assigned to killing Jews in Poland. Christopher Browning, *Ordinary Men: Ordinary Men: Reserve Police Battalion 101 and the Final Solution in Poland* (New York: Harper Collins, 1992).

3. Goldhagen, *Hitler's Willing Executioners*, 23, 69, 72, 447–48.

4. See also David Bankier's study of public opinion in Germany during the Nazi period. David Bankier, *The Germans and the Final Solution: Public Opinion under Nazism* (Oxford, UK & Cambridge, Mass.: B. Blackwell, 1996).

5. Stanley Milgram, *Obedience to Authority: an Experimental View* (New York: Harper & Row, 1974), 123, 138.

6. Solomon E. Asch, "Opinions and Social Pressure," *Scientific American* 193, no. 5 (1955): 2-6.

7. Milgram, *Obedience to Authority*, 6; Stanley Milgram, "Behavioral Study of Obedience," *Journal of Abnormal and Social Psychology* 163, no. 67, 371–78. Browning, *Ordinary Men*, 172–73. Asch defines a social man as a moral "somnambulist." Asch, "Opinions," 2. See also Milgram, *Obedience to Authority*, 8, 133–34, 143, 155.

8. Zygmunt Bauman, in *Modernity and the Holocaust* (Ithaca, N.Y.: Cornell University, 1989), also states that responsibility arises out of the proximity of the other: "Proximity means responsibility, and responsibility is proximity," 184.

9. I am indebted to Eliott Aronson, *The Social Animal* (San Francisco: W.H. Freeman, 1972), for this interesting insight; see particularly 51, 53.

Chapter 1 – The Historical Setting

1. On Hitler's antisemitism, see Adolf Hitler, *Mein Kampf* (New York: Fredonia Classics, 2003); George Stein, *Hitler* (Englewood Cliffs, NJ: Prentice-Hall, Inc., 1968), chapters 1, 2, 5; Ian Kershaw, "The Persecution of the Jews and German Popular Opinion in the Third Reich," *The Leo Baeck Yearbook* 26 (1981): 261–89; Eberhard Jaeckel, *Hitler's World View: A Blueprint for Power* (Cambridge, Mass.: Harvard University, 1981).

2. Historians dispute Goldhagen's statement that "the anti-Semitism of tens of thousands of upper-class Germans was not all that different from that of the Nazis themselves" (316), as well as his statement that by the 1920s, the German people "were more dangerously oriented toward the Jews than they had been during any other time since the dawn of modernity" (79), since "the vast majority of them subscribed to the underlying Nazi model of Jews" and were thus already "Nazified" in their views of the Jews (87). For Goldhagen, all Hitler did was to whip up and inflame the already existing emotional antisemitism of the people (443). For disagreement with this assessment, see Robert S. Wistrich, "Helping Hitler," *Commentary* 102, no. 1 (1995): 27–31. David Bankier

(in a public lecture at Yad Vashem, August 1995) and Yehuda Bauer (at a similar lecture at Yad Vashem, July 24, 1966) also questioned this assessment by Goldhagen.

3. In this study, we use "antisemitism" as a single and non-hyphenated term, as strongly urged by Franklin H. Littell, since it does not denote anything against Semites that would include Arabs, but simply hatred of Jews. The spelling "anti-Semitism" is a misnomer, since it gives the impression of being opposed to a supposedly Semitic culture and influence. Antisemitism is plain and simple hatred of Jews – not hatred of Semitic culture and ideas. The variant spelling "anti-Semitism," is used here only when quoted from other sources.

4. Goldhagen quotes Walter Laqueur, who notes that during the Weimar period, Jews were in the forefront of every new, daring, revolutionary movement and were prominent in the media, arts, and entertainment, in *Hitler's Willing Executioners*, 249. Others have noted the disproportionate number of Jews in the practice of law, especially in the larger cities.

5. Avraham Seligmann, "An Illegal Way of Life in Nazi Germany," *The Leo Baeck Year Book* 37 (1992): 327–61, 333.

6. Goldhagen, *Hitler's Willing Executioners*, 137. Goldhagen notes in this regard that whereas slaves were historically also transformed into the "socially dead," there was a utilitarian purpose behind it, whereas Jews were reduced to being "socially dead," not to derive material advantages for their masters, but to deprive them of their freedoms and to inflict suffering, starvation, and psychological disorientation as to their ultimate fate, and make them more amenable to their eventual murder; 169.

7. Henry Friedlander, "The Deportation of the German Jews: Post-War German Trials of Nazi Criminals," *The Leo Baeck Year Book* 29 (1984): 201–26, 208.

8. Friedländer, "The Deportation of the German Jews," 209, 212.

9. Friedländer, "The Deportation of the German Jews," 211, 217.

10. The Nazis feared that harming the half-Jews, a population fully assimilated into German life, would draw attention and even arouse resentment among friends and relatives of these people – at a time when the government sought to preserve calm on the home front, in the midst of a difficult war.

11. Kershaw, "The Persecution of the Jews," 286.

12. It should be noted that most Austrians enthusiastically welcomed annexation to Nazi Germany, which was accompanied by extensive popular anti-Jewish riots on a scale unknown even in Germany proper. Throughout the eight years of its annexation to Germany, Austria failed to produce an anti-Nazi movement of any mark.

13. The respective figures of Jewish casualties as a percentage of the total Jewish population for other countries, apart from Germany and Austria, are: Soviet Union – 1 million (30%); Lithuania – 140,000 (83%); Latvia – 70,000 (77%); the Czech protectorate – 78,000 (66%); Slovakia – 68,000 (76%); Romania – 271,000 (44%); Hungary – 550,000 (66%); Yugoslavia – 56,000 (71%); Greece – 60,000 (78%); the Netherlands – 100,000 (71%); Belgium – 29,000 (44%) - France – 77,000 (22%). Figures taken from, Israel Guttman, ed., *Encyclopedia of the Holocaust*, Vol. 5 (Jerusalem: Yad Vashem, 1990), 1282.

14. Goldhagen, *Hitler's Willing Executioners*, 448.

15. Kershaw, "The Persecution of the Jews," 231.

16. Kershaw, "The Persecution of the Jews," 263–64, 287.

17. Kershaw, "The Persecution of the Jews," 238, 273–74, 269. Bankier, *The Germans and the Final Solution*, 74, 84, 120. Otto Dov Kulka, "Public Opinion in Nazi Germany and the 'Jewish Question,'" *Zion* 40 (1975): 186–290, 205. It has also been noted that the Catholic population, in the south and west of the country (with the notable exception of Austria), was generally less hostile toward Jews than the majority Protestants, perhaps because Catholics feared that as a minority, they too might be in line for similar harsh measures by the new regime, though not as drastic as those awaiting the Jews. Kershaw, "The Persecution of the Jews," 270, 278.

18. Bankier, *The Germans and the Final Solution*, 69, 81.

19. Kershaw, "The Persecution of the Jews," 273, and, Kulka, "Public Opinion," 214–15, 218–19, 228–29.

20. Bankier, *The Germans and the Final Solution*, 85ff; Goldhagen, *Hitler's Willing Executioners*, 102; Kershaw, "The Persecution of the Jews," 275–77, 279–80; Kulka, "Public Opinion," 234–35, who notes that the deportation of Jews to concentration camps during this pogrom did not arouse similar misgivings.

21. Quoted in Bankier, *The Germans and the Final Solution*, 127.

22. Bankier, *The Germans and the Final Solution*, 131, 133, 135; Kershaw, "The Persecution of the Jews," 359; Kulka, "Public Opinion," 245.

23. Kershaw, "The Persecution of the Jews," 283, 289, 364–65; Kulka, "Public Opinion," 256–57; Bankier, *The Germans and the Final Solution*, 105–14.

24. Bankier, *The Germans and the Final Solution*, 134, 144, 147; Kershaw, "The Persecution of the Jews," 368–70.

25. John Weiss, *Ideology of Death: Why the Holocaust Happened in Germany?* (Chicago: I.R. Dee, 1996), 382. See for instance the fulmination of Petty Court Judge Beinert, of Wernigrode, in 1924: "The German people are coming to recognize more and more that the Jews bear the heaviest guilt for our misery. There can be no thought of improving the lot of our people if we do not crush the power of the Jews;" Benno Mueller-Hill, *Murderous Science* (New York: Oxford University, 1988), 19. I am indebted to Mueller for this eye-opening account on the dispensing of justice in Nazi Germany, by jurists who stayed on the bench in postwar West Germany until their retirement.

26. Mueller-Hill, *Murderous Science*, 37. This was especially disastrous for Jewish attorneys, since they made up 22% of all attorneys, and were even more overrepresented in the larger cities, such as Berlin – 60%; Vienna – 80%; 59–60. On the same day (April 7, 1933), all Jewish professors of law at prestigious universities were summarily and humiliatingly dismissed; 69.

27. These court case examples are listed in Mueller-Hill, *Murderous Science*, 65, 104, 111, 114. One of the anomalies of Nazi Germany was that a Jewish person who had married a non-Jewish woman, before the onset of the 1935 race laws, could remain married to her and was not charged with the severe offence of "race defilement," whereas entertaining a casual friendly relationship with an unmarried Aryan woman could land the man in jail, if not a concentration camp.

28. Mueller-Hill, *Murderous Science*, 196–97; John Weiss, *Ideology of Death*, 251–52.

29. John Weiss, *Ideology of Death*, 251-52, 397.

30. John Weiss, *Ideology of Death*, 296, 358–59. After the war Verschuer served on the editorial board of a journal with the name *Mankind Quarterly*; 393.

31. John Weiss, *Ideology of Death*, 348–49.

32. Kershaw, "The Persecution of the Jews," 166–77. See also, Nathan Stoltzfus, *Hitler's Compromises: Coercion and Consensus in Nazi Germany* (New York: W.W. Norton, 1996), chapters 2 and 3.

33. Stoltzfus, *Hitler's Compromises*, 86–108; Kershaw, "The Persecution of the Jews," 347–48, 353.

34. Kershaw, "The Persecution of the Jews," 339, 354. At the same time, Catholic bishops, while condemning the euthanasia program, hailed the invasion of Russia as a crusade and holy war, "for the Christian faith, for Christ and his most holy Cross"; 340.

35. Kershaw, "The Persecution of the Jews," 247.

36. Kershaw, "The Persecution of the Jews," 249–50. A German Christian church election pamphlet of November 1932 stated: "And it is God's will that we maintain our Race and our *Volkstum* in purity, that we remain German men, and do not become a bastard-Volk of Jewish Aryan blood. That is why we oppose un-Christian humanitarianism, pacifism, the Internationale, Freemasonry and Christian cosmopolitanism, and confess with Martin Luther: 'For Germans was I born, them will I serve.'" Richard Gutteridge, *Open Thy Mouth for the Dumb!: The German Evangelical Church and the Jews, 1879–1950* (Oxford: Basil Blackwell, 1976), 48.

37. Kershaw, "The Persecution of the Jews," 287.

38. Gutteridge, *Open Thy* Mouth, 108, 111–13, 273.

39. Goldhagen, *Hitler's Willing Executioners*, 108.

40. John Weiss, *Ideology of Death*, 312–313.

41. Gutteridge, *Open Thy Mouth*, 92–93.

42. Gutteridge, *Open Thy Mouth*; Weiss, *Ideology of Death*, 226; Goldhagen, *Hitler's Willing Executioners*, 112–14.

43. Gutteridge, *Open Thy Mouth*, 104

44. Gutteridge, *Open Thy Mouth*, 102.

45. John Weiss, *Ideology of Death*, 314–15, 351.

46. Kershaw, "The Persecution of the Jews," 253–54; Gutteridge, *Open Thy Mouth*, 190.

47. Gutteridge, *Open Thy Mouth*, 183. In response to the action against Pastor von Jan, Bishop Wurm of the Lutheran church counseled pastors to withhold from delivering sermons that could be construed as being in league with Jews, and to see to it that pronouncements and prayers have a purely pastoral character, not political; Gutteridge, *Open Thy Mouth*, 185.

48. Gutteridge, *Open Thy Mouth,* 251.

49. Compare this silence with the pastoral letter of the Roman Catholic Archbishop Jules-Géraud Saliège, of Toulouse, France, in the summer of 1942: "Jews are men, Jewesses are women. . . . They cannot be maltreated at will. They are part of the human race. They are our brethren as much as are many others. Christians cannot forget that." Gutteridge, *Open Thy Mouth,* 267, 269.

50. Gutteridge, *Open Thy Mouth,* 64, 71, 93; Bankier, *The Germans and the Final Solution,* 122–23.

51. Gutteridge, *Open Thy Mouth,* 186, 268; Goldhagen, *Hitler's Willing Executioners,* 114.

52. Gutteridge, *Open Thy Mouth,* 312.

53. Nathan Stoltzfus, *Resistance of the Heart: Intermarriage and the Rosenstrasse Protest in Nazi Germany* (New York: W.W. Norton, 1996), 260.

54. Stoltzfus, *Hitler's Compromises,* chapter 8. See also Wiener Library, Tel Aviv University, file AR 600, for a comprehensive list of the women protesters and related information.

55. Kershaw, "The Persecution of the Jews," 275, 277.

CHAPTER 2 – FRIENDS, ACQUAINTANCES AND VARIOUS RELATIONSHIPS

1. Avraham Seligmann, "An Illegal Way of Life in Nazi Germany," *The Leo Baeck Yearbook* 37 (1992): 327–61; 327–28, 332, 340–41, 351, 359–61.

2. Seligmann, "An Illegal Way of Life," 338–39.

3. Seligmann, "An Illegal Way of Life," 338–39, 354.

4. Seligmann, "An Illegal Way of Life," 346–47, 349, 359.

5. Seligmann, "An Illegal Way of Life," 351.

6. Seligmann, "An Illegal Way of Life," 355–56, 360.

7. Emma Richter was honored by the Berlin Senate in 1960. Yad Vashem Archives (henceforth, YVA) M31.2/53.

8. Frieda Adam, YVA M31.2/5540.

9. On May 8, 1945, the day the war was officially over, drunken Russian soldiers burst into the Hagemann home, penetrated the cellar where

both the Hagemanns and Kahanes were seeking shelter from marauding soldiers, and began to abuse Hagemann's grownup daughters. Jacob and his daughter offered stiff resistance and were severely beaten. The Russian military police intervened in time. This incident made a strong impression on the Hagemanns. In a diary entry on that day, Gerhard wrote: "Hahne and his wife displayed great courage. That moment he became my best friend. Dear Jacob, he was beaten for our sake; this we should not forget. 1 o'clock at night. Our nerves were to some extent stilled. We went to sleep." Gerhard Hagemann, YVA M31.2/6038.

10. Angela Pohl, YVA M31.2/5151.

11. Mina Kuttelwascher, YVA M31.2/1880; Konstantin Müller & mother Anna, YVA M31.2/877; Charlotte Weiler, M31.2/553.

12. Walter Czok, YVA M31.2/567. Czok's membership in the SA prevented him from being awarded Yad Vashem's Righteous title, as further explained in Appendix A.

13. Valeska Buchholdz, YVA M31.2/2830.

14. Ernst's father died while in hiding of a stroke, in February 1945, and his body was secretly removed and discharged into the Spree River, which was not too far from their house. Sotscheck/Cassier and Pissarius files, YVA M31.2/11988-11989.

15. Esther-Maria Seidel, YVA M31.2/2422.

16. Heinrich Wilmes, YVA M31.2/1253.

17. Ludwig Walz, YVA M31.2/894.

18. Maimi von Mirbach, YVA M31.2/2040.

19. Paula Huelle, YVA M31.2/653.

20. Erich Buengener, YVA M31.2/4788.

21. Reinhold Duschka, YVA M31.2/4537.

22. Walter Rieck, YVA M31.2/670.

23. Marie-Luise's soldier son Martin was not harmed. He fell into Russian captivity and was freed in 1948. Marie-Luise Hensel, YVA M31.2/763.

24. Gustav & Agnes Zubeil, YVA M31.2/1080. After leaving the Zubeil boat home, the Witkowskis were sheltered by Hertha Mueller until the war's end. YVA M31.2/678.

25. After the war, in the 1950s, the Arndts helped the Gehres emigrate to the U.S.A. Max & Augusta Gehre, YVA M31.2/3984.

26. Anni Schulz, YVA M31.2/3984.

27. Maria Meier and parents Albert & Maria; Ludwig & Elisabeth Weeg, YVA M31.2/4365. A slightly similar story is that of Maria Saidler, from Vienna, who once worked as a cleaning woman for Anna Sommer. Later, when Anna needed help, Maria sheltered her in her home; YVA M31.2/1390.

28. Hubert Pentrop, YVA M31.2/463.

29. Two other work colleagues also helped Lilli Wolff during various stages of her life under the Nazis: Metta Schmitt, originally from Bonn, Lilli's business partner in the stage costume designing business, and Martha (Matti) Driessen, an employee at Lilli's shop. After the war, Martha moved with Lilli for a new life and another dress designing venture to Dallas, Texas. Dorothea Neff, YVA M31.2/1652.

30. See Appendix A on the debate by the Commission for the Designation of the Righteous on Gailer's qualification for the Righteous title. Leonhard Gailer, YVA M31.2/5645.

31. As for Strauss, he managed to flee before the arrival of the police at List's farmhouse and successfully crossed into Switzerland. After the war, he kept in touch with Maria List and offered her financial assistance, which she politely turned down. She never told him about her husband's fate. Strauss moved to Jamaica, where he died in 1983. The story was brought to Yad Vashem's attention in 1992 by a delegation of students from Michelstadt, who researched the Darmstadt municipality files. Heinrich & Maria List, YVA M31.2/5525.

32. Wanda Feuerherm, YVA M31.2/3782. See also the file of Dr. Fritz Aub, YVA M31.2/3783, for the story of Gerda's parents rescue.

33. Christa Beran, YVA M31.2/3221.

34. Edith Berlow, YVA M31.2/5444.

35. After the war, economic troubles and health ailments caused her to be addicted to morphine, and her medical veterinary license was revoked. She underwent three drug-weaning attempts. After her divorce from Hans, she joined a circus and tended some 200 animals. For the next ten years, she wandered with the circus across Europe. In 1963, her veterinary license was reinstated and she opened an animal clinic in Berlin in 1972. She met again Hans, who was divorced from his second wife, and remarried him. He died in 1975. Maria von Maltzan, YVA M31.2/3545.

36. Elisabeth Wust, YVA M31.2/6097.

37. Also included are the other dramatis personae involved in the rescue operation of Walter Posiles and his brothers: Charlotte Fritz, Friederike

Buchetter, Alois and Josephine Kreiner, Maria Fasching, Lydia Matouschek, and Olga Holstein; YVA M31.2/1423-1429.

38. Adele Puetz, YVA M31.2/3114.

39. Johanna Eck, YVA M31.2/841.

40. Josef Cammerer, YVA M31.2/396. See also Karl Schoerghofer, YVA M31.2/390.

41. Ludwig Clauss, YVA M31.2/1683. Clauss may have felt that in light of Landé's dedicated work for him during a fifteen-year period, he was personally responsible for her survival, even if it meant jeopardizing his professional career and his carefully tailored pro-Nazi opportunistic stance. He never publicly recanted his prewar racist apologetics. Clauss was at first mistakenly awarded the Righteous title. When I learned of this, I asked the commission to reconsider in light of all the data pertaining to this man, and the Righteous title was withdrawn.

42. Artur Jacobs, YVA M31.2/3112.

43. Ernst-Otto Motzko, YVA M31.2/520.

44. Paul Kerner, YVA M31.2/3069; Leo Tschoell, YVA M31.2424.

45. Helmut Bittner, YVA M31.2/650.

46. Marianne Golz-Goldlust, YVA M31.2/3845.

47. Fritz Heine, YVA M31.2/3533.

CHAPTER 3 – HELP THROUGH THIRD PARTIES

1. Lydie Forsstroem, YVA M31.2/1874.

2. Hedwig Schroedter, YVA M31.2/5870.

3. Erna's daughter, Gerda, was sheltered intermittently in the house of Wanda Feuerherm, whom she knew from before, in her little wooden house, in the Lichtenberg section, on the outskirts of Berlin; YVA M31.2/3783.

4. After the war, Ursula Meissner married the Greek ambassador to Germany, P. Calogeras; YVA M31.2/6275.

5. Anastasia Gerschuetz, YVA M31.2/3257.

6. Ewald Kleisinger, YVA M31.2/188; Herbert Vogt, YVA M31.2/606.

7. Eva Gaebler, YVA M31.2/1803.

8. Paul David, YVA M31.2/2372. Margit married in 1943 her cousin Fritz David, a communist who fought in the Spanish civil war, then was

turned over to the Nazis and imprisoned before being pardoned in 1942 on Hitler's birthday.

9. Willi Friedrichs, YVA M31.2/502. See Appendix A for Friedrichs' imprisonment after the war and his involvement in a robbery that cost the life of a bank clerk and precluded his nomination to the Righteous title.

10. Elisabeth Bornstein, YVA M31.2/2311.

11. According to Ernst Ehrlich, Schuerholz was a *Luftwaffe* (German Air Force) officer and was court-martialed for making anti-Nazi statements. Through the help of a friend, a member of the SS, the charge was dropped, and Schuerholz was released from the *Luftwaffe*. Franz Schuerholz, YVA M31.2/808.

12. Herbert & Erika Patzschke, Gertrud Kochanowski, Albert & Dorle Heuer, YVA M31.2/1088-1090.

13. Hanning Schroeder, YVA M31.2/1252. See also Ilse Rewald, "Berliner, die uns halfen, die Hitlerdiktatur zu ueberleben," *Landeszentrale für Politische Bildungsarbeit Berlin*, from the series *Beitraege zum Thema Widerstand*, March, 14, 1975.

14. Wilhelm Buerger, YVA M31.2/1469-1471.

15. Sibylle Dierke, YVA M31.2/4061. Not recognized under the Righteous program, because of the uncertainty of Clara von Methenheim's Jewishness at the time of the hiding. See discussion of the "Jewishness" issue in Appendix A.

16. Maria & Gerhard Mueller; YVA M31.2/3157.

17. Theodor Görner, YVA M31.2/387; Lisa Holländer, YVA M31.2/669; Klara Grueger, YVA M31.2/3425.

18. Viktoria Kolzer, YVA M31.2/2029. In 1960, Kolzer was honored by the Berlin Senate under the *Unbesungener Helden* program.

19. Hertha Mueller, YVA M31.2/678. Hertha Mueller was honored by the Berlin Senate in 1961.

20. Ursula Treptow, YVA M31.2/3984. Ken Lindenberg relates that, through his Jewish girlfriend, he was able to find shelter in the flat of Thea Streckfuss. This lasted until Thea's husband deserted from the army and went into hiding. To protect herself, Thea denounced her husband's action and joined the Nazi party while secretly aiding her husband at his hiding place. This new development forced Ken to switch to another hiding place for himself. YVA M31.2/3340.

21. Irene Block, YVA M31.2/1196. In August 1944, Irene Block divorced
     her husband, Hans, then in the army. The reason as given by Fulda: "so
     as not to endanger him." She does not elaborate. In a slightly similar
     story taking place in Vienna, Trude Fritz, upon receiving her deporta-
     tion summons in September 1941, was referred by a Jewish friend to Dr.
     Rudolf Wertz. He diagnosed her as suffering from a severe abdominal
     inflammation and ordered her to remain in bed for six weeks. She paid
     the customary five marks for the visit and went home. Two doctors from
     the Jewish community office, accompanied by a Gestapo doctor, came
     to see her, and she showed Dr. Wertz's prescription. Much later she was
     deported to Theresienstadt (instead of Poland, as in the original sum-
     mons), and survived. After the war, she learned that Wertz had acted
     likewise in several cases, and as a result was arrested and sent to a certain
     camp, which he luckily survived. YVA M31.2/159.
22. Maria vvyon Maltzan, YVA M31.2/ 3545; Erik Myrgren, YVA
     M31.2/3546.
23. Fritz Strassman, YVA M31.2/ 3010.
24. Otto Mörike, YVA M31.2/412. See also Max Krakauer, *Lichter um
     Dunkel* (Stuttgart: Calver, 2012), which has been translated into
     English by Hans M. Wuerth as *Lights in Darkness*. Albrecht Goes,
     YVA M31.2/5074; Richard Goelz, YVA M31.2/5039; Alfred Dilger,
     YVA M31.2/4882. Earlier, Goelz gained prominence when, in 1933,
     he introduced Gregorian chants in evangelical churches. After the
     war he underwent a mental crisis and later passed into the Russian
     Orthodox church, moving to Milwaukee, Wisconsin, where he served
     as a monk.
25. Harald Poelchau, YVA M31.2/965; Ruth Wendland, YVA M31.2/9.
26. Gertrud Luckner, YVA M31.2/280. See also Gertrud Luckner,
     Freiburger Rundbrief 49, no. 12 (1959–1960): 29-44. There are not many
     reports of the Catholic clergy's help to Jews. Included among the few is
     Pater Heinrich Kreutz, of the Herz-Jezu church in Berlin, and his suc-
     cessor there, Horst Rothkegel, who sheltered Erich Wolff in the church
     compound; YVA M31.2/1978. Also, Pater Heinrich Middendorf, head
     of a monastery in Stegen, who sheltered *Mischlinge,* baptized Jews, and
     Jewish intermarried spouses; YVA M31.2/5837.
27. Elisabeth Abegg, YVA M31.2/345.
28. Gerhard & Ilse Schwersensky, YVA M31.2/3201.

CHAPTER 4 – FOREMEN, SUPERVISORS, AND WORK COLLEAGUES

1. Otto Weidt, YVA M31.2/671.

2. Willi Daene also helped Emilie Korn, a worker at Teves, with new credentials under which she appeared as a Belgian laborer. This made it possible for her to "return" to Belgium, after her tour of duty as a forced laborer was over. Mrs. Schulze, one of the forewoman in the company, also sheltered several Jewish persons in her home, two of which (Gertrude Sachs and her daughter) she hid for two years. YVA M31.2/1250a.

3. Kurt Zabel, YVA M31.1/3340.

4. Josef Niessen, YVA M31.2/1841.

5. In similar stories, Margot Bloch was helped by Herbert Patzschke, a foreman at the Flohr lift firm in Berlin, where she worked for a while. Margot stayed in his home for three crucial weeks, giving her time to make other arrangements with friends in Hannover; M31.2/1090. Ella Bernhardt, in charge of the Jewish forced laborers section in a Berlin firm producing uniforms, used her authority to warn them of approaching danger and occasionally provided temporary shelter in her home; M31.2/2502. Also Helmuth Sell, owner of a Berlin mechanics factory, who aided a Jewish errand boy with arrangements to flee Germany to Hungary, via Vienna; M31.2/2075. Ludwig Knapp, YVA M31.2/452.

6. Karl Dangelmeier, YVA M31.2/769. Also worth mentioning is the story of Liselotte Flemming, who passed food to several people in the Riga ghetto, friends of Bertha Eichhorn, whom she met at Bertha's workplace in a hostel for German women secretaries assigned to the Wehrmacht. Liselotte's husband was at the time a major in the army; YVA M31.2/2828.

7. Konrad Schweser, YVA M31.2/288.

8. Willi Ahrem, YVA M31.2/102.

9. Hans Sürkl, YVA M31.2/1808.

10. Fritz Muehlhof, YVA M31.2/1419. Some additional rescue stories of German nationals in charge of Jewish labor in Eastern Europe include the following. In Stanislawow, Franz Weschenfelder was a medical orderly with the *Schutzpolizei* (military police). He met and befriended

Abraham Liebesman, a bacteriological physician in a lab that the German authorities took over. Franz helped Liebesman's family and some friends to ward off Nazi liquidation raids. In February 1943, Franz facilitated Liebesman's departure to Strij with the help of false credentials. The two met again after the war; YVA M31.2/343. In Strij, Gertrud Steinl, a forewoman at the Karpathen Oel Gesellschaft, befriended Sarah Shelomi, whom she later learned was Jewish. At this point, Gertrud's concern for Sarah grew to the point where she arranged for her to move in with her parents, who lived in Graslitz/ Graslice, in the Sudeten region of Czechoslovakia. Sarah worked as a maid in their home, without them knowing of her Jewish origin; M31.2/1618. Finally, in Tarnów, some Jews enlisted Franz Fritsch in 1943 to help them flee to Hungary, via Slovakia. He had previously headed a uniform-producing company, utilizing Jewish labor, which was later acquired by Julius Madritsch, a Viennese entrepreneur active in Kraków. Arrested by the Gestapo on various charges, Fritsch escaped to Hungary in 1944 and lived under an assumed name until the war's end; M31.2/279. In Skolpje, Macedonia, Georg Ufer, who dealt in the mines industry on behalf of a German company, helped a Jewish business colleague from before the war flee to Albania in 1942, then under Italian occupation, where he was safe; M31.2/1809.

11. Bernhard Falkenberg, YVA M31.2/1531. In July 1964, Falkenberg testified in a trial in Hanover against the SS commanders who were involved in the liquidation of the Włodawa Jews; M31.2/198. In an analogous story, in Jagelnice (near Czortków), Poland, Ludwig Semrad, from Vienna, was the German-appointed trustee of a tobacco-producing firm. Together with his Polish wife, Wanda, the Semrads spirited a group of Jews from the Czortków ghetto and brought them to his tobacco firm where he employed them in various nonessential, related jobs. When the Gestapo appeared and asked to release the Jews to them, Semrad claimed that these Jewish workers were essential for the functioning of his factory. While suspecting his true motivations, and constantly harassing him with visits and interrogations, the Gestapo (for unknown reasons) did not lay their hands on him, and he was not removed from his *treuhander* post. YVA M31.2/1531.

12. Otto Busse, YVA M31.2/469. After the war, Busse was considered by many of his countrymen a traitor, and had to leave his position as a

department manager in a big Darmstadt store. In 1969, he came to Israel to live in Nes Ammim (a Christian settlement), and "to atone, even if only in a very small way, for the collective guilt of Christianity for the atrocities committed against the Jewish people in our age." He returned to Germany in 1973; YVA M31.2/469.

13. Artur Schade, YVA M31.2/6619.

14. Karl Laabs, YVA M31.2/1914.

15. Hermann Graebe, YVA M31.2/116. See also Miriam Peleg, "Testimony of Herman F. Graebe, Given in Israel," *Yad Vashem Studies* 6 (1967): 283–313, and Douglas D. Huneke, *The Moses of Rovno* (New York: Dodd, Mead & Co., 1985).

16. Johann Pscheidt, YVA M31.2/2.

17. Alfred Rossner, YVA M31.2/6239.

18. Berthold Beitz, YVA M31.2/299.

19. Julius Madritsch, YVA M31.2/21-23. In November 1944, Madritsch was arrested in Vienna and hauled to Montelupich prison in Kraków on charges of helping the Polish underground, and of passing information on conditions in Plaszów to outside sources (which was true). After three days, he was conveyed to Berlin. The charges could not be substantiated, and he was released after two weeks' confinement.

20. Oskar Schindler, YVA M31.2/20. To author Grossman, Schindler described his motivation as follows: "The strongest motivation for my behavior and the reason of my inner transformation was the daily sight of ongoing sufferings of Jewish persons, and the brutal treatment of the Prussian Supermen in the occupied region – a group of lying hypocrites, sadistic murderers, who with an efficient propaganda promised to free my homeland, the Sudeten region, but in reality turned it into a degraded and plundered colony. . . . An important compelling urge for my behavior was the feeling of a moral obligation towards my numerous Jewish schoolmates and friends from my glorious race-free youthful period." In Kurt R. Grossmann, *Die Unbesungenen Helden* (Berlin: Arani, 1957), 41-2. Interestingly, and quite paradoxically, after the war, the man who could talk his way out of the most difficult situation could not operate a business even of moderate means and needed to be supported by those he helped survive. His several enterprises, in Argentina and Germany, failed. His marriage broke up, and his heavy drinking finally took a toll on his

health. He died at the relatively young age of sixty-four, a disoriented man, with no family, no goals, no ambitions – nothing to look forward to, but with the pleasant feeling of having singlehandedly saved so many lives. Jewish survivors from Israel continued to support him until his dying day. During one of his many visits to Israel, he planted a tree in Yad Vashem. On his deathbed, he asked to be buried as close as possible to his Israeli survivors, and he was interred in the Latin cemetery, on Mt. Zion, Jerusalem. His pallbearers were many of those he saved from the Nazis several decades earlier.

21. The quotes are from John Weiss, *Ideology of Death*, 343–44.

22. As earlier noted, von Reichenau's sister-in-law, Maria von Maltzan, was a major rescuer of Jews in the Berlin area.

23. Hugo Armann, YVA M31.2/3254.

24. Anton Schmid, YVA M31.2/55.

25. Eberhard & Donata Helmrich, YVA M31.2/154. See also the book by the Helmrichs' daughter: Cornelia Schmalz-Jacobsen, *Zwei Bäume in Jerusalem* (Hamburg: Hoffman und Campe, 2002).

26. Max Liedtke & Albert Battel, YVA M31.2/1979.
The letter by Heinrich Himmler to Martin Bormann reads as follows: "The Reichsführer-SS, 8 October 1942 – Field Headquarters, Secret Matter, 5 copies.
To Herr Reichsleiter Martin Bormann! Dear Party comrade Bormann! Enclosed for your information is a copy of the file of attorney Dr. Albert Battel. I intend to have Battel arrested immediately after the war. I, moreover, recommend that at the appropriate time an examination be undertaken by the Party for the purpose to have him expelled from the Party. I have also informed the Silesian Gau authorities, to which Battel once belonged, concerning this matter. Heil Hitler! H. Himmler."
Battel, it turned out, had a Jewish brother-in-law (Eduard Heims), whom he helped to emigrate from Germany in 1933. Battel had joined the Nazi party in 1933, but in 1936, he was reprimanded by the party for extending a loan to a Jewish lawyer, whom he then allowed to pay off by doing work in his office. Later, in Przemyśl (before the incident described here), a reprimand was entered into his military papers, because "during negotiations with the leader of the *Judenrat* (Council of Jewish Elders), he had cordially shaken the hand of the man, a Dr. Duldig."

27. Oskar Schoenbrunner, YVA M31.2/1167.

28. Fritz Müller, YVA M31.2/2892.
29. Herbert Coehn, YVA M31.2/2390a. Stefania Dobrowolska was also recognized as among the Righteous. YVA M31.2/2390.
30. Wilhelm Hosenfeld, YVA M31.2/8589.
31. Herbert Haardt, YVA M31.2/2132.
32. Goldhagen, *Hitler's Willing* Executioners, 167; he places the number of all types of camps at 10,000; 168.
33. Goldhagen, *Hitler's Willing* Executioners, 171.
34. Goldhagen *Hitler's Willing* Executioners, 312.
35. Goldhagen, *Hitler's Willing* Executioners, 312, 314.
36. Gerhardt Marquardt, YVA M31.2/3161. Some labor foremen helped by providing additional food to their Jewish laborers, such as Emil Willmann, a foreman in a textile spinning factory in a camp in Neustadt-bei-Neisse that employed Jewish forced labor from Poland. He smuggled additional food to several of the workers, which his wife prepared at home; YVA M31.2/1503.
37. Hans Scheidling, YVA M31.2/4727.
38. Walter Groos, YVA M31.2/5871.
39. Artur Lanc, YVA M31.2/3385.
40. Willi Bleicher, YVA M31.2/65.
41. Wilhelm Hammann, YVA M31.2/2725. In his endeavor to rescue children, Hammann was aided by Herbert Siewert, Walter Vielhauer, and Franz Leitner – all German political prisoners since the early years of Nazi rule (Hammann was in Nazi jail since 1935) and assigned administrative positions in Buchenwald.
42. Ludwig Wörl, YVA M31.2/1. Also, Hermann Langbein, *People in Auschwitz* (Chapel Hill: University of North Carolina, 2004), 220–21.

CHAPTER 5 - RANDOM MEETINGS AND SUDDEN ENCOUNTERS

1. Rosa & Paul Mayer, YVA M31.2/394.
2. Otto Noerenberg, YVA M31.2/1373. Otto Noerenberg was honored by the Berlin Senate in 1962, under the *Unbesungene Helden* program.
3. Peter Friedrich, YVA M31.2/3187. In October 1944, Erika gave birth to a son, from her liaison with Ismar during the hiding period.

4. Ellen-Latte Brockmann, YVA M31.2/ 1404.
5. Elsa Ledetsch, YVA M31.2/ 3740. A similar random Berlin street encounter, in October 1942, between Kurt Markus and a police officer, Albert Juergens, eventually led to both fleeing across the border into Switzerland in December 1942, with two other persons. Suspected of being spies for Germany, Juergens and his non-Jewish companion were held imprisoned for the duration of the war. Kurt and his wife were sent to a Swiss detention camp; YVA M31.2/479.
6. Maria Nickel, YVA M31.2/474.
7. Willi Otto, YVA M31.2/2328.
8. Rudolf Bertram, YVA M31.2/1729.
9. Roman Erich Petsche, YVA M31.2/2265. Slightly to the south, in Belgrade, newly arrived Lieutenant Gerhard Radke helped the Pincas family, in April 1941, to acquire the necessary documentations, making it possible for them to leave the country and head for Turkey. They left in time, just before the start of anti-Jewish measures in that area; YVA M31.2/1162.
10. Richard Abel, YVA M31.2/510.
11. Walter Rosenkrantz, YVA M31.2/1054-1045. See also files of Rosalia Winczewicz – YVA 31.2/972 – and the Wojtowicz brothers: Alojzy, Kazimierz, Antoni – YVA 31.2/5664 – for details of Polish help to Jews in Hanaczów, Przemyślany region, where the story took place. In Warsaw, Kripo agent Rolf Peschel helped two Jewish sisters to survive undetected on the Aryan side. His assassination in June 1944, by the Polish underground is still shrouded in mystery; YVA M31.2/2813.
12. Kurt Reinhardt, YVA M31.2/2012.
13. Imgard Wieth, YVA M31.2/403. In the same city, Konrad David, who worked for a German building firm repairing the city's airstrip, helped Nusia Koerner and her young daughter. Nusia worked for David as a housekeeper. When in April 1944 she felt threatened by a Pole who recognized her as Jewish, Nusia disclosed to her employer her true origin. From that moment, he dedicated himself to saving her and her daughter through various ways; YVA M31.2/1621. A similar initial encounter between rescuer and rescued took place in Rava Ruska, Ukraine. Abraham Weinfeld relates that one day a German came to the pharmacy where he was working asking to buy razor blades. Pharmacies did not sell such items, but Abraham promised to bring some from home. The next day, the German

returned. Abraham gave him the blades but did not ask for money in return, "and at that moment a very close friendship between us was initiated and to him primarily four of us owe our survival of the Holocaust." The man returned often, introducing himself as Robert Krysinski, and claiming he was working for the Gestapo as a translator from German to Polish. One day, he appeared in the ghetto in disguise and knocked on several doors and in broken Yiddish, yelling, "*Yiden behalt eich.*" In June 1943, at Abraham's prodding, Krysinski agreed to hide a Jewish man. The man's wife was able to pass as a Christian, with Robert introducing her as his cousin. Then Abraham and his wife came to seek shelter in Krysinski's place. The three hid in a small space under the bed. Robert was suspected of hiding Jews, and his home was raided by the Gestapo, who came to investigate with a hound dog. The three wrapped themselves with old rags and the dog failed to pick up their scent. In the meantime, Robert served the Gestapo liquor, and after several hours they left. It turned out that Robert was really Leonard Bartlakowski, and although born in Berlin and a German national, he was also partly of Polish origin; YVA M31.2/1621.

14. Golhagen, *Hitler's Willing Executioners*, 348ff.

15. Erna Härtel, YVA M31.2/243.

16. Albert & Loni Harder, YVA M31.2/225. On the same Death March, near Steegen (off Elblong), Haya Baran and her mother collapsed in the snow. Screaming for help in her delirium, she was approached by a young woman, Christl Gerbrand, who calmed her, then returned with a snow sledge. Mother and daughter were taken to the woman's family's farm, where they found another hidden Jewish girl, and there they remained until the area's liberation. To outsiders, the fugitive women were introduced as Polish hand laborers on the farm. Thus they survived. Christl's brother Herbert served in a Nazi military unit but kept his silence. He died in the war. SS men came to search for straggling survivors, threatening to shoot anyone who had hidden them. Similarly, in the same region, Franz Leibl reports that during the retreat of his unit (the 7th Munich Division), he with the other soldiers approached a Gasthof (inn) near Seegen, where they saw the death marchers pass by. They were able to help six women, who pleaded for help, by instructing them to lay close to the snow-covered ground until the column had passed. Before leaving, Leibl asked the people in the Gasthof to help these women with food. Christl Gerbrand, YVA M31.2/4507.

17. Karl & Walburga Zacherl, YVA M31.2/1776.
18. Maria Grausenburger, YVA M31.2/1332.
19. Anna Ehn, YVA M31.2/1432.
20. Anna Frissnegg, YVA M31.2/2831.
21. Henny Brunken, YVA M31.2/491.
22. Josef Dinzinger, YVA M31.2/30.
23. Wilhelm & Maria Seitz, YVA M31.2/4593. See also the stories of Oskar Chaskiel Eissland, who escaped from a death march near Buchenwald camp and was hidden by the farmer Josef Maciejok; YVA M31.2/6027. Also, the fourteen-year-old Moshe Prusk, who managed to jump from a train taking prisoners from the camps of Kaufering to Dachau and was sheltered by two German women, Victoria Wanner and Maria Walch, in the Bavarian village of Weil; YVA M31.2/5386.
24. Kurt Fuchs, YVA M31.2/5964.
25. Arno Bach, YVA M31.2/3726.

Chapter 6 - Mixed Marriages, *Mischlinge* and Baptized Jews

1. Otto Springer, a German national residing in Prague (which, since March 1939, was part of the German protectorate of Bohemia and Moravia), was married to a Jewess. In 1944, the authorities asked Otto to divorce his wife. Refusing, he was sent to a forced labor camp in Klettendorf, Silesia, thence to other camps. Wife Hanna was not harmed, mainly as a result of bribery to a Gestapo official. Both survived; YVA M31.2/3402.
2. For more on mixed marriages, see Ursula Büttner, "The Persecution of Christian-Jewish Families in the Third Reich," *The Leo Baeck Year Book* 34 (1989): 268-89; Jeremy Noakes, "The Development of Nazi Policy towards the German-Jewish 'Mischlinge' 1933-1945," *The Leo Baeck Year Book* 34 (1989): 291-354. See also Friedlander, "The Deportation of the German Jews," 224; Gutteridge, *Open Thy Mouth*, 257; and Seligmann, "An Illegal Way of Life," 346. Also, the interesting, and somewhat apologetic, account of a German official in the Ministry of the Interior, who was personally involved in drafting the provisions with regard to the *Mishlinge*. Bernhard Loesener, "Das Reichsministerium des

Innern und die Judengesetzgebung," *Vierteljahrshefte für Zeitgeschi*chte 9 (1961): 262–313.

3. Marie Grünberg, YVA M31.2/2824.
4. Charlotte Weiler, YVA M31.2/553.
5. Trude Wisten, YVA M31.2/6053.
6. Lisa Holländer, YVA M31.2/669; Elisabeth Bornstein, YVA M31.2/2311.
7. Maria Steiner, YVA M31.2/431; Anna-Maria Haas, YVA M31.2/2266.
8. Marianne Golz, YVA M31.2/3845.
9. Marie-Luise Hensel, YVA M31.2/3845.
10. Werner Krumme, YVA M31.2/33.
11. Carl Strecker, YVA M31.2/3010; Walter Groos, YVA M31.2/5871; Hanning Schroeder, YVA M31.2/1252d.
12. Werner Sylten, YVA M31.2/1614. The previously mentioned Gerhard Schwersensky, a Quaker who sheltered for a time two Jewish sisters in his Berlin home, was reported to have been earlier dismissed from his public service post because he was a *Mischling.* His wife, Ilse, was non-Jewish; YVA M31.2/3201.
13. Theodor Görner, YVA M31.2/387; and Gertrud Kochanowski, YVA M31.2/1088. In a related story, Karl Groeger was an Austrian medical student who fled the country to Holland after the country's annexation to Germany in March 1938. When the Germans occupied the Netherlands, in 1940, Groeger was conscripted into the army but was soon dismissed after it was revealed that he was a quarter-Jew. He returned to Holland and joined an underground cell. In March 1943, his unit blew up the population registration office in Amsterdam, to frustrate the deportation of Jews as well as Dutch persons sent for forced labor in Germany. The building and thousands of registration cards were destroyed. This was considered a high point in the underground's operations. Anne Frank, then in hiding with her family, noted in her diary that the explosion almost threw her out of her bed. Betrayed to the authorities, the whole group, including Groeger, was caught and sentenced to death by an SS and police court; YVA M31.2/3381b.
14. Heinrich Middendorf, YVA M31.2/5837.
15. Heinrich Hamer, YVA M31.2/3358.

16. Joseph Neyses, YVA M31.2/2093. In Munich, when Rosl Vetter learned in early 1945 that all Jewish persons in mixed marriages were about to be deported to Theresienstadt, she went into hiding in the home of her friends, Gisela Scherer and her sister Josy Hoffmann, leaving a suicide note to distract the authorities. Her bank account was consequently frozen, and this made it impossible for her to contribute to the expenses of her two rescuers; YVA M31.2/694.

17. Ernst Pfau, YVA M31.2/263.

18. Eberhard Schnellen, YVA M31.2/3492.

19. Sibylle Dierke, YVA M31.2/4061.

20. Gerhard Mueller, YVA M31.2/3157. See also Jovy/Jülich/Schink, YVA M31.2/2264. Adolf and Maria Althoff, already described, operated a circus in the Darmstadt area and sheltered Alice Danner, born Jewish, who was married to Hans, a soldier on the Russian front. The Althoffs sheltered Alice and her half-Jewish daughter Irene in their circus; YVA M31.2/6433. Herbert and Ella Bernhardt helped Rosa Kahler, married to a non-Jew, to find an apartment in Berlin, to where she moved from Bublitz, Pomerania. Ella was in charge of the Jewish section of a firm producing uniforms and used her position to forewarn the 80 Jewish women of Gestapo raids. Some of them were temporarily sheltered in the Bernhardt home; YVA M31.2/2502.

21. Otto Kessel, YVA M31.2/1905.

22. Erich Buengener, YVA M31.2/4788.

23. Elisabeth Flügge, YVA M31.2/986. In Cologne, Dr. Albert Grüneberg was married to Philomene (non-Jewish) and had previously worked for the German railroads. In October 1943, both were arrested by the police and taken to a transit camp in Köln-Bocklemünd. Friends organized their escape, and they were sheltered in several places in Cologne. See Mathias Niessen, YVA M31.2/1841, on the evolution of this case and the contest in court between those who claimed to have helped the Grüneberg couple. In Mannheim, the Jewish Karl Herzberg was married to a non-Jewish woman. In February 1945, when they received deportation summons for Theresienstadt, they were helped by Wilhelm Buerger, a former business associate, who arranged for both to stay, first with the Georg Hammer, then with the Mathias Mueller families; YVA M31.2/1469-71. In Züschen, near Kassel, Pastor Walter Disselnkötter, a member of the Confessing Church, sheltered a woman

claiming to be fleeing the advancing Russians in East Prussia, but whom he and his wife, Anna, suspected to be Jewish. She was "fully" Jewish and married to the "Aryan" dentist Dr. Ernst Plüer, from Kassel. When in January 1945 she received the dreaded deportation summons, she was dissuaded from committing suicide by a friend who urged her to try seeking shelter with the pastor in nearby Züschen; YVA M31.2/9648.

24. The Reich Citizenship Decree of November 14, 1935 (which followed the Nuremberg Laws of two months earlier) defined a Jew as someone descended from at least three grandparents who were racially full Jews. A person was also classified Jewish even if an offspring of only two full Jewish grandparents, if he belonged to the Jewish religion or was married to a Jewish person, or was the offspring of an extramarital relationship with a Jew.

25. For an in-depth study of the *Mischlinge* issue, see the previously mentioned articles—Noakes, "The Development of Nazi Policy"; and, Büttner, "The Persecution of Christian-Jewish Families in the Third Reich. Also, Friedlander, "The Deportation of the German Jews," 223.

26. Gregor Johann Mendel, a nineteenth-century scientist and Augustinian friar, gained posthumous fame as the founder of the modern science of genetics. His pea plant experiments conducted between 1856 and 1863 established many of the rules of heredity, now referred to as the laws of Mendelian inheritance. He claimed that the influence of invisible factors – later called genes – showed visible traits in predictable ways, and this ushered in the new science of genetics.

27. Noakes, "The Development of Nazi Policy, " 354.

28. Elsa Blochwitz, YVA M31.2/137. In 1960, she was honored by the Berlin Senate under the *Unbesungene Helden* program.

29. Hans Sieber, YVA M31.2/2055.

30. Helmut Karnop, YVA M31.2/1254. Interestingly, Herta Thiemke's sister, Lotte, was married to a non-Jew who was drafted in the army, and the authorities pressured him to divorce Lotte (who continued practicing the Jewish religion, whereas Herta had gone over to Christianity). Upon Karnop's advice, he declined to do so.

31. Gitta Bauer, YVA M31.2/3138; Paula Huelle, YVA M31.2/653; and Leonhard Gailer, YVA M31.2/5645.

32. Maria von Maltzan, YVA M31.2/3545.

33. See Hans von Dohnányi, YVA M31.2/4605; Hans Georg Calmeyer, YVA M31.2/4997; and Gerhard Wander, YVA M31.2/925.

34. Adolf Althoff, YVA M31.2/6433.

35. Maimi von Mirbach, YVA M31.2/2040; Walter Czok, YVA M31.2/567; Anastasia Gerschuetz, YVA M31.2/3257; Michael Jovy, YVA M31.2/2264a.

36. Heinrich Grüber, YVA M31.2/75. For more on the baptized Jews, see Werner Cohn, "Bearers of a Common Fate? The 'Non-Aryan' Christian 'Fate-Comrades" of the Paulus-Bund, 1933–1939," *The Leo Baeck Yearbook* 33 (1988): 327–66; especially, 331, 337, 345, 351, 353. Also, Gutteridge, *Open Thy Mouth*, 206–07.

37. Gertrud Luckner, YVA M31.2/280. See also *Freiburger Rundbrief* 49, no. 12 (1959/1960): 29-44.

38. Konrad von Rabenau, YVA M31.2/625; Richard Goelz, YVA M31.2/5039. See the brochure by Beate Steckan in YVA M31.2/625, "*Nacht Über Deutschland*," which ends with words by Dietrich Bonhoeffer: "I believe that God can and wants to produce goodness out of everything. For this, he needs people who will endure everything, in the hope it will serve the good cause."

39. Wilma Groyen, YVA M31.2/3852.

40. In 1965, Mrs. Forck turned down the German government citizenship courage award *Verdienstkreuz Erster Klasse*, offered by the President of West Germany. In her letter to President Dr. Heinrich Luebke, she wrote: "The whole congregation of St. Stephani-South, in Bremen, to which I belong, with its pastor Dr. Gustav Greiffenhagen, has since the beginning of the Nazi rule protested against injustice and violence in the Church and State, and was therefore in many ways exposed to much suffering. Out of Christian responsibility, the Church unanimously protected and helped the Jewish members of the congregation, as long and as far as it was possible. A number of congregants were either arrested or were suspended from their jobs. I see myself as just one member of this Confessing Congregation who, each according to his capacity, tried to fulfill the Christian command of brotherly love for those in greatest need. For reasons of conscience, I cannot accept a special public decoration for what I consider as a Christian obligation. I, therefore, beg of you to cancel the bestowing of this award." Elisabeth Forck, YVA M31.2/400.

41. Esther-Maria Seidel, YVA M31.2/2422; Alfred Dilger, YVA M31.2/4882; Maria Hueren, YVA M31.2/3492; Sibylle Hueren, YVA M31.2/4061; and Heinrich Middendorf (mentioned in chapter 6), YVA M31.2/5737. Pastor Guenther Brandt, of the Confessing Church, similarly helped the Jewish Christian Gertrud Leupold in early 1945. Brandt reportedly also extended temporary shelter in his Potsdam home to Susanna Vogel in late 1943. She was a *Mischling*; YVA M31.2/1867.

CHAPTER 7 - SUBVERTING THE SYSTEM – PERSONS IN POSITIONS OF AUTHORITY AND INFLUENCE

1. Otto Weidt, YVA M31.2/671; Hermann Graebe, YVA M31.2/116; Berthold Beitz, YVA M31.2/299; Julius Madritsch, YVA M31.2/21; Raimond Titsch, YVA M31.2/22; Oskar Schindler, YVA M31.2/20. As we shall see later, Calmeyer saved 2,800 Jews, and in this he was helped by a loyal staff of Germans and Dutch confidantes. As for Schindler, he acted alone, except for the help by his wife, Emilie, in Brünnlitz. At the same time, his Jewish confidantes in Kraków (Abraham Bankier) and in Plaszów/Brünnlitz (Isaac Stern) were also of much help to him in his rescue efforts.
2. Josef Meyer, YVA M31.2/157.
3. Hans von Dohnányi, YVA M31.2/4605.
4. Ferdinand G. Duckwitz, YVA M31.2/679. After the war, Duckwitz became West Germany's first ambassador to Denmark. Later he was director of the East European division in the German Foreign Ministry. See Hans Hedtoft's Foreword in Aage Bertelsen, *October '43* (New York: G.P. Putnam's Sons, 1954).
5. Eduard Schulte, YVA M31.2/3842. See Walter Laqueur and Richard Breitman, *Breaking the Silence: The Secret Mission of Eduard Schulte, Who Brought the World News of the Final Solution* (London: Bodley Head, 1987).
6. Wilhelm von Hahn, YVA M31.2/761. In her memoirs, Mrs. Ullman, wife of Rabbi Solomon Ullman, dedicated a song to von Hahn, which I freely translated as following: "1943, to von Hahn; A Righteous among all the Unrighteous. No war medal adorns your breast. No combat medal was bestowed on you; and in the Nazi Iliad you will not be lauded as a

hero. Yet, there where to be a human being is of value; where no false idols are worshipped; where people still pray to and worship God; there a higher reward is awaiting you. All those saved by you, who were not crushed by hostile hands, with humility will bow before God. All will testify on your behalf when the honors will be distributed. The Almighty remains eternal." See also, Leon Platteau, YVA M31.2/229.

7. Jacob Presser, *Ashes in the Wind; the Destruction of Duth Jewry* (London: Souvenir Press, 1965), 299.
8. Presser, *Ashes in the Wind,* 311.
9. Presser, *Ashes in the Wind,* 305-11.
10. Benno Stokvis documents, in Gerhard Wander, YVA M31.2/925.
11. Hans G. Calmeyer, YVA M31.2/4997; Gerhard Wander, YVA M31.2/925; Cornelis Teutscher, YVA M31.2/2478; Antonius Mom, YVA M31.2/2477; and Jaap Van Proosdij, YVA M31.2/7763. Presser, *Ashes in the Wind,* 297–98, 301–04, 308–11.

CHAPTER 8 - OPEN DEFIANCE OF NAZI ANTISEMITISM

1. Otto Krayer, YVA M31.2/5531. See Avram Goldstein, *Otto Krayer: 1899–1982,* reprinted from *Biographical Memoirs* 57, (The National Academy Press, Washington, D.C, 1987), and Mueller-Hill, *Murderous Science.*
2. Armin T. Wegner, YVA M31.2/306. See also Sybil Milton, "Armin T. Wegner: Polemicist for Armenian and Jewish Human Rights, *Armenian Review,* 42, no. 4/168 (1989): 17–40. In April 1996, his remains were reinterred in Armenia, as a gesture to the man who had sounded the alarm on the massacre of the Armenians during World War I. (Report in *Ha'aretz,* April 19, 1996; Weekly Supplement section, 25-28).
3. In the Gestapo report, her words are given as follows: *"Das Vorgehen gegen die Juden halte ich jedoch nicht für richtig. Mit diesen Massnahmen kann ich mich nicht einverstanden erklären.... Mir ist ein jeder anständige Mann recht, ganz gleich welcher Nationalität er eingehört."* Ilse S. Totzke, YVA M31.2/6335.
4. Ilse S. Totzke, YVA M31.2/6335.
5. Gutteridge, *Open Thy Mouth,* 184-185; Wolfgang Gerlach, *And the Witnesses Were Silent: The Confessing Church and the Persecution of the*

Jews (Lincoln: University of Nebraska, 2000), 107, 144–45, 147–48; Heinz D. Leuner, *When Compassion was a Crime: Germany's Silent Heroes* (London: Wolff, 1978), 114.

6.   Kevin P. Spicer, *Resisting the Third Reich: The Catholic Clergy in Hitler's Berlin* (DeKalb, Ill.: Northern Illinois University, 2004), 160–82.

7.   Spicer, *Resisting the Third Reich*, 167.

8.   Spicer, *Resisting the Third Reich*, 177.

9.   Spicer, *Resisting the Third Reich*, 175.

10. Spicer, *Resisting the Third Reich*, 178. Otto Ogiermann, *Bis zum letzten Atemzug: das Leben und Aufbegehren des Priesters Bernhard Lichtenberg* (Leipzig: St. Benno-Verlag, 1983), 131.

11. Gotthard Klein, *Berolinen Canonizationis Servi Dei Bernardi Lichtenberg* (Rome: Congregation de Causis Sanctorum, 1992), 165–66. Ogiermann, *Bis zum letzten* Atemzug, 142–43, 152, 161.

12. Klein, *Berolinen,* 330.

13. Klein, *Berolinen,* 166.

14. Guenther Lewy, *The Catholic Church and Nazi Germany* (New York: McGraw-Hill, 1965), 284.

15. YVA M31.2/10292; Spicer, *Resisting the Third Reich,* 453–60.

CHAPTER 9 – POSSIBLE MOTIVATIONS

1.   Tec Nechama, *When the Light Pierced the Darkness: Christian Rescue of Jews in Nazi-Occupied Poland* (New York: Oxford University, 1986).

2.   Tec, *When the Light Pierced*, 154, 160, 180.

3.   Tec, *When the Light Pierced*, 153.

4.   Tec, *When the Light Pierced*, 164.

5.   Tec, *When the Light Pierced*, 188–89.

6.   Tec, *When the Light Pierced*, 190.

7.   Samuel and Pearl Oliner, *The Altruistic Personality: Rescuers of Jews in Nazi Europe* (New York: Free Press, 1988), 199, 203, and especially chapter 10.

8.   Oliner, *The Altruistic Personality*, 222.

9.   Oliner, *The Altruistic Personality*, 189.

10. Fogelman Eva, *Conscience and Courage: Rescuers of Jews During the Holocaust* (New York: Anchor/Doubleday, 1994).

11. Fogelman, *Conscience and Courage*, xiv, xvii.

12. Fogelman, *Conscience and Courage*, 57.

13. Fogelman, *Conscience and Courage*, 59. See also articles in Elizabeth Midlarsky and L. Baron, ed., *"Altruism and Prosocial Behavior,"* *Humboldt Journal of Social Relations* 13, no. 1/2 (1986).

14. Fogelman, *Conscience and Courage*, 66

15. Fogelman, *Conscience and Courage*, 41.

16. Fogelman, *Conscience and Courage*, 58.

17. Fogelman, *Conscience and Courage*, 61.

18. Fogelman, *Conscience and Courage*, 65.

19. Fogelman, *Conscience and Courage*, 150.

20. Fogelman, *Conscience and Courage*, 68–69.

21. Fogelman, *Conscience and Courage*, 81.

22. Fogelman, *Conscience and Courage*, 76–77.

23. Fogelman, *Conscience and Courage*, 68.

24. Fogelman, *Conscience and Courage*, 161–64.

25. Fogelman, *Conscience and Courage*, 254.

26. Fogelman, *Conscience and Courage*, 257–58.

27. London, "The Rescuers: Motivational Hypotheses about Christians who Saved Jews from the Nazis," J. Macaulay and L. Berkowitz, ed., *Altruism and Helping Behavior* (New York, Academic Press, 1970), 241–50.

28. London, "The Rescuers," 244.

29. London, "The Rescuers," 245, 249.

30. London, "The Rescuers," 247.

31. Kristen Renwick Monroe, "A Different Way of Seeing Things: What We Can Learn from the Rescuers of Jews," in John Michalczyk, ed., *Resisters, Rescuers, and Refugees: Historical and Ethical Issues* (Kansas City: Sheed & Ward, 1997), 243–48.

32. Monroe, 244.

33. Monroe, "A Different Way of Seeing," 245, 247. Elsewhere, she terms rescuers as "John Donne's people," after the sixteenth-century English poet, author of "No man is an island."

34. Monroe, "A Different Way of Seeing," 248.

35. Daniel Fraenkel, "The German Righteous Among the Nations," *Lexicon of the Righteous Among the Nations: Europe, Part 1* (Jerusalem: Yad Vashem 2007): lii-lxiii.

36. Fraenkel, "The German Righteous," lxii.

37. For more by Levinas, see Emmanuel Levinas, *Total and Infinity*, trans. Alphonso Lingis (Pittsburgh: Duquesne Uni., 1969), and *Alterity and Transcendence*, trans. Michael B. Smith (London: Athlone, and New York: Columbia University, 1999). See also Ze'ev Levy, "The Concept of 'the Other' in Levinas' Ethics," *Daat* 30 (1993): 21–40.

38. James Mensch, "Rescue and the Face-to-Face," St. Francis Xavier University, Antigonish, Nova Scotia, Canada (unpublished), 12.

39. Mensch, "Rescue," 12. See also James Mensch, "Death and the Other: A Shared Premise" (unpublished). I am particularly indebted to Prof. Mensch for his insightful interpretation of Levinas's thought.

40. In interpreting Levinas's philosophy, Mensch advances the interesting observation that according to Levinas it is God that the Holocaust rescuer confronts in the face-to-face encounter. The God that cannot be represented, the God that transcends the natural world, appears in the form of the Jew who knocks on the door. God's being, as totally other-worldly, can only appear as a lack of worldly content (such as poverty and persecution). Such worldly privation is God's manifestation – in the guise of the abandoned, the unfortunate, and the wretched. It is the God who appears as an appeal, and a call to respond. This God was present during the Holocaust; "he appeared each time the Jew knocked on the door." However, only a precious few, the rescuers, recognized this" (Mensch, "Rescue and the Face to Face," 10). Somewhat similar, yet different, is Pastor John Cazalis's personal Christological interpretation of his help to Jews in France – the Jew in the form of the Crucified. "In every one of them, whoever he was, it was the Christ who came toward us, in the form of the rejected one, the condemned and crucified. In loving them, it is His love that we received. When they invaded our homes and lives . . . , it was His mercy and joy that came into play. . . . On each occasion as well, we knew afterwards that He had blessed us." Georges Casalis, in Emile C. Fabre, ed., *Les Clandestins de Dieu* (Paris: Fayard, 1968), 203–204).

41. On the Rosenstrasse incident, see Stoltzfus, *Resistance of the Heart*.

42. Browning, *Ordinary Men*.

43. Milgram, *Obedience to Authority*.

44. Goldhagen argued that the perpetrators were persons capable of making moral choices, but he disregards the fact that the group was a

pressure-cooker, which may have precluded such moral choices. He also challenges the carrying-out-of-orders theory: "Would the perpetrators have carried out an order to kill the entire Danish people, their own Nordic cousins, just as they did the Jews? Would they have exterminated, root and branch, all the people of Munich?" Surely not. "The perpetrators' conception of the victims was a critical source of their willingness to kill them." Yet this is not entirely a convincing argument. U.S. soldiers could be led to kill with greater ease village inhabitants in Vietnam, but would have disobeyed orders to wipe out inhabitants of an American city. That does not prove that U.S. soldiers had an "eliminationist" concept vis-a-vis the Vietnamese people. However, Goldhagen is correct in pointing out that in Germany, people had been captive for close to a decade to a vicious form of demonological anti-semitism. The Jew was portrayed as the ultimate enemy, and this no doubt contributed in silencing moral scruples, allowing perpetrators to deal harshly with the Jews. But it was the group context that facilitated it and removed personal responsibility from arbitrarily shooting men, women, and children, time and again, coupled with a deep hatred of the Jewish people, the result of a centuries-old demonological depiction of Jews. Goldhagen, *Hitler's Willing Executioners*, 14, 380, 390, 392.

AFTERWORD

1. Saul Friedländer, *The Years of Extermination: 1939–1945* (New York: HarperCollins, 2007), xiiii–xix.

2. Words spoken during the Hebrew University (Jerusalem) conference on the German *Sonderweg* and the Final Solution, November 26–28, 1996.

3. John Weiss, *Ideology of Death*, chapters 23, 24; Goldhagen, *Hitler's Willing Executioners,* chapter 16.

4. Bankier, *The Germans and the Final Solution*, 153–56.

5. No radical antisemitism was evident during the Weimar period, and before the Nazi rise to power, antisemitism was stronger and more widespread in France. At the same time, one has to differentiate between concepts and political action. The Social Democrats, for instance, were

not free from antisemitic views, but their political philosophy left them no room but to favor civil rights to Jews.

6.   Elisabeth Abegg, YVA M31.2/345.

APPENDIX A - THE RIGHTEOUS TITLE AND ITS CRITERIA

1.   Hans von Dohnányi, YVA M31.2/4605. See also Yehuda Bauer, *Jews for Sale?: Nazi-Jewish Negotiations* (New York: Yale University, 1994), 108–09.
2.   Hans Walz, YVA M31.2/497.
3.   Walter Czok, YVA M31.2/567.
4.   Alfons Zuendler, YVA M31.2/5831.
5.   Willi Friedrichs, YVA M31.2/502.
6.   Wilhelm von Hahn, YVA M31.2/761.
7.   Hans Georg Calmeyer, YVA M31.2/4997. Jacob Presser, *Ashes in the Wind: The Destruction of Dutch Jewry* (London: Souvenir Press, 2010), 297–98.
8.   Wilm Hosenfeld, YVA M31.2/8589. Filmmaker Roman Polanski integrated this story of the German officer into his film of the Jewish musician, in *The Pianist*.
9.   Berthold Beitz, YVA M31.2/299.
10.   Julius Madritsch, YVA M31.2/21.
11.   Alfred Rossner, YVA M31.2/6239.
12.   Oskar Schindler, YVA M31.2/20.
13.   Karl Plagge; YVA M31.2/9557.
14.   Ludwig Wörl, YVA M31.2/1; Hermann Langbein, YVA M31.2/305.
15.   Willi Bleicher, YVA M31.2/65; Wilhelm Hammann, YVA M31.2/2725.
16.   Otto Krayer, YVA M31.2/5531.
17.   Armin T. Wegner, YVA M31.2/306.
18.   Ilse Sonja Totzke. YVA M31.2/6335.
19.   Max Liedtke and Albert Battel, YVA M31.2/1979.
20.   Bernhard Lichtenberg; YVA M31.2/10292.
21.   Eduard Schulte, YVA M31.2/3842.
22.   Gustav Schroeder, YVA M31.2/5353.

23. Konrad von Rabenau, YVA M31.2/625.

24. Elisabeth Forck, YVA M31.2/400.

25. Hannelore Bach, presently living in the United States, responded angrily to her rescuer's disqualification: "I find it ironic that the Nazi regime under Hitler looked for me, wanted to put me in a concentration camp and exterminate me as a Jew – never mind that Mother was a Protestant and I was baptized the same. And yet, the Commission for the Designation of the Righteous considers me as a non-Jew who had left the Jewish fold. And where did that put me under the Nazi regime? My father's sister was killed in Auschwitz with many members of his family. His brother, my uncle lives in Israel in a kibbutz with his extended family. . . . Leonhard and Maria Gailer's family and the whole village will find it hard to believe that the 'Jiddishe Maedele' that the Gailer family took in and hid is not considered a Jew after these years by her own people." I wrote back, explaining the Commission's logic and ruling, adding that this was no reflection on the humanitarianism of the Gailer family. Leonhard Gailer, YVA M31.2/5645.

26. Heinrich Middendorf, YVA M31.2/5837.

27. Dietrich Bonhoeffer; M31.2/8908. For Bonhoeffer's 1933 article, see Dietrich Bonhoeffer, *No Rusty Swords,* vol. 1, ed. Edwin H. Robinson (London: Collins, 1965), 223–27, 241. On Bonhoeffer's theological anti-Judaism, see Emil L. Fackenheim, *The Jewish Return to History* (New York: Schocken, 1978), 36. See also Saul Friedländer, *Nazi Germany and the Jews,* vol. 1 (New York: HarperCollins, 1997), 45–46.

28. Alexandre Glasberg, M31.2/9792.

APPENDIX B: BERLIN SENATE'S UNBSESUNGENE HELDEN

1. Dennis Riffel, *Unbesungene Helden: Die Ehrungsinitiative der Berliner Senats 1958 bis 1966* (Berlin: Metropol, 2007).

2. Riffel, 37.

3. Riffel, 40.

4. Riffel, 38–40.

5. Riffel, 40–2.

6. Riffel, 49.

7. Riffel, 50.

8. Riffel, 51–4.

9. Riffel, 69. There are no definite accounts of how many Jews in Berlin survived the Nazi period while remaining in that capital city. In 1947, 1,379 Jewish Berliners came forward to report on their survival. Another estimate places the Jews hidden or living illegally in Berlin at 3,500, of whom only half survived, while still another estimate suggests that the figure may be as much as 5,000. Consideration must also be given to those hidden in Berlin who did not regard themselves Jewish, only so by Nazi definition. Moreover, what makes the count even more difficult is that half of the rescued persons had left Germany right after the war, whereas most rescuers remained in the city; Riffel, 22, 29, 43.

10. Riffel, 46. Some suggested a less bombastic title than *Unbesungene Helden*, which they felt could make some recipients feel uncomfortable, but this was rejected by Lipschitz, who held fast to the UH title. Others preferred the term "Silent Heroes" (*Stille Helden*); Riffel, 11, 87.

11. Riffel, 66, 104.

12. Riffel, 106, 78–9, 116, 118. In 1198 out of 1,864 cases, rescuers who had initiated a request were asked by UH to provide witnesses. A total of 186 rescuers had difficulties doing so as the rescued persons either had already died or had left Germany, or their testimonies were found to be lacking in vital and incontrovertible information; Riffel, 170.

13. Riffel, 95, 73. On thirty-three occasions, Lipschitz, who always retained the final word, overruled the recommendations of his team, by allowing a more liberal decision, especially when involving compensation costs. See for instance Lipschitz's ruling in the Margaret F. and Bruno Fredrich cases; Riffel, 94, 96–7.

14. Riffel, 138. Persons living in East Berlin were not processed by Lipschitz's organization but turned over to the Jewish community for further examination and financial assistance; Riffel, 71, 76. This prevailed until the erection of the Berlin Wall in August 1961, which led to a total communications cutoff, including petitions by East Berliners with regard to the UH program; Riffel, 98.

15. Riffel, 112, 114.

16. Riffel, 117.

17. Riffel, 116. In 1986, she was also posthumously honored by Yad Vashem.

18. Riffel, 115. A total of 123 persons asked for the closure of their cases due to the length of time in processing their requests; Riffel, 118.

19. Riffel, 25, 33, 72, 92–3. Persons asking for financial assistance were required to submit documents as to their income and assets, including taxes paid; Riffel, 80. In some cases, petitioners asked for their file to be closed after they were awarded monetary benefits of one sort or another from other governmental agencies, and therefore they did not need any additional emoluments. A total of eighteen honorees declined financial assistance; all others accepted it; Riffel, 120–1.

20. "Ehrung von Berliner Bürgern, die in der NS-Zeit verfolgten uneigennützig Hilfe gewährt haben," Riffel, 89. Another definition stated "uneigennützig Verfolgten während der Zeit der nationalsozialistischen Gewaltherrschaft in nicht unerheblichem Masse Schutz und Hilfe gewährt hat," Riffel, 140.

21. Riffel, 141.

22. Riffel, 91–2.

23. Riffel, 157–9.

24. Riffel, 162. Strangely, sheltering Jews in the period after the July 20, 1944 assassination plot on Hitler's life was considered less risky for rescuers than before it, since after that event the Nazi regime had become preoccupied with other pressing needs, and these were the first signs of the disintegration of the regime. Many cases of this period were consequently resolved with only one-time financial assistance. As explained by an UH employee in response to such a query, in the post–July 20, 1944 period the Gestapo was busy with keeping the peace and calm within the population, and not that anxious to catch helpers of Jews. As noted by Riffel, it was a very strange explanation; Riffel, 161.

25. Riffel, 84, 137, 164–5. For example, a certain woman continuously supplied a Jewish family with food until that family's arrest and deportation in July 1943. During that period, she had to face abuse and maltreatment by neighbors, which impaired her health. She was recognized and awarded a monthly stipend of 100 DM; Riffel, 162.

26. Riffel, 154–5. Also worth noting is the story of Helene Jacobs, who belonged to the Confessing Church, and was a member of the Kaufmann circle, which helped many Jews with sheltering places and false credentials; she was arrested and imprisoned. She was recognized (later, by Yad Vashem as well); Riffel, 155, 197. Maria Nickel, who turned over

her personal identities to Ruth Abraham, after changing the photos on them, was also honored; Riffel, 156. Years later, she was also recognized by Yad Vashem.

27. Riffel, 176. See other similar cases; Riffel, 152, 166.

28. In light of this, the UH recognition of Gertraut von Cleve is indeed surprising. She worked as secretary in the army command and was an important contact person for the conspirators. She was fortunate not to have been identified and avoided arrest. Lipschitz insisted that she be recognized, and so it was, topped with a monthly stipend of 200 DM. Similarly for fellow conspirator Fritz Neubecker, who was also recognized, although in his case he also reportedly afforded help to some Jews; Riffel, 167–8.

29. Riffel, 185.

30. Riffel, 188. For similar romantically involved cases, see Riffel, 186–90.

31. Riffel, 191–2. See the interesting case of a so-called "full" Jewess, who sheltered for a long time in her home a Jewish man. She managed to convince the authorities that her son, who was serving in the army, was the product of an illicit affair with a non-Jewish man, while herself being at the same time married to a Jewish man. By special decision of Hitler, the son was allowed to stay in the army, and thus his mother was protected from arrest. She was not recognized, for in the words of the UH staff, "it was her moral obligation to help two persons of her faith," Riffel, 198–9.

32. Riffel, 193, 195.

33. The original German reads: "Herr...hat sich in selbstloser Weise mit den ihm zu Gebote stehenden Mitteln und unter Gefährdung seine eigenen Person gegen die von den nationalsozialistischen Machthabern erbarmungslos geübte Missachtung menschlicher Würde und die kaltblütige Vernichtung unschuldiger Opfer des Rassenwahns aufgelehnt. Durch sein Verhalten, das besonderen persönlichen Mut voraussetzte, hat er dem Nationalsozialismus Widerstand geleistet. Sein Beispeil muss als Anzeichen dafür gelten, dass es in jenem Deutschland der äussersten Gewaltherrschaft noch wertvolle und opferbereite Kräfte gegeben hat," Riffel, 74–5.

34. In the German original: "teil ich Ihnen mit, dass ich mich sehr darum bemüht habe, die Bedeutung ihrer Hilfeleistungen für bedrängte Verfolgte voll zu würdigen. Ich verkenne nicht, dass Ihre Haltung mit

dazu beigetragen hat, das Schicksal der verfolgten Mitbürger seinerzeit zu erleichtern. Ich möchte aber darauf hinweisen, dass die Zahl der Berliner Bürger, die seinerzeit den Verfolgten beigestanden haben, sehr gross ist, so dass ich gezwungen bin, im Rahmen dieser Ehrung für die Anerkennung einen fest umrissenen und sehr strengen Massstab anzulegen. Massgebend für die Entscheidung ist daher der Umfang der eigenen Gefährdung und das Ausmass der geleisteten Hilfe. Bei Anwendung dieses strengen Massstabes kann daher für die Ehrung nur ein sehr beschränkter Personenkreis in Betracht kommen. Ich bitte Sie, versichert zu sein, dass die Auswahl dieser verdienten Bürger sehr sorgfältig getroffen wird. Dannach muss ich Ihnen aber zu meinem Bedauern mitteilen, dass Sie nach diesen Grundsätzen für eine Ehrung leider nicht in Betracht gezogen werden können," Riffel, 124–5.

35. Riffel, 127.
36. Riffel, 118–9, 130–2.
37. Riffel, 133–5. Requests originating in East Berlin were not automatically rejected but were turned over to the Jewish community's *Arbeitsgemeinschaft* association, for further processing, unless they had in the meantime moved to West Berlin; Riffel, 136–7.
38. Riffel, 29, 195–6. Grüber and Poelchau were both later honored by Yad Vashem. Margarete Sommer was likewise declined the UH honor. She had worked for the Catholic diocese of Berlin and referred Jews to persons prepared to hide them, providing them with life provisions. She had already been honored by the West German government, in 1953, with the *Bundesverdienstkreuz*, first class; Riffel, 30. She was also later honored by Yad Vashem.
39. Riffel, 80, 200–3.
40. Riffel, 205–6, 210.
41. Riffel, 147.
42. Riffel, 152.
43. Riffel, 152–3. See also Denis Riffel, "Flucht über das Meer," in Benz Wolfgang, ed., *Überleben im Dritten Reich* (Munich: C.H. Beck, 2003), 153–165.
44. In the rejection letter, the UH office left out the customary positive acknowledgment at the end of the nonacceptance letter, which stated that "this decision has in no way any bearing on your behavior during the Nazi period, and ask for your understanding of this determination." In

summary, forty-seven compensation cases were rejected, while twelve others were recognized. Riffel, 174–5, 179–81.

45. Riffel, 218–20. A person known for homosexual relations could also forfeit the UH title. In total five such cases were rejected, also due, for some, to a prior sentence against them for sexual misconduct, such as sexual relations with a minor; Riffel, 212.

46. Riffel, 211, 213–17.

47. See also Riffel, 222–51 for more examples of false statements submitted.

48. Riffel, 223.

49. Riffel, 26–8, 171–3.

50. Riffel, 12, 18, 23, 100-1, 110, 129, 142, 235, 245.

51. Riffel, 241, 242–4. In August 1960 Siegmund and Marga Spiegel, who were aided by a group of Münsterland farmers (eventually recognized by Yad Vashem), appealed to the provincial authorities of Nordrhein-Westfallen to have their rescuers honored—a request that was declined due to "verification" problems; Riffel, 241.

52. Riffel, 246–8. The *Bundesverdienstkreuz* program was instituted in 1951 and has been awarded to some 2,10,000 persons for various social, philanthropic, and church work, "away from the public eye."Awards were given for efforts to improve employment and create jobs, entrepreneurial and scientific achievements, fostering peaceful interaction and mutual tolerance with other religions and cultures, and for enhancing Germany's image abroad. It is the country's highest tribute to individual persons. Three thousand to five thousand awards are handed out each year. No pecuniary payment is necessarily attached.

53. Riffel, 75, 249.

54. In 1969, the Berlin Senate transmitted to Yad Vashem microfilm records of 450 UH honorees. See, Der Senator für Inneres; I Wg 3-0254/810; letter by Mr. Fritz to Dr. Kermisz, at Yad Vashem, of November 2, 1972.

BIBLIOGRAPHY

*   *   *

PRIMARY SOURCE

Yad Vashem Archives (Righteous Among the Nations). YVA M31.2/file number.

PUBLISHED WORKS

Aronson, Elliot. *The Social Animal*. San Francisco: W.H. Freeman, 1972.

Asch, Solomon E. "Opinions and Social Pressure." *Scientific American* 193, no. 5 (1955): 2-6.

Bankier, David, *The Germans and the Final Solution: Public Opinion under Nazism*. Oxford, UK; Cambridge, Mass.: B. Blackwell, 1996.

Bauer, Yehuda. *Jews for Sale?: Nazi-Jewish Negotiations*. New York: Yale University, 1994.

Bauman, Zygmunt. *Modernity and the Holocaust*. Ithaca, N.Y.: Cornell University, 1989.

Bertelsen, Aage. *October '43*. New York: G.P. Putnam's Sons, 1954.

Bonhoeffer, Dietrich. *No Rusty Swords*. Edited by Edwin H. Robinson. Vol. 1. London: Collins, 1965, 223–27.

Browning, Christopher. *Ordinary Men: Reserve Police Battalion 101 and the Final Solution in Poland*. New York: HarperCollins, 1992.

Büttner, Ursula. "The Persecution of Christian-Jewish Families in the Third Reich." *The Leo Baeck Year Book* 34 (1989): 268–89.

Cohn, Werner. "Bearers of a Common Fate? The 'Non-Aryan' Christian Faith Comrades of the Paulus-Bund, 1933–1939." *The Leo Baeck Yearbook* 33 (1988): 327–28.

Fabre, Emile C., ed. *Les Clandestins de Dieu*. Paris: Fayard, 1968.

Fackenheim, Emil L. *The Jewish Return to History*. New York: Schocken, 1978.

Fogelman, Eva. *Conscience and Courage: Rescuers of Jews during the Holocaust*. New York: Anchor/Doubleday, 1994.

Fraenkel, Daniel. "The German Righteous Among the Nations." *Lexicon of the Righteous Among the Nations: Europe, Part 1*. Jerusalem: Yad Vashem, 2007.

Friedlander Henry. "The Deportation of the German Jews: Post-War German Trials of Nazi Criminals." *The Leo Baeck Yearbook* 29 (1984): 201–26.

Gerlach, Wolfgang. *And the Witnesses Were Silent: The Confessing Church and the Persecution of the Jews*. Lincoln: University of Nebraska, 2000.

Goldhagen, Daniel. *Hitler's Willing Executioners: Ordinary Germans and the Holocaust*. New York: Knopf, 1996.

Goldstein, Avram. *Otto Krayer: 1899–1982*. Vol. 57 of *Biographical Memoirs*. Washington, D.C.: The National Academy Press, 1987.

Grossmann, Kurt R. *Die Unbesungenen Helden* [Unsung heroes]. Berlin: Arani, 1957.

Gutteridge, Richard. *Open Thy Mouth for the Dumb!: The German Evangelical Church and the Jews, 1879–1950*. Oxford: Basil Blackwell, 1976.

Guttman, Israel, ed. Vol. 5 of *Encyclopedia of the Holocaust* (Hebrew Edition). Jerusalem: Yad Vashem, 1990.

Haaretz. April 19, 1996. Weekly Supplement section, pp. 25–28.

Hitler, Adolf. *Mein Kampf*. Boston: Houghton Mifflin Company, 1971.

Huneke, Douglas. *The Moses of Rovno: The Stirring Story of Fritz Graebe*. New York: Dodd, Mead & Co., 1985.

Jaeckel, Eberhard. *Hitler's World View: A Blueprint for Power*. Cambridge, Mass.: Harvard University, 1981.

Kershaw, Ian. "The Persecution of the Jews and German Popular Opinion in the Third Reich." *The Leo Baeck Institute Year Book* 26 (1981): 261–89.

Klein, Gotthard. *Berolinen Canonizationis Servi Dei Bernardi Lichtenberg*. Rome: Congregation de Causis Sanctorum, 1992.

Krakauer, Max. *Lichter um Dunkel*. Stuttgart, 1947. Stuttgart: Calver, 2012.

Kulka, Otto Dov. "Public Opinion in Nazi Germany and the 'Jewish Question'." *Zion 40* (1975): 186–290.

Langbein, Hermann. *People in Auschwitz.* Chapel Hill: University of North Carolina, 2004.

Laqueur, Walter, and Breitman, Richard. *Breaking the Silence: The Secret Mission of Eduard Schulte, Who Brought the World News of the Final Solution.* London: Bodley Head, 1987.

Leuner, Heinz David. *When Compassion Was a Crime: Germany's Silent Heroes.* London: Wolff, 1978.

Levinas, Emmanuel. *Total and Infinity.* Translated by Alphonso Lingis. Pittsburgh: Duquesne University, 1969.

Levinas Emmanuel. *Alterity and Transcendence.* Translated by Michael B. Smith. New York: Columbia University, 1999.

Levy, Ze'ev. "The Concept of 'the Other' in Levinas' Ethics." *Daat* 30 (1993): 21–40.

Lewy, Guenter. *The Catholic Church and Nazi Germany.* New York: McGraw-Hill, 1965.

Loesener, Bernhard. "Das Reichsministerium des Innern und die *Judengesetzgebung.*" *Vierteljahrshefte für Zeitgeschichte* 9 (1961): 262–313.

London, Perry. "The Rescuers: Motivational Hypotheses about Christians who Saved Jews from the Nazis." In J. Macaulay and L. Berkowitz, eds., *Altruism and Helping Behavior,* New York: Academic Press, 1970, 241-50.

Luckner, Gertrud. *Freiburger Rundbrief* 49, no. 12 (1959–1960): 29-44.

Mann, H.G. *Prozess Bernhard Lichtenberg: Ein Leben in Dokumenten.* Morus: Berlin, 1977.

Michalczyk John, ed., *Resisters, Rescuers, and Refugees: Historical and Ethical Issues.* Kansas City: Sheed & Ward, 1997.

Midlarsky Elizabeth, and L. Baron. "Helping During the Holocaust: The Role of *Political,* Theological, and Socioeconomic Identifications." *Humboldt Journal of Social Relations* 13, nos. 1–2 (1986): 285–305.

Milgram Stanley. *Obedience to Authority: An Experimental View.* New York: Harper & Row, 1974.

Milgram, Stanley. "Behavioral Study of Obedience." *Journal of Abnormal and Social Psychology* 67, no. 4 (1963): 371–78.

Milton, Sybil. "Armin T. Wegner: Polemicist for Armenian and Human *Rights.*" *Armenian Review* 42, no. 4 (1989): 17–40.

Mueller-Hill, Benno. *Murderous Science.* New York: Oxford University, 1988.

Noakes, Jeremy. "The Development of Nazi Policy towards the German-Jewish 'Mischlinge' 1933–1945." *Leo Baeck Year Book* 34 (1989): 291–354.

Ogiermann, Otto. *Bis zum letzten Atemzug: das Leben und Aufbegehren des Priesters Bernhard Lichtenberg.* Leipzig: St. Benno-Verlag, 1983.

Oliner, Samuel, and Pearl Oliner. *The Altruistic Personality: Rescuers of Jews in Nazi Europe.* New York: Free Press, 1988.

Peleg, Miriam. "Testimony of Herman F. Graebe, Given in Israel." *Yad Vashem Studies* 6 (1967): 283–313.

Presser, Jacob. *Ashes in the Wind: The Destruction of Dutch Jewry.* London: *Souvenir* Press, 2010.

Renwick Monroe, Kristen. "A Different Way of Seeing Things: What We Can Learn from the Rescuers of Jews." John Michalczyk, ed. *Resisters, Rescuers, and Refugees: Historical and Ethical Issues.* Kansas City: Sheed & Ward, 1997; 243-48.

Rewald, Ilse. "Berliner, die uns halfen, die Hitlerdiktatur zu ueberleben," Landeszentrale für Politische Bildungsarbeit Berlin. From the series *"Beitraege zum Thema Widerstand,"* March 14, 1975.

Riffel, Dennis. Unbesungene Helden: Die Ehrungsinitiative der Berliner Senats *1958 bis 1966.* Berlin: Metropol, 2007.

Riffel, Dennis. "Flucht über das Meer." Benz Wolfgang (ed.), *Überleben im Dritten Reich.* Munich: C.H. Beck, 2003; 153–65.

Schmalz-Jacobsen, Cornelia. *Zwei Bäume in Jerusalem.* Hamburg: Hoffman und Campe, 2002. Translated into English, *Two Trees in Jerusalem.* New York: Humanity in Action, 2015.

Seligmann, Avraham. "An Illegal Way of Life in Nazi Germany." *The Leo Baeck Yearbook* 37 (1992): 327–61.

Spicer, Kevin P. *Resisting the Third Reich: The Catholic Clergy in Hitler's Berlin.* DeKalb, Ill.: Northern Illinois University, 2004.

Stein, George H. *Hitler.* Englewood Cliffs, NJ: Prentice-Hall, Inc., 1968.

Stoltzfus, Nathan. *Hitler's Compromises: Coercion and Consensus in Nazi Germany.* New Haven: Yale University, 2016.

Stoltzfus, Nathan. *Resistance of the Heart: Intermarriage and the Rosenstrasse Protest in Nazi Germany.* New York: W.W. Norton, 1996.

Tec, Nechama. *When the Light Pierced the Darkness: Christian Rescue of Jews in Nazi-Occupied Poland.* New York: Oxford University, 1986.

Weiss, Aharon, ed. *Yad Vashem Studies* 19 (1988).

Weiss, John. *Ideology of Death: Why the Holocaust Happened in Germany.* Chicago: I.R. Dee, 1996.

Wistrich, Robert S. "Helping Hitler." *Commentary* 102, no.1 (1995): 27–31.

Archives/Manuscript Materials/Private Letters

Mensch, James. "Rescue and the Face to Face." St. Francis Xavier University, Antigonish, Nova Scotia, Canada (unpublished), page 12.

Mensch, James. "Death and the Other: A Shared Premise" (unpublished). I am particularly indebted to Prof. Mensch for his insightful interpretation of *Levinas's* thought.

Steckan, Beate. *"Nacht Über Deutschland,"* in YVA M31.2/625.

INDEX

*   *   *

CPSIA information can be obtained
at www.ICGtesting.com
Printed in the USA
BVHW03s1734080518
515641BV00011B/255/P